Teaching Social Foundations of Education: Contexts, Theories, and Issues

Sociocultural, Political, and Historical Studies in Education
Joel Spring, Editor

For a complete list of titles in LEA's Communication Series, please contact Lawrence Erlbaum Associates, Publishers, at www.erlbaum.com.

Teaching Social Foundations of Education: Contexts, Theories, and Issues

Edited by

Dan W. Butin
Gettysburg College

LAWRENCE ERLBAUM ASSOCIATES, PUBLISHERS

2005   Mahwah, New Jersey   London

Lawrence Erlbaum Associates, Inc., Publishers
10 Industrial Avenue
Mahwah, New Jersey 07430
www.erlbaum.com

Cover design by Kathryn Houghtaling Lacey

Library of Congress Cataloging-in-Publication Data

Teaching social and foundations of education : contexts, theories, and issues / edited by Dan W. Butin
    p. cm. — (Sociocultural, political, and historical studies in education)
    Includes bibliographical references and index.
    ISBN 0-8058-5145-3 (cloth : alk. paper)
    ISBN 0-8058-5146-1 (pbk. : alk. Paper)
    1. Educational sociology—Study and teaching—United States. 2. Teachers—Training of—United States. I. Butin, Dan W. (Dan Wernaa) II. Series.

LC191.425 200
306.43'071'1—dc22
                                             2004054108
                                                CIP

Books published by Lawrence Erlbaum Associates are printed on acid-free paper, and their bindings are chosen for strength and durability.

Printed in the United States of America
10 9 8 7 6 5 4 3 2 1

Contents

Preface

Dan W. Butin

It happens every semester. I begin my social foundations of education course by bringing in a large, framed poster of a Sioux Medicine Man. It is a striking black-and-white photograph of a man standing alone on a hill, looking off into the distance, holding a long wooden pipe, a buffalo skull at his feet. It is a noble, saddening, and vivid picture.[1]

So I ask my students to go through what I say will be the standard routine of description, reflection, and critical analysis. They accurately describe the photograph, noting the distant yet proud look on the man's face. They reflect on how little they truly know of Native American culture and how sad the history of these peoples has been. And they (tentatively) critique American society for wantonly destroying such a people.

I tell them that they did a wonderful job: a wonderful job, that is, of articulating exactly what the photographer Edward Curtis (1868–1952) wanted them to see. I explain how Curtis, already a well-known photographer at the time, went to see a Montana Blackfeet Indian Sundance in 1900. How, from that encounter, he convinced President Theodore Roosevelt and J. P. Morgan to fund a multiyear odyssey around the North American continent to photograph, paint, and describe for future generations every single Indian tribe still in existence at the time. How, after 30 years, he had made 10,000 recordings, 40,000 photographs, 20 volumes of text, a full-length motion picture with Kwakiutl people, and several

---

[1]See www.gettysburg.edu/~dbutin for the actual photo.

books of Indian stories; how he had also destroyed his health, ruined his marriage, and become financially destitute.

I then tell them that Curtis wanted you to answer exactly as you did—he wanted to convey the sadness that came with seeing what he believed to be the final breaths of a dying culture. He was not interested in questions of identity, of politics, of legal sovereignty, or of American racism and its consequences of human, social, and structural degradation. For "behind" the photograph is a whole other picture: Curtis staged his photos by paying the subjects to put on the clothes and paraphernalia that they did; by the time Curtis started his odyssey, most traditional Native American patterns of being had all but disappeared due to legislation forbidding such practices, the forced relocation of tribes to reservations or urban environments, the total destruction of the buffalo herds in the Plains, the surge of missionary activity in the West and Pacific Northwest, and the use of boarding schools to separate children from their families, language, and culture (Faris, 1996; Lyman, 1982; Sandweiss, 2002).

Some students nod their heads in seeming sympathy and/or agreement; some seem confused; some are silent. I then explain that the social foundations of education will be about learning to not only describe, reflect on, and critically analyze the picture of American education; it will fundamentally be an exploration of what the "photographer" did not care to or did not know how to make visible.

I immediately tell the class to form groups of threes and fours and brainstorm a list of answers to the following question: "Why do youth drop out of school (K–12)?" I encourage them to think out of the box, share suggestions with other groups, reflect on their own personal experiences. After several minutes I ask the groups to decide on the top two reasons from the list and write them up on the blackboard.

I have been doing this opening routine, more or less as just articulated, for 4 years. I am yet to be surprised by students' answers. Students almost always cite youths' lack of motivation and/or cognitive ability, lack of parental support, the negative influence of peer groups, and pregnancy. Occasionally students focus on the school: The materials are too boring, the teacher has low expectations.

These are wonderful answers, I tell them. The only problem is that they are exactly the answers that are allowed to be visible in our educational system: The answers are, to go back to the analogy, the ones that the photographer wanted to be seen. The point, I explain, is that every single answer on the blackboard succumbs to a "blame the victim" approach by focusing on the individual or the individual's local environment as the source of the problem (cf. Hernstein & Murray, 1994; Lewis, 1967). Such perspectives are ubiquitous in a culture that fosters the myths of radical individualism and meritocracy. I then suggest that the "dropout problem" may be productively viewed in other ways: Historically, dropping out of school was the norm, which suggests that we have only recently decided it was a "problem" (Dorn, 1996); anthropologically, cultures could not survive if youth consistently failed their rites of passage, which suggests that something else besides school "failure" is going on (Spindler & Spindler, 1989); philosophically and politically, how we define success determines not only how we come to define failure, but ultimately how we come to define ourselves (Varenne & McDermott, 1999).

Finally, I intone to my students, some youth fail because other youth such as yourselves succeed. Because you got into this prestigious, small, liberal arts school, somebody else didn't. Your success has (whether directly or not) caused her failure. I glare. I nod knowingly. I repeat that last phrase. I am finished. This performance (for it is a performance), I should note, is done with (at least from my perspective) humor, irony, self-deprecation, and a large dose of encouragement. My goal is to make a point, not to break it.

I spend the rest of this first class going through the syllabus, explaining the journals, the classroom observations, the quizzes, the importance of the service learning, and so on. I tell students to expect discussions, debates, silence, and frustration. I suggest that we are about to embark on a stormy journey; I, for one, think it is well worth the ride, but please make sure to hold on and keep your eyes open. I then dismiss them.

***

There are over 1,400 teacher education programs throughout the United States. Teachers may be certified in traditional 4-year undergraduate programs, either with a major or minor in education; others enter a masters of teaching program (MAT) directly linked to a 4-year baccalaureate degree or enroll in a stand-alone MAT program, sometimes after completing a bachelor's degree; more recently, a host of alternative certification programs have arisen to fulfill the need for ever more teachers. Overall, such diverse programs produce well over 300,000 new certified teachers every year (US Department of Education, 2002).

Most of these new teachers have taken some coursework in the social foundations of education. Yet what is it that has been taught and learned? Other courses—for example, educational psychology, elementary and secondary methods, reading seminars, the student-teaching practicum—are all seemingly able to articulate clear and definable objectives that are aligned to a coherent and consistent curriculum that, in turn, can be adequately assessed. What about social foundations?

The history of social foundations seems to be one of eclecticism. No singular texts, no definitive methodology, no "best practice" formulations are to be found. The lack of a foundation within foundations in fact seems to be a foundational theme (Butin, 2004; Talburt, 2001; Warren, 1998). In one respect such a lack of calcification fosters an ongoing dialogue within and across educational disciplines, allowing for the questioning, rethinking, and reworking of theory and practice. Aronowitz (2001), speaking of academicians' freedom of action and reflection more generally, referred to this as the "last good job in America."

Yet such a lack of certitude within foundations is troubling when linked to other dilemmas in the field: A surprisingly small percentage (less than two-thirds) of all faculty members teaching foundations courses have doctoral degrees in the field (Shea & Henry, 1986; Shea, Sola, & Jones, 1987); there is a heavy overreliance on textbooks (Butin, 2004); the supposed "bread and butter" of foundations—the philosophy and history of education—is actually the least enjoyable for most instructors to teach (Towers, 1991).

This volume offers a more deliberate and deliberative model of the social foundations of education. It addresses how we teach, what we teach, and why we teach the way we do. And it suggests that each of these is inextricably linked in multiple social, cultural, and political webs of meaning.

The social foundations of education is, if nothing else, an exploration into the layered contexts of our educational process. Whether it is approached through diverse disciplines, theoretical perspectives, or pedagogical practices, the social foundations classroom is supposed to help students understand the complex, intertwined, and deep roots of why we do what we do in contemporary schooling.

Yet how exactly do we as professors begin to open the lens by which students come to understand these contexts of education? How do we encourage a thoughtful, reflective, incisive, and critical awareness in our students? How do we help students see other perspectives, other peoples, other modes of being? How do we, as Clifford Geertz (2000) suggested, come to see that "foreignness does not start at the water's edge but at the skin's" (p. 76)?

This is not about "sage on the stage" versus "guide on the side" methodology debates. Rather, this is about the inherent tension of teaching social foundations of education: At the same time that I explicitly support my students' reflection, analysis, and critique of the present educational system, I am implicitly constrained by the very same structures, systems, and policies. Does my class decenter my students' world enough to make them realize that there may be more than a singular normative framework by which to understand how we do schooling? Or do I provide—in the context of a required, 75-minute class—an enjoyable, perhaps intellectually stimulating way to get through a 14-week semester? To what extent am I complicit in perpetuating and/or reinscribing the very structures and practices I am critiquing?

Yes, I allow students the opportunity to engage with and begin to confront their preconceptions. Yes, I foster and support an active classroom where students have a voice and a stake in what they learn and how they learn it. And yes, I promote a pedagogy that acknowledges and works within the complexity and contradictions of multiple traditions, disciplines, and knowledges. Yet for all of this work (and it is a lot of work), this fundamental tension remains; put simply, do I disrupt my students' world or do I tame it?

Is it enough to lecture about social justice, or do we actually have to do it? To what extent can we offer students the freedom to discover the limits of authority in the classroom without reneging on our duties as professors of actually teaching the fundamentals of our discipline? How do we coax our students into understanding the boundaries of their own perspectives and the need to take into account a larger picture of our communities, our cultures, and our world without leaving them bereft of any grounding? And how are these theories operationalized in the day-to-day realities of the higher education classroom?

I believe that these issues are critical to examine for both new and seasoned faculty within the social foundations field. The topics addressed do not go away. Our students come to us wanting to become teachers, experts, scholars. This volume thus offers professors an opportunity to expand the hermeneutics of the possible within the social foundations classroom through deep investigations of such complexities and potentials.

OVERVIEW OF THE BOOK

This edited volume is an opportunity to begin a dialogue both within and for the social foundations field. It is an attempt to discuss, through multiple perspectives and differing strategies, not only what it means to teach social foundations, but how we can go about doing it thoughtfully and coherently. So how do we do it?

Part I—*Defining and Contextualizing Social Foundations*—provides an important entrance into these discussions. In chapter 1, Steve Tozer and Debbie Miretzky offer a historical contextualization of the status of the social foundations field. "How do social foundations teachers represent to themselves and others," they ask, "the distinctive contribution their field can make to the professional preparation and development of teachers and school leaders in an era that appears inhospitable to foundations coursework in the professional curriculum?" Tozer and Miretzky argue that the foundations field has found itself uncomfortably positioned between the professional standards movement and the conservative "market-driven" paradigm, where neither path is conducive to foundations scholars. Yet, they argue, a historical understanding of the social foundations field offers greater clarity of how the field is situated to weigh in on the paramount philosophical and political issues of contemporary education debates around diversity, democracy, and the contexts of teaching and learning. The foundations field, they conclude, must be willing to offer thoughtful critique and clearer articulations of who we are and what we teach.

Chapter 2 takes up exactly such issues. It is an edited transcript of a panel discussion and subsequent e-mail correspondences between four senior scholars within the social foundations field. The panel begins with an opening question: "Is there a social foundations canon?" This question immediately opens up a much broader and deeper dilemma—namely, what constitutes social foundations: Is it a curricular emphasis? A theoretical orientation? An interdisciplinary and/or thematic coherence? The ensuing discussions focus quickly and ably on the implications and assumptions of these questions. Definitions of the social foundations are taken up, modified, and debated. The panel explores how boundary conditions for the field are both necessary and exclusionary and how such boundaries become manifest in the construction of social foundations courses and textbooks. There is a pragmatic and political urgency to these discussions: Each of us has to construct a syllabus every semester, and the particularities of this act will determine what we teach, what students learn, and how we come to articulate our field; more troubling is the reality that if we do not go about defining such specificities, others will. The debate touches on the heart of what it means to teach within the social foundations field.

Part II—*Models of Social Foundations Practice*—offers concrete examples of how the theoretical discussions in the preceding chapters actually begin to play out in diverse social foundations classrooms. In chapter 3, Eugene Provenzo positions the social foundations of education as social activism through the enactment of oral history research projects. Provenzo provides a forceful exemplar of practices that genuinely link the classroom to local communities. He shows how students become engaged in the construction of their own learning and their own histories through the construction of oral history projects, thereby also demonstrating how neither the professor nor the students stand in isolation from each other as learners and teachers. Through oral histories, Provenzo demonstrates, students begin to grasp how knowledge becomes constructed and how the social, political, and cultural contexts of schools and society are deeply enmeshed.

In chapter 4, Rebecca Martusewicz and Jeff Edmundson explore how the social foundations of education can be enacted within a cultural ecological framework. Grounding their work in the ecojustice literature (Bowers, 1997, 2001), Martusewicz and Edmundson suggest that we must teach through a "pedagogy of responsibility." We must be cognizant of the very language in which we frame our practices and thoughts, language that all too often uncritically succumbs to assumptions of industrialization, mass production, and exploitation. Martusewicz and Edmundson provide a telling analogy: Much like 30 years ago when teachers engaged in denying voice to girls and women in the classroom, so today do educators ignore the technological and industrial mentality to the detriment of the environment and our interconnected relationship to the world around us. They provide an important critique of critical "liberation pedagogy" and offer fertile examples of how to develop classroom pedagogy that is respectful of non-commodified traditions. A pedagogy of responsibility, they suggest, "exists in the tension between two necessary ethical questions: What do we need to conserve, and what needs to be transformed?" These are crucial questions the social foundations may need to examine closer.

In chapter 5, Mary Bushnell Greiner explores a similar dynamic through the role of art and, specifically, aesthetic education within social foundations. By emphasizing the role of out-of-classroom and nontextual modes of learning and teaching, Bushnell Greiner introduces an issue all too often absent from curricular and pedagogical discussions: To what extent do our educational practices reconfirm, and thus reinscribe, static educational patterns? "I promised to be a loyal American," writes a first-generation student in Bushnell Greiner's class, "but I found myself in great confusion and uncertainty after watching the documentary 'Children in America's Schools' based on Kozol's book 'Savage Inequalities.' I couldn't believe my eyes." Bushnell Greiner suggests that aesthetic education may be able to both support and disrupt students' notions of American education. Aesthetic education allows two critical moves in the social foundations classroom: It acknowledges and embraces the role of emotions within the educational process and it uses works of art to subvert our implicit resistance to questioning. Bushnell Greiner argues that to "live in art" is to accept that education is dynamic, difficult, contested, and emotionally engaging. Bushnell Grenier thus shows us how a multistep process of description, analysis, and inquiry allows art and the creation of art works to open alternative modes of perception within educational discourses. This is a radical move, one with far-reaching implications for social foundations and teacher education.

Part III—*Developing Teacher Educators With/in Social Foundations*—offers insights about how social foundations works within teacher education programs. In chapter 6 I examine student resistance: the *how* and *why* of students unwilling and/or unable to grapple with the issues raised in a social foundations classroom. Although some students are open to discussions and analysis of politically volatile and culturally sensitive issues—for example, affirmative action, inequities due to race, ethnicity, class, and gender—many are not. I explore how such resistance gets played out in the classroom, how it is linked to students' attempts at identity maintenance, and some implications and suggestions for working with and through such resistance in a teacher education program.

In chapter 7, Kathleen Knight Abowitz delves further into this issue through a thoughtful examination of student autonomy. Abowitz argues that "A definition of autonomy is needed that can help instructors view students as subjects requiring respect and that can help them shape pedagogy that positions students as subjects-in-process." How do we reconcile our sense of individual free will with the cultural, political, and social structures and systems that inhibit and form how we think and act? To focus on the former is to fall prey to an insidious deficit model exemplified in a blame-the-victim mentality; to overemphasize the latter is to succumb to a hopelessness that inhibits any positive action towards greater voice and action. Abowitz provides an excellent theoretical and pragmatic balance. She extends Baxter Magolda's (1999) work on self-authorship to think through what it means to be a self-in-process, and what kinds of learning environments are necessary to foster the explicit acknowledgment of individual autonomy within determining structures. This is an extremely helpful articulation of how to facilitate student discussion and growth without rejecting students' voices.

Chapters 8 and 9 more formally explore the role of social foundations within teacher education programs. In chapter 8, Mary Bushnell Greiner and Jeff Edmundson explore the role of social foundations within teacher education programs. They begin with the fundamental premise that the social foundations of education can "widen the reach of justice, that our schools are ideal locations to conduct such an enterprise, and that the social foundations classroom sets the path for prospective teachers to embark on that journey." Bushnell Greiner and Edmundson directly confront the need for social foundations within teacher education to provide a rigorous theoretical grounding within a program committed to practical usefulness. Their answer is that social foundations can provide powerful theoretical tools for extremely practical purposes. Through numerous examples and ideas, Bushnell Greiner and Edmundson offer the reader a viable means to infuse social foundations throughout teacher education.

In chapter 9, Kathleen deMarrais continues this discussion by putting forward a model of how social foundations can be more centrally positioned within teacher education, particularly as this relates to the performance-based standards movement. She offers a comprehensive articulation of the Urban/Multicultural Teacher Education Program in the College of Education at the University of Tennessee to demonstrate the viability of collaborating across departmental boundaries within education. Further, deMarrais forcefully argues for a greater social foundations role within the ongoing standards movement. In so doing, she mirrors and supports Tozer and Miretzky's contention that social foundations scholars have much to gain from increasing involvement with policy, research, and educational groups focused on developing powerful models of teacher education.

Finally, in Part IV I conclude by providing an overview and synthesis of the discussions within and across these chapters. I suggest that the social foundations of education may be best understood as the passionate engagement with contested positions. Specifically, I suggest that the future of social foundations lies with the deep and sustained engagement of issues of diversity, of demonstrating democracy, and of defining social foundations for ourselves and for others.

MOVING FORWARD

Two additional points are important to make. The first concerns the book's appendix, which contains actual syllabi from Kathleen Knight Abowitz, Rebecca Martusewicz, Eugene Provenzo, and myself. This allows the reader to move between a particular chapter and the corresponding syllabus to gain a sense of how certain issues play out in the linkages between theory and practice. Moreover, it is an opportunity to share specific texts, practices, and formats, for all too often theoretical insights within the social foundations are discussed and propounded without a corresponding sense of how they may be enacted. I cannot claim that the syllabi included here are able to span all or even most of the topics in this volume; nevertheless, they offer readers an opportunity to see the breadth and diversity by which a social foundations classroom may be conceptualized and enacted.

The second point is that this book is part of an ongoing discussion. These chapters offer an opportunity for reflection and action within a social foundations classroom. One of the main goals of such an approach is to demonstrate that the issues that come up in our classrooms are not isolated and situation specific; rather, the topics addressed in this volume are paramount across the social foundations landscape. We are not alone in grappling with these weighty issues.

In a now-classic critique, Michael Huberman (1993) suggested that our educational system promotes, for better or for worse, a teachers-as-artisans model of education: teachers devoted to constructing and developing an engaging classroom environment in the privacy and freedom of their personal creative space. The implication is that education is not a shared or communitarian endeavor; in fact, there is a strong tendency in the exact opposite direction—of constructing boundaries between one's own classroom and external political, social, and cultural pressures.

Notwithstanding the conceptual clarity of the artisan metaphor, the notion of the secluded teacher is a highly romantic sentiment. One may look at this through the constraining lens of the standards movement defining what and how we teach, or one may look at this through the enabling lens of collaborations and intersections. Talbert and McLaughlin (2002) suggested that there are schools that are able to construct "strong collaborative artisan communities" that create spaces for improving practice, fostering dialogue, and enhancing collaborative endeavors all centered around engaging students and inventing repertoires of effective classroom practice.

I hope that this volume offers a step toward informing the latter perspective. The ideas, theories, and practices developed and shared within the context of this volume speak to the potential and power of collaboration across time, space, and perspectives. To this end, I invite the reader to partake in the dialogue through the companion web site to this volume, www.gettysburg.edu/~dbutin. You will find more information about the issues discussed in this volume, detailed bibliographies of the history and present of social foundations, additional syllabi, and links to social foundations of education resources such as conferences, journals, and publication opportunities. I encourage you to join and extend the conversations begun here as a means to sustaining and bettering the scholarship and practice within the social foundations of education classroom.

ACKNOWLEDGMENTS

This book was made possible by Naomi Silverman's patience and vision. I appreciate Joel Spring's early supportive comments and willingness to have this book within his series. Most of all, this book has been sustained by two intellectuals. The first is Eric Bredo, who never tired of my questions, always gave freely with his time, and consistently provided me with thoughtful and thought-provoking arguments and suggestions. The second is my wife. It is hard to argue with someone who not only understands poststructuralism better than I do, but has had 11 years to figure out all my faults. This book owes much to both of them.

REFERENCES

Aronowitz, S. (2001). *The last good job in America: Work and education in the new global technoculture.* Lanham, MD: Rowman & Littlefield.

Baxter Magolda, M. B. (1999). *Creating contexts for learning and self-authorship.* Nashville, TN: Vanderbilt University Press.

Bowers, C. A. (1997). *The culture of denial: Why the environmental movement needs a strategy for reforming universities and public schools.* Albany: State University of New York Press.

Bowers, C. A. (2001). *Educating for eco-justice and community.* Athens: University of Georgia Press.

Butin, D. (2004). The foundations of preparing teachers: Are education schools really "intellectually barren" and ideological? *Teachers College Record online.* www.tcrecord.org

Dorn, S. (1996). *Creating the dropout: An institutional and social history of school failure.* Westport, CT: Praeger.

Faris, J. (1996). *Navajo and photography: A critical history of the representation of an American*. Albuquerque: University of New Mexico Press.

Geertz, C. (2000). *Available light: Anthropological reflections on philosophical topics*. Princeton, NJ: Princeton University Press.

Herrnstein, R. J., & Murray, C. A. (1994). *The bell curve: Intelligence and class structure in American life*. New York: Free Press.

Huberman, M. (1993). The model of the independent artisan in teachers' professional relations. In J. W. Little & M. W. McLaughlin (Eds.), *Teachers' work: Individuals, colleagues, and contexts* (pp. 1–50). New York: Teachers College Press.

Lewis, O. (1966). *La vida: A Puerto Rican family in the culture of poverty—San Juan and New York*. New York: Vintage Books.

Lyman, C. (1982). *The vanishing race and other illusions: Photographs of Indians by Edward S. Curtis*. New York: Pantheon Books.

Sandweiss, M. (2002). *Print the legend: Photography and the American West*. New Haven, CT: Yale University Press.

Shea, C., & Henry, C. (1986). Who's teaching the social foundations courses? *Journal of Teacher Education, 37*, 10–15.

Shea, C., Sola, P., & Jones, A. (1987). Examining the crisis in the social foundations. *Educational Foundations, 2*, 47–57.

Spindler, G., & Spindler, L. (1989). There are no dropouts among the Arunta and Hutterites. In E. Trueba, G. Spindler, & L. Spindler (Eds.), *What do anthropologists have to say about dropouts* (pp. 3–15). New York: Falmer Press.

Talbert, J. E., & McLaughlin, M. W. (2002). Professional communities and the artisan model of teaching. *Teachers and Teaching: Theory and Practice, 8*(3/4), 325–343.

Talburt, S. (2001, Summer). Dewey, identity politics, and the parvenue: Some questions facing the social foundations of education. *Educational Foundations*, 47–62.

Towers, J. (1991). How and why social foundations of education are taught at Minnesota's private four-year colleges. *Journal of Social Studies Research, 15*(1), 30–35.

U.S. Department of Education. (2004). *The secretary's Third Annual Report on Teacher Quality*. Washington DC: www.ed.gov/about/report/annual/teachprep/2004/index.html

Varenne, H., & McDermott, R. (1999). *Successful failure: The school America builds*. Boulder, CO: Westview Press.

Warren, D. (1998). From there to where: The social foundations of education in transit again. *Educational Studies, 29*(2), 117–130.

About the Contributors

Kathleen Knight Abowitz is an associate professor in the Department of Educational Leadership at Miami University. She teaches courses in ethics, philosophy, and social foundations of education, and her research interests are in the field of political philosophy. Her recent scholarship on citizenship appears in *TCRecord.org* and *Philosophical Studies in Education.*

Eric Bredo is a professor in the Department of Leadership, Foundations and Policy at the University of Virginia where he has been program coordinator in Social Foundations and is currently Co-Director of the UCEA Center for Ethics and Leadership. His work focuses on the relationship between classical American pragmatism and contemporary theory in sociology, psychology, and education. A recent book is *William James and Education*, coauthored/edited with Jim Garrison and Ron Podeschi. He also coauthored/edited *Knowledge and Values in Social and Educational Research* with Walter Feinberg. His articles have appeared in *Harvard Education Review, Sociology of Education, Educational Psychologist, Educational Theory, Educational Foundations, Educational Studies, Journal of Aesthetic Education*, and *Journal of the Learning Sciences*, among others. He is currently working on an article on philosophy of science for educational researchers.

Dan W. Butin is an assistant professor of education at Gettysburg College. Dr. Butin's research focuses on teacher education, alternative pedagogical strategies, and educational theory. He is the editor of *Service-Learning in Higher Education* (Palgrave), and is presently at work on a new book, *The limits and possibilities of teaching for social justice.*

Kathleen deMarrais is a professor in the Department of Educational Psychology at the University of Georgia and is the chair of the Department of Social Science Education. She is the editor of, most recently, *Foundations for Inquiry: Methods and Perspectives in Education and the Social Sciences* (Lawrence Erlbaum Associates), and the author of *The Way Schools Work: A Sociological Analysis* (Longman) and *Inside Stories: Reflections on Qualitative Research* (Lawrence Erlbaum Associates). DeMarrais is the series book editor for *Inquiry and Pedagogy Across Cultural Contexts* at Lawrence Erlbaum Associates.

Jeff Edmundson is assistant professor in the Curriculum and Instruction Department at Portland State University, where he works with preservice and inservice teachers. His research and writing focus on developing a deep understanding of culture and ecology within teacher education programs.

Mary Bushnell Greiner is associate professor in the Department of Elementary and Early Childhood Education at Queens College, City University of New York. She is also a member of the Urban Education faculty at the Graduate Center of the City University of New York. Dr. Bushnell Greiner teaches courses in social foundations of education, school and community, and anthropology and education. Her research interests are in aesthetics and education as well as teacher professionalism, and her recent scholarship appears in *Educational Studies, Anthropology and Education Quarterly*, and *Education and Urban Society*.

Wendy Kohli is associate professor and department chair of curriculum and instruction in the Gradual School of Education and Allied Prpfessions at Fairfield University in Fairfield, Connecticut. She is the author of *Critical Conversations in Philosophy of Education*, by Routledge, and her scholarship appears in such journals as *Harvard Educational Review, Educational Theory, Educational Studies, Studies in Philosophy and Education*, and the *International Journal of Social Education*. Wendy has been President of the American Educational Studies Association, on the Board of the John Dewey Society, active in the Philosophy of Education Society, and a former member of the NCATE Board of Examiners.

Rebecca Martusewicz is professor of social foundations of education at Eastern Michigan University. She is the editor of *Educational Studies* as well as the new online journal the *EcoJustice Review: Educating for the Commons* (www.ecojusticeeducaiton.org). Rebecca has recently published *Seeking Passage* (2001, Teachers College Press). Here present research is focused on issues of eco-justice and education.

Debra Miretzky is the Program Director of the National Society for the Study of Education in Chicago. She also teaches classes in Social Foundations at the University of Illinois. Her research interests include school-family relationships and civic education.

Joe Newman is professor and chair of Educational Leadership of Foundations at the University of South Alabama. Active throughout his career in higher education in the History of Education Society and the American Educational Research Association, Newman served the American Educational Studies Association as program chair in 2002 and president in 2003. His scholarly work has appeared in *Educational Studies, Educational Foundations, History of Education Quarterly, History of Education Review, Education Week, Professing Education, Phi Delta Kappan*, and other journals. Newman is the author of *America's Teachers: An Introduction to Education*, 5th edition (in press).

Eugene Provenzo is professor of education at the University of Miami. He is the author, most recently, of *Teaching and Learning in American Society: A 21st Century Perspective* (Allyn & Bacon), and editor of *DuBois on Education* (Altamira Press). Currently he is editing a four volume *Encyclopedia of the Social and Cultural Foundations of Education* (Sage Publications).

Barbara Thayer-Bacon is a professor at the University of Tennessee. She is a faculty member in the Cultural Studies Program and teaches undergraduate and graduate courses on philosophy and history of education, social philosophy, and cultural diversity. Her primary research areas are philosophy of education, pragmatism, feminist theory and pedagogy, and cultural studies in education. Dr. Thayer-Bacon is the author of *Relational "(e)pistemologies"* (Peter Lang Publishers, 2003), *Transforming Critical Thinking: Constructive Thinking* (Teachers College Press, 2000), and (with Charles S. Bacon) *Philosophy Applied to Education: Nurturing a Democractic Community in the Classroom* (Prentice-Hall, 1988). She has written several book chapters and more than 50 referred articles in journals including *The Journal of Thought, Educational Theory, Studies in Philosophy and Education, Inquiry*, and *Educational Studies*.

Steve Tozer is professor and chair of policy studies in the College of Education at the University of Illinois at Chicago. Dr. Tozer is the author, coauthor, or editor of five books and numerous articles on the social contexts of schooling, including *Philosophy of Education 1998* and a textbook for teachers, *School and Society*, now in its fourth edition. His articles appear in such journals as *Journal of Aesthetic Education, Educational Studies*, and *Educational Theory*. In 1999 Dr. Tozer received the Stevenson Award from the Association for Teacher Educators for outstanding leadership and dedication to the education profession. He recently completed a 2-year term as Chair of the Governor's Council on Teacher Quality in Illinois and is immediate past President of the Council for Social Foundations of Education.

Part I

DEFINING
AND CONTEXTUALIZING
SOCIAL FOUNDATIONS

Chapter 1

Social Foundations, Teaching Standards, and the Future of Teacher Preparation

Steve Tozer and Debra Miretzky

A new libertarianism has developed on the right, a point of view hostile to social spending and inimical to proposals for social justice and a welfare state. Radical critiques of public education have subsided as financial support has decreased. Schools are being directed to focus upon discrete "competencies," on basic skills. The focal preoccupations are with efficiency, with accountability in terms of what is measurable. There is continual talk of behavioral engineering, of the values of management expertise. Less and less attention than ever is paid to emancipatory thinking or any type of critique. Technology and the free enterprise system are ascribed an implacable reality, along with explanations that legitimate them, even in economic decline. The most obvious concerns are with economic survival, with "making it," in the face of unemployment, inflation, oil crises, and presumably inexorable decay. Hopelessness is expressed; there is a grim cynicism with respect to possibilities of reform. (1978, p. 57)

With few revisions, Maxine Greene's description of the social context of schooling could be written about conditions in the United States today.[1] First published in *Educational Studies* in 1976 as "Challenging Mystification: Educational Foundations in Dark Times," the article addressed the need for teacher educators to respond critically to their political-economic envi-

---

[1]This chapter began as the Stevenson Lecture, which Steve Tozer presented at the 1999 annual meeting of the Association of Teacher Educators in Chicago. It was then revised for Tozer and Miretzky (2000). This collaborative paper is a thorough reconsideration of both earlier pieces.

ronment.[2] Greene urged educators to confront the "mystification" of lived experiences that were distorted and tamed by the efforts of the powerful to protect and justify their privilege:

> The responsibility for critical understanding of the language of functional rationality, its premises, its origins, its distortions falls heavily on the educator. Perhaps it falls most heavily on the foundations specialist in teacher education, since he/she is distinctively obligated to equip teachers-to-be to reflect critically upon and identify themselves with respect to a formalized world .... There must be efforts made to reflect critically on the numerous modes of masking what is happening in our society—the numerous modes of mystifying, of keeping people still. (1976, p. 19)

Clearly, this is not the language that dominates contemporary teacher education reform. Social foundations educators are caught between two powerful and competing movements, neither of them very compatible with the historically critical traditions of social foundations research and teaching. One of these movements is the standards-based movement in pre-K–12 teaching, with its emphasis on standardized achievement tests, curricular alignment with state and national standards, and professional teaching standards (Darling-Hammond & Snyder, 2000). The opposing position is a market-driven orientation that emphasizes the deregulation of teacher preparation and the elimination of the "monopoly" of colleges and universities on teacher certification programs (Ballou & Podgursky, 1999, 2000). As Cochran-Smith and Fries described it, the agendas of both movements are "driven by ideas, ideals, values, and assumptions about the purposes of schooling, the social and economic future of the nation, and the role of public education in a democratic society" (2001, p. 3), and both movements seek to assert legitimacy through their use of evidentiary, political, and accountability claims. Although these two camps are at war with one another in state and national policy arenas, they both largely ignore social foundations of education as an essential part of teacher preparation programs.

This recent turn of events is serious business for social foundations educators. On the deregulators' side, alternative routes to certification and "fast tracks to teaching" seek to reduce teacher education coursework to an absolute minimum. Advocates embrace the view that subject-matter knowledge and classroom experience are the most effective combination to produce teachers. The opposing standards movement is driven by outcomes measures, both for teacher candidates and for students, that offer little attention to social foundations of education in the teacher preparation curric-

---

[2]Greene (1976) readers may be familiar with the article under a different name, "The Matter of Mystification: Teacher Education in Unquiet Times," published in Greene (1978).

ulum. In the absence of a compelling case for the foundations, it is a fairly safe bet that the curricular space for social foundations coursework will be in jeopardy in many states. The politics of the matter are such that quoting Maxine Greene, no matter how passionately one might agree with her position, will not likely communicate to most policymakers and even many teacher educators why social foundations of education should be studied. Moreover, our students will ask, as they have asked for decades, "How will coursework in the foundations of education make me a better teacher?" Increasingly, in this period of standards-based, assessment-driven professional preparation, they can also ask, "How will this course help me on the standards-based teacher certification exam in my state?"

In sum: How do social foundations teachers represent to themselves and others the distinctive contribution their field can make to the professional preparation and development of teachers and school leaders in an era that appears inhospitable to foundations coursework in the professional curriculum?

SOCIAL FOUNDATIONS IN HISTORICAL PERSPECTIVE

We have found that the best way to understand the distinctive contribution that social foundations can make to professional preparation is to examine the historical origins of social foundations instruction. Before the 1930s, if teacher and administrator candidates took foundations courses, they tended to be of two kinds. One was single-discipline coursework such as philosophy of education, history of education, or sociology of education. Scholars like R. M. MacIver in sociology, Elwood Cubberley in history, and W. H. Kilpatrick in philosophy used the lenses of the social sciences and humanities to study and teach about education in cultural context. The other kind of foundations course at the turn of the century used a different meaning of foundations: more akin to "fundamentals" or "basics." Thus, New Jersey State Normal School Professor Levi Seely's 1901 book *The Foundations of Education* was really an introduction to teaching practice, rather than an effort to use foundational disciplines to study school and society.

In 1934, however, George S. Counts published *The Social Foundations of Education*, which focused not on teaching or schools at all, but on the cultural base, or foundations, on which education must rest in any context. The opening words of his introduction signaled his perspective:

> The historical record shows that education is always a function of time, place, and circumstance. In its basic philosophy, its social objective, and its program of instruction, it inevitably reflects in varying proportion the experiences, the condition, and the hopes, fears, and aspirations of a particular people or cultural group at a particular point in history .... While the biological inheritance of the race presumably remains practically unchanged from

age to age and thus gives a certain stability to the learning process, education as a whole is always relative, at least in fundamental parts, to some concrete and evolving social situation. (p. 1)

And in the United States, for Counts, educational objectives and programs of instruction had to take account of the democratic inheritance of the nation, especially because that promise had been imperfectly kept. He began chapter 1 with the words, "The highest and most characteristic ethical expression of the genius of the American people is the ideal of democracy" (p. 9). He then went on to say:

> The point is at once conceded that the history of the United States has been marked by many contrary influences and tendencies. The legions of democracy, not infrequently battered and leaderless, have always had to fight for their existence; and the ideal has often been confused with the reality. (p. 11)

For Counts, then, students of education needed to study the cultural substrata on which all educational processes must ultimately rest. This meaning, not foundations as the fundamentals or basics of education, permeates the 1934 volume. The book found a welcome audience among his colleagues at Teachers College, Columbia. In fact, they had influenced his thinking. Beginning in 1928–1929, a multidisciplinary group of faculty at Teachers College had begun to meet regularly to examine the social contexts of educational ideals and practices. Three participants in that discussion group who subsequently wrote about that experience went on to write very similar accounts, each different in emphasis and particulars. Harold Rugg (1952), Kenneth D. Benne (1974, 1984, as described in footnote), and R. Freeman Butts (1993) wrote about the origins of the Social Foundations Division at Teachers College, Columbia, in this period, but we quote at some length from Benne, as this piece of private correspondence has not previously been published as completely.

> I know rather accurately the origins of "educational foundations" instruction at Teacher College, Columbia U. The first semester of the yearlong educational foundations course, Ed200Fa, was focused on issues of social policy in their bearing on "educational" policy and programs. (Ed200Fb was more individually oriented, dealing with psychological issues of human development in their bearing on controverted questions of curriculum, guidance and school administration.)

> About the time of the depression of 1929 .... Professor W. H. Kilpatrick instituted a discussion group. Its members came from various disciplinary backgrounds—Kilpatrick, [Bruce] Raup and [John] Childs philosophy, [George] Counts and [Edmund de S.] Brunner sociology, Harold Clark economics, Goodwin Watson social psychology, Harold Rugg the arts, Jesse Newlon educational administration and political science. They met periodically—not less than once a month, sometimes more often. They had no fixed agenda—ques-

tions of foundering economy, a socio-economic crisis, intense political controversy—which were current and had a bearing, so they believed, on the task, orientation and policies of education.

They came to believe that all teachers should become students of the issues of contemporary society and culture and of the relations of these issues to questions of educational aims, methods, and programs. They also believed that a cross-disciplinary approach was conducive to adequate treatment of these issues.

In keeping with this thinking, they brought the psychological, sociological, economic, historical, and philosophical professors together into a division of educational foundations ....

It was the same group (Kilpatrick's) which hatched the idea of the radical educational journal, *The Social Frontier*. It was probably at its greatest height in 1936 when I went to Teachers College. We used it frequently in Social Foundations courses (Ed 200F). (Benne to Tozer, 1984)[3]

Rugg's earlier account confirmed Benne's, although he indicates the discussion group began in 1928. He noted the cultural context, that, as we later note, seems regularly to attend key turning points in the evolution of the social foundations field.

In the long run, the formation of the Teachers College Discussion Group may prove to be one of the chief contributions of this period. They rediscovered the prior role of *the art of disciplined conversation* in the cooperative building of a theory and a program of education for a culture in crisis. (p. 515)

One of the major outcomes of the Kilpatrick discussion group was that it devised a two-semester curriculum, culminating in *Readings in the Foundations of Education*, for which Rugg served as lead editor (1941). The Counts and the Rugg volumes shared a common approach to foundational study in professional preparation: They sought to provide a critical, cross-disciplinary study of education, including schooling, as a cultural process grounded in the social institutions, processes, and ideals that characterize particular cultures. It was critical in its explicit effort to test social and educational institutions and processes against democratic ideals. This critical, cross-disciplinary view of social foundations of education, not the "introduction to teaching" approach, marked the development of the field from the 1940s onward, and it led to the founding of the American Educational Studies Association (AESA) in the 1960s and the Council of Learned Societies in Education (CLSE) in the 1970s.

---

[3]Benne, Kenneth D.; Personal correspondence to Steve Tozer, January 10, 1984. In this correspondence, Benne also mentioned that he had written about this topic in Benne (1974), *The Education Professoriate*, Society of Professors of Education Monograph #4.

The turning points in the history of the development of the field are tied to historical moments when social inequities and instrumental rationality were ascendant. The social foundations movement originated when the Great Depression had ravaged the nation and teacher preparation was still locked in a social transmission model that Rugg called "the Conforming Way." In the late 1960s the American Educational Studies Association was founded amidst a tension between the forces of social protest and a conservative techno-rationalist school reform movement symbolized in the work of James B. Conant. And when Maxine Greene wrote her remarks cited earlier in this chapter, the competency-based teacher education movement threatened to take over teacher preparation entirely.

Partly in response to the behaviorism of the competency-based movement, foundations organizations had by 1978 published the *Standards for Academic and Professional Instruction in Foundations of Education, Educational Studies, and Educational Policy Studies*. The sponsoring organization for the *Standards*, the Council of Learned Societies in Education, changed its name in 2000 to the Council for Social Foundations of Education to communicate its mission more accurately. Through 2003–2004, it has been the official voice of some 20 social foundations organizations (e.g., History of Education Society, Philosophy of Education Society, AESA) in the governing structure of the National Council for Accreditation of Teacher Education (NCATE).

The CSFE *Standards*, like the Foundations Division at Teachers College in the 1930s, presents an explicit rationale for the role of social foundations in the professional preparation of educators: that social foundations uses the lenses of the social sciences and humanities to help teacher candidates develop "interpretive, normative, and critical perspectives on education" and that such perspectives are important to interpreting educational practice in cultural context. The knowledge, skills, and dispositions indicated in the *Standards* are those that help teachers develop the sociocultural understandings, critical skills, and habits of mind to interpret and critically evaluate educational aims, practices, and problems in their institutional and cultural context (Tozer, 1993; Tozer & Avcioglu, 2001). The *Standards* were revised in 1996, partly in response to the professional standards-based movement in teacher preparation.

A PERSISTENT TENSION:
CURRICULAR PURPOSES VERSUS CURRICULAR SPACE

Before leaving this brief historical overview of the social foundations of education, one other tension must be noted: between efforts to articulate the distinctive role of the foundations and the effort to minimize that role in the curriculum. This is not a new phenomenon, as Butts told us in his account of the 1949–1950 academic year at Teachers College, during his tenure as department chair. This little-remarked passage is worth quoting at length.

> Aside from the competition for staffing in a resurgent college blessed with the enrollment booms of the late 1940s and guided by the strong leadership of Dean Caswell, the movement to dilute the eight-point [credit] requirement in the foundations fields for the M.A. degree was already under way. First, certain other courses in the Department could be substituted at will for the 200F without our permission. Then a college-wide committee appointed by Dean Caswell and dominated by members of Division IV (Instruction) got the faculty to approve general courses in administration, guidance, and curriculum in place of two points of foundations courses .... This creeping dilution and ultimately virtual defeat of the foundations requirement are among my principal regrets. I think I did my best to counteract the trend, but I never quite succeeded. I have always felt guilty about this.
>
> It's ironical, too, because the whole department turned to and devoted twenty-four two-hour meetings to reexamining the foundations idea and the role of the Department in the College and formulating guidelines for the future policy, program, and personnel of the Department. This was a genuine joint project, hammered out in lively department meetings ... over the academic year of 1949–1950 .... I'm actually very proud of the documents that emerged by May, 1950. I believe they are still basically sound .... "The task of educational foundations centers upon a basic and comprehensive study of the culture and of human behavior as these are related to the total educational enterprise. It assumes that every member of the educational profession should have a fundamental understanding of the relations of education to the deepest values, traditions, and conflicts in society and to the basic characteristics of human behavior .... The foundations process ... is one which (1) deals with questions of educational direction, policy, and action in areas of unresolved problems in the culture, in such way (2) that every available, pertinent, and scholarly resource is brought authentically into the effort, (3) with a definite view to attaining the greatest possible personal commitment to democratic beliefs, purposes, and goals, and (4) to extending the effort to gain the maximum possible community of understanding, purpose, and commitment. It need hardly be said that this is an effort to make a discipline of the democratic process, particularly as this becomes the concern of educators in a democracy. (Butts, 1993, pp. 23–24)

Even while social foundations coursework at Teachers College was being articulated in terms of a cross-disciplinary study of culture and behavior that emphasized the ideals and practices of democratic life, its curricular space was being squeezed. We should not be surprised to see that same tension today, played out under new historical circumstances.

ALIGNMENT AMONG STANDARDS: A "NEW ORTHODOXY"?

Since publication of the Carnegie Commission report, *A Nation Prepared: Teachers for the 21st Century* (Carnegie Forum on Education and the Economy, 1986), the professional teaching standards movement has built up a considerable head of steam. The standards movement in teaching has been fueled by national organizations such as the National Council for Accreditation of Teacher Education (NCATE), the Interstate New Teachers Assessment and Support Consortium (INTASC), the National Board for Professional Teaching Standards (NBPTS), and the National Commission on Teaching and America's Future (NCTAF), and by close collaboration among these four entities. The first three of these organizations cooperatively assumed standards-based leadership in the domains of teacher preparation, new teacher support, and experienced teacher recognition, respectively.

Further, nearly all of the 50 states are embracing the professional standards movement in one form or another, either through formal partnerships with NCTAF or NCATE, incentives for teachers to participate in NBPTS certification, adoption of INTASC standards, legislation leading to standards-based teacher certification, or some combination of these. The number of states with partnerships with NCATE, for example, has grown to all 50 in the last few years. The number of states with experienced teachers who have successfully achieved National Board Certification has grown since the spring of 1994 from a handful to all 50; the number of board-certified teachers has grown in that time from 177 to 32,144 (NBPTS, 2004).

In addition to these collaborative efforts focusing on the standards-based development and assessment of teachers, the Interstate School Leaders Licensure Consortium developed *Standards for School Leaders* (1996) so that school principals may be prepared, professionally developed, and assessed according to professional standards (these standards have been adopted by most states for leadership preparation and development). Further, from the Goals 2000 initiative of the first Bush administration to the No Child Left Behind act of the second, the federal government has emphasized the need for rigorous learning standards in the nation's public schools. Since the 1983 *Nation at Risk* report, in fact, most states have formally passed K–12 (or P–12) learning standards. Typically these are based on the content standards articulated by professional subject matter organizations such as the National Council on the Teaching of Mathematics or National Council on the Teaching of English. Kendall and Marzano (1996) documented newly developed standards in over a dozen subject-matter domains, including the arts, civics, and life skills, in addition to the more traditional academic subjects of math, science, history, and language arts.

One of the first things that one notices about the work of the Carnegie- and Rockefeller-funded National Commission on Teaching and America's Future (NCTAF) is the effort to bring alignment to the mix of standards confronting educators. The first recommendation of their first report, *What*

Matters Most (1996), is, "Get serious about standards, for both students and teachers." NCTAF supports a collaborative alignment among standards-generating organizations and state educational agencies, and to some extent that alignment is already taking place. A clear division of labors has been established among the organizations generating standards for teaching. NCATE has generated standards for the development and assessment of teacher education units in higher education institutions, with greatest emphasis on the initial preparation of teachers (National Council for Accreditation of Teacher Education, 1995). INTASC, as its name indicates, focuses on new teacher assessment and development, and the National Board for Professional Teaching Standards has generated standards for the assessment and development of experienced teachers. Each of these organizations has worked with the others to make sure that these various standards—for teacher preparation, early-career development, and experienced teacher development—will work coherently to support the growth of teachers throughout their careers. At the same time, NCTAF urges that state professional standards boards be formed, so that each state will develop teacher certification aligned with national subject-matter standards and with the learning goals for students in that state's schools.

These efforts at aligning student learning standards, teaching standards, and career-path assessments represent an organized and systematic approach to the professional preparation, induction, development, and assessment of teachers emergent over the past decade. It is this systematic approach that has led some to refer to a "new orthodoxy" in the field of teacher preparation and development (Beyer, 1999). The notion of a "new orthodoxy" alerts us to the dangers of falling too quickly into a line that leads to an uncertain destination, following an organized leadership that is seeking a "holy grail" of effective teaching but may only be generating a new dogma that will prove counterproductive for teachers and students alike (Raths, 1999). Despite the concerns about a new orthodoxy, the standards-based movement in professional development of teachers continues to gain momentum. It does so in state boards of education, in rapidly increasing NBPTS certifications, in schools and colleges of education turning to standards-based performance assessments of teacher candidates, and in standardized testing services generating new standards-based assessments of teachers. Over $200M in federal and private funds has been spent to support NBPTS, and well over $150M in addition has been spent on application fees and financial incentives for successful board applicants (Goldhaber, Perry, & Anthony, 2004). Currently, NCTAF has developed formal partnerships with 20 states and numerous municipalities to pilot standards-based teacher development and to demonstrate that the NCTAF agenda can work. Virtually all other states are pursuing standards-based teacher quality reform independently of formal NCTAF partnerships, and were doing so before the No Child Left Behind Act raised the bar for accountability (Furhrman, 2001).

THE CONSERVATIVE RESPONSE:
IS TEACHER EDUCATION NECESSARY?

The new orthodoxy of the professionalization movement may be questioned by such social foundations scholars as Beyer, but it is under more vigorous attack from conservative political groups and private foundations, including the Heritage Foundation, the Manhattan Institute, and the Thomas B. Fordham Foundation—as well as the U.S. Department of Education under Education Secretary Rod Paige. As the 2002 Annual Report on Teacher Quality concluded:

> Leaders in the teaching profession sought to boost the professional image and prestige of teaching, seeking to elevate it to the status of law or medicine, by controlling entry into the teaching ranks through increasingly prescriptive state laws and regulations. Did the reforms improve the prestige of the profession and the quality of the teaching force? Judging by today's data, it seems they did not. (U.S. Department of Education, 2002, p. 2 of 11 in chap. 2)

Education Secretary Paige contended that the research shows that verbal ability and content knowledge are "the only measurable teacher attributes that relate directly to improved student achievement" (p. 2 of 6, chap. 4); knowledge of pedagogy or time spent student teaching is presented as making little difference (p. 6 of 7, chap. 1). Alternate routes to certification, at least those programs that require their teacher candidates to pass the same licensure or certification exams as traditionally certified peers, clearly emerge as the option of choice for teacher candidates, as they "streamline the process of certification to move qualified candidates into the classroom on a fast-track basis .... A model for tomorrow would be based on the best alternate route programs of today" (p. 9 of 11, chap. 2).

Such a forthright challenge to the teacher education establishment prompted vigorous rebuttal (Darling-Hammond & Sykes, 2003; Darling-Hammond & Youngs, 2002; National Commission on Teaching and America's Future, 2003) as proponents of the professionalization agenda charged that "an accurate review of rigorous research on teacher qualifications and their relationship to student achievement could provide useful guidance to state policymakers, [but] such a review is not to be found in this report" (Darling-Hammond & Youngs, 2002, p. 13), and that Paige offered "a fictionalized account of what research says about what effective teachers know and how they come to know it" (p. 23).

It is difficult to link discrete teacher preparation components clearly with outcome measures for student achievement. Although there are a few studies that show that knowledge of subject matter as represented by coursework or majors does seem to have some effect on student achievement (Goldhaber & Brewer, 2000; Guyton & Farokhi, 1987; Monk & King, 1994), there is little published research evidence that other aspects of teacher preparation—instructional methods, learning theories, foundations of education, classroom management, or student teaching—have an impact on student achievement. At this point, "There is no research that directly assesses what teachers learn in their pedagogical preparation and then evaluates the relationship of that pedagogical knowledge to student learning or teacher behavior" (Wilson, Floden, & Ferrini-Mundy, 2001, p. 22).

Although this is largely due to the fact that research on teacher education itself is a relatively new field of study, there are other factors, as Wasley and McDiarmid (2003) pointed out, that contribute to the complexity of linking teacher preparation components with student achievement. For example, it is not difficult to document coursework taken by teachers, but this does not tell us what teachers actually *learned*. Clinical experiences as a student teacher are obtained as a "guest" in someone else's classroom; it is hard to know how much a student teacher moderated his or her own tendencies or responses as a result. There are the influences of 16 years of informal "observation" as a student as well as the need to cope with the overwhelming demands of early teaching that are thrown into the mix of knowledge, skills, and dispositions teachers possess. Given all this, how can we possibly know when professional choices and behaviors reflect what was learned in teacher preparation without intensive and costly observations and interviews? If it is difficult enough to connect content knowledge with student achievement, how likely can it be that the importance of social foundations knowledge can be demonstrated empirically? And if not empirically, how do foundations scholars make the argument that practicing teachers need a course in social foundations of education to understand the social contexts of their practice?

TWO CHALLENGES TO SOCIAL FOUNDATIONS OF EDUCATION

Although the debate between the standards-based professionalizers and the conservative deregulators continues, neither position offers much comfort for programs in social foundations of education, at either the teacher preparation or the advanced graduate levels. One reason that social foundations educators may be concerned about the standards movement is the emphasis on "performance" assessments. The standards-based movement emphasizes program *output* measures, such as teaching performance, rather than program *inputs* such as course requirements. State policymakers, then, can reasonably reduce or eliminate required curricular components of teacher preparation in favor of holding programs and their graduates accountable to professional standards and performance-based assessment. If state curriculum requirements are reduced in favor of output assessments, teacher preparation programs have incentive to eliminate or reduce those elements that do not have a strong effect on assessed performance—or do not readily lend themselves to performance assessment. State-mandated coursework will become less a priority in teacher development (a) as colleges of education are asked primarily to produce candidates who are able to demonstrate that they can teach well, and (b) as performance standards become the yardstick for measuring the value of the various components of teacher preparation.

This is now happening in many states. In Illinois, for example, the state's detailed specifications for teacher education coursework are being replaced by assessments based on the work of INTASC, NCATE, ETS (Educational Testing Service), and others who are working in the professional standards paradigm. The state requirements for social foundations instruction in every teacher education program in Illinois are already history. Like Illinois, the majority of states have until now required coursework in social foundations of education (usually framed in terms of history or philosophy of education, or school and society, or foundations of education) as part of teacher preparation. When state-mandated curriculum requirements are reduced or eliminated in favor of output assessments, there is no reason to assume social foundations coursework will be required. Nor is the foundation-oriented language of NCATE standards strong enough or specific enough to mandate courses in social foundations. It becomes particularly difficult to defend the continued inclusion of social foundations classes in a teacher preparation program when we recognize that these classes have historically received the lowest ratings in terms of usefulness by teacher candidates, and their value to teachers is often not readily apparent (Sirotnik, 1990). How will familiarity with philosophy or history or sociology of education make any real contribution, not only to teaching but also to performance on a standards-based assessment of teaching?

Social foundations components of teacher education programs in the era of No Child Left Behind now confront two challenges. The first of these is the loss of the protection of social foundations courses when state curriculum requirements are reduced or eliminated in favor of outcome assessments. The second is to show how social foundations preparation actually contributes to success in these outcome assessments. If no such demonstration is forthcoming, we predict grim times ahead for social foundations instruction in professional preparation programs—for teachers and school administrators as well.

Setting aside the issues of curricular space and the self-interest of the foundations instructor, there are other reasons to expect social foundations educators to express concerns about the rising tide of standards in teacher preparation and development. These concerns reside in the historical commitment of social foundations to critical inquiry—an orientation to inquiry that invites normative assessments of social and educational phenomena against competing notions of democratic life. The professional *Standards* in social foundations, first published in 1978, define social foundations of education partly in terms of "developing interpretive, normative, and critical perspectives on education, both inside and outside of schools." Those *Standards* were developed expressly to resist "a narrowly behaviorist, competency-based evaluation movement in education," one that was gaining momentum in the 1970s (Council of Learned Societies in Education, 1996). It is not surprising that a generation later, social foundations educators might look askance at a new professional standards movement, especially one that emphasizes performance evaluation. How does a teacher manifest a critical and normative social foundations perspective in his or her teaching performance? How do we know that the critical, interpretive, and normative skills, knowledge, and dispositions gained in a foundations class make a difference in what a teacher does or in why he or she does it? And even if we could make visible such a difference, is it problematic to reduce the teacher education curriculum to that which can be measured in performance assessments?

SOCIAL FOUNDATIONS RESPONSES TO THE PROFESSIONAL STANDARDS MOVEMENT

It must be said at this point that there are several important contexts in which social foundations inquiry takes place. Preservice teacher certification is just one of these. A second is preservice preparation, at the graduate level, of school administrators, whose role is increasingly recognized as essential in school improvement. A third context is graduate-level coursework for practicing teachers, usually pursuing a master's degree or postbaccalaureate coursework. Finally, the pursuit of research and the production of social foundations researchers is another important domain for social foundations inquiry. Several hundred faculty and graduate students representing this kind of work convene each year for the American Educational Studies Association annual meeting. Some social foundations researchers have little or nothing to do with preservice preparation; many faculty members who teach social foundations in one of the hundreds of preservice teacher education programs nationwide conduct no foundations research.

In response to the standards movement, social foundations educators of various stripes have a number of options before them, three of which are:

(a) largely to ignore these developments, as "this too shall pass"; (b) to use the lenses of the social sciences and humanities to critically interpret and resist these developments through scholarship and collective professional action, as social foundations scholars did with competency-based teacher education in the 1970s; (c) to critically interpret these developments while at the same time working to strengthen the potential of the professional teaching standards movement to achieve its stated goal of providing caring and qualified teachers for every classroom in the nation. We consider each of these briefly in turn.

1. *"This too shall pass."* In our view, this response has high risk for the future of social foundations of education and low insight into the current debate over teacher professionalism. It is high-risk because even if the current standards-based developments in performance assessment do lose momentum over the next decade, this will provide ample time for social foundations components of teacher preparation programs to become more marginalized than they now are, unless action is taken to counter that trend. Second, there are good reasons to believe that the current movement marks a long-lasting if not permanent change in the evolution of teacher preparation. In *Teaching in America: The Slow Revolution*, Grant and Murray (1999) offered an intriguing thesis: that public school teaching today is in the midst of a "slow revolution" that can best be understood in comparison to the "academic revolution" that established distinctive status, rewards, and conditions of work for college teachers in the first half of the 20th century. Although the ultimate outcome of this "slow revolution" cannot be predicted, say the authors, it will not likely be stopped because "teachers will not give up the gains they have made" (p. 215). These gains may be described as increases in teachers' education, social and professional consciousness, and voice in educational decision making. As Grant and Murray (1999) wrote, "The conviction is growing among teachers that the kinds of outcomes that are being demanded for children—that all of them become competent problem-solvers and critical thinkers—can't be achieved if the teachers themselves are not similarly empowered to inquire into the nature of their own practice, and to have the ability to change its course" (p. 215). This position is hospitable to the professional standards movement in teaching, because the standards movement makes visible and debatable the terms and definitions of high quality professional practice, thus potentially empowering teachers to influence the conditions that affect that practice.

2. *Critique in service of resistance to standards-based professional development.* Our view is that this alternative, like the first, is high-risk to social foundations and high-risk to teaching because it underestimates the power of the current professionalization movement in two ways. First, it

underestimates the substantial support among political leaders at the state level (governors, legislators, and state school officers), within both national teachers unions, among influential teacher educators, and in the business community. The collapse of the competency-based teacher education movement of the 1970s came about in part because of its ill-conceived theoretical base and in part because of a weak stakeholder base. The situation is different this time around. Second, a strategy of resistance underestimates the power of the current movement to genuinely inform and change teacher practice to meet the needs of children. The empirical base for this observation is still weak, but growing in strength as new studies are completed (Goldhaber et al., 2004). Finally, although social foundations scholars can, should, and will provide serious and valuable critique to the standards movement in teacher development, to put that critique to the service of resisting the trend instead of addressing its weaknesses will likely further marginalize social foundations components of professional preparation by giving aid to the conservative effort to reduce teacher education curricula. Like Ralph Nader in the 2000 presidential campaign, a "third-party" position among foundations scholars is likely to serve the more conservative stance.

3. *Critique in service of improving the model.* In our view, this option offers an opportunity to strengthen the inevitable weaknesses of the standards movement and at the same time to demonstrate the value of social foundations to teaching practice. This presents a considerable challenge to social foundations educators, however. One part of the challenge is to sustain an effective critique of the standards movement that will prove compelling to nonfoundations scholars—and to suggest ways that the standards model can be improved in theory and in practice. A second part of the challenge is to demonstrate that social foundations experiences can make a difference to teaching practice and to assessed teacher performance.

Why take on these two challenges? Our experiences with national standards in Chicago schools lead us to believe that the teacher standards movement genuinely has the potential to make a significant impact on the quality of teaching in the classrooms of the future. After seven years working collaboratively with the Chicago Teachers Union, the Chicago Public Schools Teachers Academy, and INTASC-based professional teaching standards, we believe that any serious plan for improving teaching on the massive scale on which it must be improved in an urban center like Chicago must include some articulated standards for what constitutes good teaching. On the other hand, we also believe that building professional communities of practice around standards-based discourse will be a surer route to success than a commitment of massive resources to teacher assessment. And finally, if the standards-based assessments are not sufficiently informed by social foundations perspectives, those standards assessments will be seriously limited in their value. To date, there is very little reason to believe that the teacher candidate or teacher assessments used by NCATE, INTASC, or NBPTS incorporate much attention at all to the "critical, normative, and interpretive perspectives" of the *CFSE Standards* for social foundations. Assessing such perspectives is laborious, costly, and requires considerable sociocultural expertise.

Although we are calling for engagement with the current standards movement, certainly it is true that critical questions need to be raised. For example, although so many teachers speak highly about their NBPTS assessment experiences, how are we to understand the disproportionately low pass rate of people of color? Is this a function of urban teaching styles that are not rewarded on the NBPTS model, or are teachers of color performing "below standard" on written portions of the assessment due to a mismatch between their cultural and educational backgrounds and the criteria of the exam? Adequate inquiry into this issue would necessarily require an analysis of educational practices within cultural contexts, and social foundations scholars have much to contribute to such an inquiry. The result could be an NBPTS process that better serves teachers of more diverse backgrounds than are, perhaps, currently being served.

SOCIAL FOUNDATIONS EDUCATORS
AND THE CHILDREN LEFT BEHIND

At the same time that the federal and state governments are holding teachers accountable for student achievement and applying sanctions to schools that do not meet expectations, America's teaching force is facing its most diverse and arguably most challenging student population ever—and the reasons for this reside in cultural context. Under NCLB, schools and teachers are held accountable for getting *every* student, not just some, to perform to high levels of achievement. Over the past 30 years, schools in the United States have become increasingly diverse, from 22% K–12 racial/ethnic minority students in 1972 to 40% in 2001. These numbers are expected to rise, and "minorities" will become the majority student population by 2035 (National Center for Education Statistics, 2002; U.S. Department of Commerce, 1996). Minority students have consistently attained lower scores on standardized tests of academic achievement (Lee, 2002), and have been long overrepresented in special education programs, in instructional groups designated as "low-achieving," and in vocational curricular tracks (Oakes & Lipton, 1994).

The challenges of working with students with greater needs may be contributing to some teachers' decisions to leave teaching which is a greater problem for the teacher workforce than teacher preparation shortages (Ingersoll, 2003). According to National Center for Education Statistics data, public school teachers who left teaching between 1993–1994 and 1994–1995 and cited dissatisfaction with teaching as a career named student discipline problems (17.9%) and poor student motivation to learn (17.6%) as the main reasons they were dissatisfied with teaching as a career (NCES, 1997). Whether teachers understand these difficulties as residing in the psychological makeup of the student independent of culture, or in deficient home environments, or in cultural mismatches between dominant (educational) and subaltern (family) institutions, is going to be largely a product of the kind of professional preparation and development such teachers receive.

More specifically, Hanushek, Kain, and Rivkin (2001) found, in their analysis of student/teacher panel data developed under the UTD (University of Texas at Dallas) Texas Schools Project with the Texas Education Agency, that

> teacher transitions are much more strongly related to student characteristics than to salary differentials, and this is especially true for female teachers. Schools serving large numbers of academically disadvantaged black or Hispanic students tend to lose a substantial fraction of teachers each year both to other districts and out of the Texas public schools entirely. (p. 3)

They went on to say:

> Higher average student achievement significantly reduces the probability of moving or exiting Texas public schools at all levels of experience. Non-black and non-Hispanic teachers are more likely to transition the higher the Black and Hispanic enrollment shares, and the effects are generally statistically significant. Exactly the opposite is true for Black and Hispanic teachers, who are significantly less likely to transition the higher the minority enrollment shares. (p. 19)

Given that minority teachers continue to be grossly underrepresented in the teacher workforce (Villegas & Lucas, 2004), these findings do not bode well for achieving the kind of success No Child Left Behind demands. And regardless of the ethnicity or race of teacher, Dennis Shirley, Professor and Chair of the Teacher Education program at Boston College, noted:

> One of the problems with teacher education is that it never really prepares the students for the challenges of being in the urban schools .... Beyond critical thinking skills, it's important that beginning teachers have at least a rudimentary ability and understanding of how to interact with constituents and parents from different cultural, class, religious, and ethnic backgrounds. There needs to be a facility and joy in cross-cultural encounters, and a lot of creative skills to go along with that. (*FINE Forum e-newsletter*, 2003)

These are the kinds of knowledge, skills, and dispositions that social foundations classes are positioned to develop and support, as Zagumny (2000) pointed out. No matter what might be claimed by proponents of fast-track teacher certification routes or by those who disparage the performance of traditional teacher training programs, it is difficult to argue against the position that teaching has gotten more, rather than less, challenging. Public school teachers are now expected to meet the needs of mainstreamed special education, non-English-speaking, low-income, homeless, neglected, migrant, and any of the other diverse and deserving populations of students who come into their classrooms, and to suggest that teachers whose expertise is purely in intellectual, subject-matter-oriented domains are prepared to address the needs of these children is a claim that social foundations scholars need to question in visible, compelling ways. A renewed emphasis on the value added by social foundations classes, taught meaningfully and well by instructors who recognize that today's educators confront a multitude of demands, gives teachers powerful knowledge, skills, and dispositions to call upon.

The Council of Social Foundations Educators (CSFE) standards—the standards NCATE expects accredited teacher preparation programs to fulfill—present an explicit rationale for the role of social foundations in the professional preparation of educators: that social foundations uses the lenses of the social sciences and humanities to help teacher candidates develop interpretive, normative, and critical perspectives on education and that these perspectives are crucial for interpreting educational practice in cultural contexts through the development of sociocultural understandings, critical skills, and habits of mind. In other words, these standards situate teachers as *professionals* who bring a repertoire of tools to their work—not only intellectual understandings, but the capacity to utilize an appreciation for diversity, critical thinking, awareness of civic and democratic principles, and understanding of the philosophical, social, and moral implications of schooling, to more effectively engage in educational practice, leadership, and governance on behalf of students and on behalf of their profession (CLSE, 1996). To excuse educators of their need for these skills while expecting them to manage the myriad of challenges they are presented with is to sell the children in today's classrooms woefully short.

TEACHER ASSESSMENT AND CULTURAL INTERPRETATION

Culture, as most educators are aware, is one of the two fundamental pillars, or foundations, of human learning. The other, of course, is the human learning organism. As Counts knew, *all adequate explanations and justifications of teaching and learning practices must ultimately rest on these two interactive foundations: the nature of the learner and the cultural context in which learning takes place*. We would never expect teachers to explain their classroom practices independent of an understanding of learning theory. How can we expect them to explain practice without an adequate understanding of cultural context?

Teachers' opportunities to develop sufficient cultural-context knowledge, critical ways of thinking and questioning, and dispositions to employ them will be greatly enhanced by serious and well-planned study in the social foundations of education. Teacher candidates need a great deal of practice in thinking, talking, and writing critically about the learner in social context if they are to learn more than to say the "right words" (e.g., "all children can learn"). More immediately, they will need such experiences if they are to apply their understanding of learning theory to the standards-based assessments now upon us.

If we were to take standards-based teacher assessment seriously, good social foundations instruction could make a significant contribution to new-teacher performance because what is measured is not just classroom performance but a teacher's *interpretation* of that performance. The NBPTS and INTASC assessments are not simply performance based; they are also heavily interpretation based. Therefore, teachers who cannot provide theoretically sound accounts of *why* they make the choices they make, and *why* certain outcomes were produced, will be seriously disadvantaged if the assessments are insightfully scored. Notice, for example, the following three INTASC principles (almost any three would do), none of which would likely be called a particularly "social foundations" principle:

> **Principle 2**: The teacher understands how children learn and develop and can provide learning opportunities that support their individual, social, and personal development.
>
> **Principle 3**: The teacher understands how students differ in their approaches to learning and creates instructional opportunities that are adapted to diverse learners.
>
> **Principle 4**: The teacher understands and uses a variety of instructional strategies to encourage students' development of critical thinking, problem solving, and performance skills. (INTASC, 1992, pp. 16, 18, 20)

In INTASC portfolio assessment, as in NBPTS assessment, teachers are called upon to demonstrate *and explain* their teaching practices, and the consequences of those practices, in ways that reflect the principles above. Social-context understandings are important to the "teacher understands" clause in each of these principles. Children learn and develop in particular cultural contexts (principle 2), they develop different learning approaches in part due to cultural context (principle 3), and the very meanings of diversity, critical thinking and problem solving are culturally constructed (principle 4). For teachers to try to explain their teaching practices adequately without reference to the importance of the cultural context of their choices is to try to achieve the impossible.

In addition, teachers can examine the fact that they are authorized to teach, ultimately, by the community, and that the "curriculum goals" already mentioned have been shaped by the standards and expectations of some community of stakeholders. The awareness that teachers cannot simply say and do whatever they want in a classroom seems almost too obvious, but the recognition that there is a responsibility to the larger community does influence the choices made in the classroom. Social foundations instruction helps equip teachers to think well about the tensions among various communities (e.g., academic research vs. neighborhood vs. school district administration) and their influences on one's teaching choices.

Social foundations classes are places where the kinds of issues and questions above can be addressed. The standards movement can help make the social foundations component of teacher preparation and development relevant and meaningful by compelling a sharper focus on understanding and process, justification and interpretation, and critical reflection. Some argue that such skills can be and have been integrated throughout teacher preparation programs without distinct social foundations courses. We argue that dedicated study in the foundations elevates the knowledge of the teacher to a distinctive professional level that is appropriate for teachers who have to make decisions in complex cultural contexts.

Study in the social foundations provides a series of forums in which teacher candidates and teachers seeking advanced degrees have access to at least two kinds of social foundations learning. One of these might be called "bits of knowledge." Such knowledge includes, for example, the recognition that schools have played a mixed role in serving the ideals of a democratic society; that speaking black English doesn't indicate a lack of ability to learn standard English, or a lack of ability to learn at all; and that student performance is tied closely to family support. But beyond such knowledge bits, social foundations classes can encourage and present *new ways of thinking*, as these converge and inform fresh understandings and generate more sophisticated questions. This type of discourse supports a language of critique and possibility, increasing the likelihood of a sense of individual power both inside and outside of the classroom.

Such new ways of thinking include learning to ask questions such as "Whose interests are served by how schools are run?" Teachers need to learn how to analyze the source of a learning problem not simply in the child or the school, but in the interaction of the child and school as a unit. Further, teachers need to know that they may want and need to attempt to play a role in the larger educational environment as an advocate or a researcher, or may want to attempt to be a change agent in the larger community of the student.

Any problem a teacher faces has multiple sources and multiple facets. The successful resolving of problems is enhanced when understanding of the historical, sociological, and philosophical influences is available to the teacher searching for solutions.

Standards-based assessments, if sophisticated enough to capture the depth of social foundations thinking, would provide a means of better understanding the linkage between integrated theories of teaching and learning and teaching performance. However, these findings are not likely to allay the doubts of those who dispute the necessity of social foundations courses for teacher preparation and development. Social foundations faculty need to begin to draw those connections in compelling ways for their students, and they need to begin to document the effect on students' conceptualizations of teaching and learning. Researchers need to explore with practicing teachers the degree to which social understandings operate significantly in their daily work, and these stories need to be told. For many foundations educators, it has long been evident that a foundations setting at the teacher education table cannot be assumed. Standards-based assessment can certainly help address this concern. But there are no guarantees.

We currently have no evidence that assessors hold candidates accountable for social foundations understandings. If assessments actually held candidates accountable for the understandings that are implied by the INTASC standards and the NBPTS principles, there would be significant implications for social foundations knowledge. However, as already noted, given the level of sophistication in design and in assessor expertise needed to assess such knowledge, it is unlikely that such assessment will become a priority anytime soon. It is arguable, as well, that concerns about teacher "shortages," despite the lack of evidence supporting these claims (Ingersoll, 2001, 2003; Levin & Quinn, 2003), will continue to undermine efforts toward teacher quality by contributing to a sense of urgency around hiring, rather than careful assessment of a teacher's suitability and capacity for the profession.

CONCLUDING REMARKS

This overview of the social foundations of education, which throughout its 75-year institutional history has been marked by purposeful efforts to justify its curricular place in professional preparation programs, raises as many questions as it seeks to address. Two remaining observations are in order here. First, if social-context perspectives are vitally important to practice, to practical theorizing, and to performance assessment, then teachers would benefit if social foundations (like psychological foundations) learning were to permeate the entire professional preparation program. Social foundations faculty would need to work together with their colleagues in a genuine learning community to make this happen optimally for all. Second, in doing so, social foundations faculty could benefit from collaborating closely with their other teacher preparation colleagues to address the following question: "How will social foundations instruction advance the goals of our program?" The INTASC and NBPTS standards can and should provide common ground for such joint inquiry.

Finally, however, these are largely standards-based, instrumentalist arguments that fall short of the oppositional, democratic ethic expressed by Maxine Greene almost 30 years ago. It is very difficult, in the present climate of conservatism, to build a strong political case for social foundations of education on the need for demystification of power and privilege in the United States. Yet the same power and privilege lie at the foundation—the social foundation—of the inequities in schooling that decade after decade limit the life chances of millions of people in the United States. Social foundations educators from Counts to Butts to Greene to today's inheritors of their mantle believe that all educators must be prepared for critical understanding of the meanings of their practice in institutional and cultural life.

The work of justifying social foundations of education in teacher preparation programs remains an intellectual and political challenge that is embedded in a persistent system of inequity. If we in social foundations education think the struggle should be easy, or that there should be no struggle, then we do not understand our own society. If Maxine Greene could talk about "dark times" in 1976, it is not pessimistic to apply a similar assessment to the future of social foundations of education today. But in the past, such times as these have fueled the resistance and resilience of social foundations educators.

REFERENCES

Ballou, D., & Podgursky, M. (1999). Reforming teacher training and recruitment: A critical appraisal of the recommendations of the National Commission on Teaching and America's Future. *Government Union Review, 17*(4), 1–53.

Ballou, D., & Podgursky, M. (2000). Reforming teacher preparation and licensing: What is the evidence? *Teachers College Record, 102*(1), 5/27.

Beyer, L. E.(1999). *A critical appraisal of the "new orthodoxy" in teacher education.* American Educational Research Association, Montreal, Quebec, Canada, April.

Butts, R. F. (1993). *In the first person singular: The foundations of education.* San Francisco: Caddo Gap Press.

Carnegie Forum on Education and the Economy, Task Force on Teaching as a Profession. (1986). *A nation prepared: Teachers for the 21st century.* New York: Carnegie Forum on Education and the Economy.

Cochran-Smith, M., & Fries, M.K. (2001). Sticks, stones, and ideology: The discourse of reform in teacher education. *Educational Researcher, 30*(8), 3–15.

Council of Learned Societies in Education. (1996). *Standards for academic and profes-sional instruction in foundations of education, educational studies, and educational policy studies* (2nd ed.). San Francisco: Caddo Gap Press.

Counts, G. S. (1934). *The social foundations of education.* New York: Charles Scribner's Sons.

Darling-Hammond, L., & Snyder, J. (2000). Authentic assessment of teaching in context. *Teaching and Teacher Education, 16*(5–6), 523–545.

Darling-Hammond, L., & Sykes, G. (2003). Wanted: A national teacher-supply pol-icy for education. *Educational Policy Analysis Archiver, 11*(33). Retrieved Sept. 17, 2003 from http://epaa.asu.edu/epaa/ulln33

Darling-Hammond, L., & Youngs, P. (2002). Defining "highly qualified teachers": What does "scientifically-based research" actually tell us? *Educational Researcher, 31*(9), 13–25.

FINE Forum e-newsletter. (2003, Fall). Program spotlight: Preparing teachers for ur-ban schools. www.gse.harvard.edu/hfrp/projects/fine/fineforum/forum7/spot-light.html

Fuhrman, S. H.(2001) Introduction. In *From the Capitol to the classroom, 100th Yearbook of the National Society for the Study of Education*, Part 2 (pp. 1–12). Chicago: National Society for the Study of Education.

Goldhaber, D. D., & Brewer, D. J. (2000). Does teacher certification matter? High school teacher certification status and student achievement. *Educational Evalua-tion and Policy Analysis, 22,* 129–145.

Goldhaber, D., Perry, D., & Anthony, E. (2004) *National Board Certification successfully identifies effective teachers.* Research brief. Seattle: Center on Reinventing Public Education.

Grant, G., & Murray, C.E. (1999). *Teaching in America: The slow revolution.* Cam-bridge, MA: Harvard University Press.

Greene, M. (1976). Challenging mystification: Educational foundations in dark times. *Educational Studies, 7*(1), 9 –29.

Greene, M. (1978). The matter of mystification: Teacher education in unquiet times. In M. Greene, *Landscapes of learning* (pp. 53–72). New York: Teachers College Press.

Guyton, E., & Farokhi, E. (1987). Relationships among academic performance, ba-sic skills, subject matter knowledge, and teaching skills of teacher education graduates. *Journal of Teacher Education, 38,* 37–42.

Hanushek, E. A., Kain, J. F., & Rivkin, S. G. (2001). *Why public schools lose teachers.* Working paper 8599. Cambridge, MA: National Bureau of Economic Research.

Ingersoll, R. (2001). Teacher turnover and teacher shortages: An organizational analysis. *American Educational Research Journal, 38*(3), 499–534.

Ingersoll, R. (2003). *Is there really a teacher shortage?* Center for the Study of Teaching and Policy, University of Washington. http://ctpweb.org

Interstate New Teacher Assessment and Support Consortium. (1992). *Model stan-dards for beginning teacher licensing and development: A resource for state dialogue.* Washington, DC: Council of Chief State School Officers.

Interstate School Leaders Licensure Consortium. (1996). *Standards for school leaders.* Washington, DC: Council of Chief State School Officers.

Kendall, J. S., & Marzano, R. J. (1996). *Content knowledge: A compendium of standards and benchmarks for K–12 education.* Aurora, CO: Mid-continent Regional Educa-tional Laboratory.

Lee, V. (2002). Racial and ethnic achievement gap trends: Reversing the progress to-ward equity? *Educational Researcher, 31*(1), 3–12.

Levin, J., & Quinn, M. (2003). *Missed opportunities: How we keep high-quality teachers out of urban classrooms.* New York: New Teacher Project.

Monk, D. H., & King, J. (1994). Multi-level teacher resource effects on pupil performance in secondary mathematics and science. In R. G. Ehrenberg (Ed.), *Contemporary policy issues: Choices and consequences in education* (pp. 29–58). Ithaca, NY: ILR Press.

National Board for Professional Teaching Standards. (2003). *Early adolescence generalist scoring guide.* Arlington, VA: Author.

National Board for Professional Teaching Standards. (2004). *NBCTs by year.* www.nbpts.org/nbct/nbctdir_byyear.cfm

National Center for Education Statistics. (1997). *Characteristics of stayers, movers, and leavers: Results from the teacher followup survey: 1994–95.* Washington, DC: Institute of Education Sciences, U.S. Department of Education.

National Center for Education Statistics. (2002). Elementary and secondary education. Racial/ethnic distribution of public school students. *Digest of Education Statistics, 2002.* http://nces.ed.gov/programs/coe/202/section1/indicator03.asp

National Commission on Teaching and America's Future. (1996). *What matters most: Teaching for America's future.* New York: Columbia University, Teachers College.

National Commission on Teaching and America's Future. (2003). *No dream denied: A pledge to America's children.* New York: Author.

National Council for Accreditation of Teacher Education (1995). *Standards, procedures, and policies for the accreditation of professional education units.* Washington, DC: Author.

Oakes, J., & Lipton, M. (1994). Tracking and ability grouping: A structural barrier to access and achievement. In J. Goodlad & P. Keating (Eds.), *Access to knowledge: The continuing agenda for our nation's schools* (pp. 187–204). New York: College Board.

Raths, J. (1999, October). A consumer's guide to teacher standards. *Phi Delta Kappan, 82*(2), 136–142.

Rugg, H. (1941). *Readings in the foundations of education, Vol. I & II.* New York: Bureau of Publication, Teachers College, Columbia University.

Rugg, H. (1952). *The teacher of teachers.* New York: Harper & Brothers.

Rugg, H., & Withers, W. (1955). *Social foundations of education.* New York: Prentice Hall.

Seeley, L. (1901). *The foundations of education.* New York: Hinds and Noble.

Sirotnik, K. (1990). On the eroding foundations of teacher education. *Phi Delta Kappan, 71*(9), 710–716.

Tozer, S. (1993). Toward a new consensus among social foundations educators. *Educational Foundations, 8*(1), 5–22.

Tozer, S., & Avcioglu, I. (2001). The social foundations of education: School and society in a century of NSSE. In L. Corno (Ed.), *National Society for the Study of Education centennial yearbook* (pp. 279–310). Chicago: National Society for the Study of Education.

Tozer, S., & Miretzky, D. (2000). Professional teaching standards and social foundations of education. *Educational Studies, 31*(2), 106–118.

U.S. Department of Commerce. (1996). *Current population reports: Population projections of the United States by age, sex, race, and Hispanic origin: 1995–2050.* Washington, DC: Author.

U.S. Department of Education. (2002). *Meeting the highly qualified teacher challenge: The Secretary's annual report on teacher quality.* Washington, DC: U.S. Department of Education, Office of Postsecondary Education, Office of Policy, Planning, and Innovation.

Villegas, A. M., & Lucas, T. (2004). Diversifying the teacher workforce: A retrospective and prospective analysis. In M. A. Smylie & D. Miretzky (Eds.), *Developing the teacher workforce. The 103rd yearbook of the National Society for the Study of Education*, Part I (pp. 70–104) Chicago: National Society for the Study of Education.

Wasley, P. A., & McDiarmid, G. W. (2003, July). *Tying the assessment of new teachers to student learning and to teacher preparation.* Paper presented at the NCTAF State Symposium. Racine, Wisconsin.

Wilson, S. M., Floden, R., & Ferrini-Mundy, J. (2001). *Teacher preparation research: Current knowledge, gaps, and recommendations: A research report prepared for the U.S. Department of Education.* Seattle: Center for the Study of Teaching and Policy, University of Washington.

Wise, A. E. (n.d.). *NCATE's emphasis on performance.* Washington, DC: National Council for Accreditation of Teacher Education.

Zagumny, L. L. (2000). *The novice and the soapbox: Moral responsibility and teaching pre-certification social foundations.* Available: http://members.aol.com/jophe00/zagumny.htm

Chapter 2

Is There a Social Foundations Canon?

An interview with Eric Bredo, Wendy Kohli,
Joseph Newman, and Barbara Thayer-Bacon

Dan W. Butin

Is there a social foundations of education canon? The assumptions and implications of this question were addressed by a group of scholars at a panel presentation at the American Educational Studies Association Conference on November 1, 2003, in Mexico City, Mexico. The participants were Eric Bredo (University of Virginia), Wendy Kohli (Fairfield University), Joseph Newman (University of Southern Alabama), and Barbara Thayer-Bacon (University of Tennessee). The panel was moderated by Dan Butin (Gettysburg College). To posit the existence of "The List"—a comprehensive summary of what comprises the core knowledge of the social foundations of education field—is to unearth and investigate deeply held assumptions, beliefs, and aspirations of what the social foundations of education is and should be. The very phrasing of the question, as if what constitutes the foundations field can be summarized by a listing of texts, may elicit fears of a Eurocentric and logocentric rigidity. Yet all social foundations professors, every semester, must pass out a course syllabus to their students. This mundane and inescapable fact may thus be taken as the underlying impetus for this starting question. What do we teach? And why? And what does this say about us as social foundations professors in specific and our field in general? The following is an edited transcription—with minor changes, additions, and deletions to enhance the flow of the text—of the panel presentation and an e-mail discussion held in the weeks prior to the panel.

Dan Butin: Welcome. I want to give a brief overview of how this panel came to be before we begin. I'm at Gettysburg College; this is my third year there and I primarily teach social foundations. In teaching social foundations as a new professor, I'm trying to figure out what exactly it is that I am teaching. With the changing demographics of K–16 education and with what I see as the marginalization and fragmentation of theory, I thought it would be appropriate to enquire as to how social foundations has or has not changed. I therefore thought I would ask some people who supposedly know something about this.

It seems to me that the best way to proceed would be to have an empirical question guide us. In the sense that this will get us down to the nuts and bolts issues, by trying to talk through what is a social foundations canon, we can begin to discuss some of the philosophical, methodological, and epistemological undertones of what it means to have edges to this discipline. By having these edges, by having these boundaries, you can start to see how that impacts your practice, and in turn how that affects your definitions: a recursive cycle, if you will. The second impetus, and I think the more pressing for me, is the pragmatic one. When I was constructing my social foundations syllabus, I was nervous: Did I leave somebody out? Did I get everybody in? Fourteen weeks; 28 sessions. Okay, I have to be fast. As I tell my students in one of the first classes, "I'm completely biased in what I'm teaching in Social Foundations, and you have no clue how biased I am in my course content." Because I want them to start thinking about what is knowledge construction, who defines it and how, and so on and so forth. And so there's this self-reflectiveness: What are my biases? What are the biases of social foundations? And how have they come about?

Let me give a final example. At the end of every semester I hand out evaluations where I write down all the texts we've read and my students give me a ranking: What did they find interesting, difficult, etcetera. And consistently one of the texts they never like is Paulo Freire's *Pedagogy of the Oppressed*. We have some excellent discussions about it in class—but as a text, my students find it completely off-putting. And so I question myself: Can I teach social foundations of education without Freire? Or, to push it further, could I do it without Dewey? So I'm hoping that we as a panel and you as an audience can help in that discussion.

Eric Bredo: If you don't mind, I'd like to respond initially with a short statement that I have prepared for this occasion: Whatever one thinks of the idea of a "canon," Dan Butin's call to consider the issue is useful for creating a moment for us to think about where we have been, where we are, and where we are going. Our field tends to be rather diffuse, like education itself. I recall an ex-dean of a prestigious education school saying that an education school is composed of "all of the units that no one else wants." In some ways social foundations is like that, although I mean no disrespect in saying so. It is similar in the sense that it represents interests that are conventionally marginalized or excluded. We tend to represent the interests of groups of people that have been marginalized or excluded, as well as subjects, such as art, emotion, other cultures, and so on and so forth, that have been treated similarly. In Burton Clark's terms, we are defenders of "precarious values." Because we represent what is not emphasized generally, we also tend to be united by what we are against: narrow, prejudicial, and thoughtlessly conventional ways of thinking and doing. Unfortunately, being united by what we oppose can make it hard to find a positive identity in common. Indeed, the very notion of being "positive" is anathema to many in social foundations.

I take this to be the dilemma of social foundations, and, indeed, of any group defending precarious values. We know what we don't want: a monofocal emphasis on what is conventionally given or "present." Yet a defense of the importance of "the fringe," "the vague," "the ideal," or the "unseen," as William James termed what is nonfocal or -ideal, can leave one with nothing central to focus upon. How, then, do we craft a common identity without losing our appreciation for what is necessarily excluded in any such effort—especially since the strongest value we share is an appreciation of the excluded?

For me this dilemma provides a context for considering Dan's question about a social foundations canon. In a sense it is the classical problem of "the one and the many" raised by the Greeks. If we find some common focus, what do we do with all the differences that do not fit within it? And if we celebrate variety or diversity or difference, how do we find a common focus? How do we unify ourselves without losing the very diversity and flexibility that are our raison d'être? And what is the role of a "canon" in such a process?

The word *canon* comes from the Greek *kanon*, meaning a ruler for or a standard of measurement. From this comes the notion of a "regulation or dogma passed by a church council," and the related notion of "an authoritative list of books accepted as Holy Scripture." This has, in turn, morphed into the secular conception of "a sanctioned or accepted group or body of related works" (Merriam Webster Collegiate Dictionary, 10th ed.). The question is, do we want or need such a holy, sanctioned, or authoritative list? And would such a list help us address the basic dilemma just outlined?

I tend to address issues of unity and diversity in populational terms, much like Darwin, Wittgenstein, or, more recently, Steven Toulmin. If we use Wittgenstein's notion of "family resemblances" as a way of making this point, it suggests that those of us in social foundations need not share any set of readings or concepts in common. We may all borrow contents from a larger common pool, making us overlap with one another in varying ways. Seen in this way, the books or concepts we use are like the traits of siblings who are all members of the same family. They may have no single set of genes unique to all of them and to no nonfamily members, no essential core, yet still share an overlapping set of traits because their genes are all sampled from the pool of genes established by their parents. We similarly don't need an essential core to have a looser form of commonality arising from sampling from the same pool of concepts, books, etcetera. This notion frees me to be able to recommend what I believe are some of the "great books" of social foundations without feeling that I am imposing my list on others as the only "sanctioned" or "authoritative" ones. It helps free me from the anxiety that Dan mentioned that I am always vulnerable for having excluded representatives of some group or orientation, no matter how inclusive I try to be.

My proposal to my colleagues, then, is basically this: "Put your preferred items in the common pot so that I will know about them and have them to draw upon." I want to know what good things you have found but do not want to feel obligated to include all of yours. I'll offer some of mine, in return, and do not expect you to feel obligated to include all of them, for neither of us has the one and only best set. But let's help each other develop a good set that all of us can draw upon as need and circumstances demands.

There's another metaphor that also helps me think through why I don't want us to create a rigid canonical list. If one thinks of ideas as tools, having a prescribed list would be like telling a mechanic to use only a prescribed set of tools. Now one tool may indeed be better than another for a given job, but we are not all doing the same job all of the time. As a result, the wider the set of tools is that we can draw upon, the better, in order to find those that are best for the job at hand. The way to attack the initial dilemma we face thus seems to me to be neither to reject the issue outright, refusing to suggest any set of works for fear of being narrow authoritarians or lifeless conventionalists; nor is it to recommend a Hirschian list of facts or books that "every culturally literate social foundations student ought to know." Rather, let's collectively generate a list of helpful works from which we can sample to our mutual benefit. Let's further give some guidance as to what's good about these works, and what they're good for. And let's admit that this is a partial and changing list, subject to continual editing and re-editing as times, issues, and availability change.

This way of thinking of curriculum materials in our field as having different degrees of overlap and nonoverlap between people, but sampled from a common pool, provides a degree of commonality without constraining variety greatly. It gives a way of having a common knowledge base while recognizing variation and change within it. This common knowledge base would likely be densely overlapping in some areas, where many people utilize some texts in common, and only weakly overlapping in others where only a small set of people give a central role to some text. In fact, some texts would have no overlap, since only a single individual would nominate them. Rather than having an essential center and a nonessential excluded set, we would have a more continuously graded field, gradually moving from things that are emphasized by a lot of people to things that are shared by only a few, to those that may have unique supporters that might still be very valuable, depending on what one is doing. I think we could adopt this way of thinking about our curricular materials as we seek, in different ways, to defend precarious values in education. The notion of a list of "good" books as a collectively generated and changing pool of resources, rather than as the holy writ, authoritative set, or unchanging canon, seems to me to be more in the spirit of social foundations. That's why we have other people here: so we can draw on one another for help. Pooling our resources in this way seems to me a much more constructive way to proceed than continually criticizing one another for not including our own favored authors.

Barbara Thayer-Bacon: I join Eric Bredo in thanking Dan Butin for bringing forward the question, "Is there a social foundations canon?" for us to debate. I agree that such a question is healthy for social foundations scholars to debate periodically.

However, I don't think it is healthy for social foundations to continue to describe itself in tragic terms as a confused and marginalized field of study that has a precarious existence. I am currently teaching an "Advanced Seminar in the Social Foundations of Education" with doctoral students from a variety of fields of study within our college of education, and we began with Steve Tozer's CASA essay from Educational Foundations, 1993, "Toward a Consensus Among Social Foundations Educators" to help the students begin to wrestle with trying to understand what social foundations is. My students were surprised to discover social foundations described as "marginalized and excluded." They know that history, sociology, and philosophy are held in high regard in the College of Arts and Sciences, and they know all students in the College of Education must take social foundations courses, so they wondered, why is the field being described as "marginalized?" Their innocent response was an "a-hah!" experience for me, for it made me realize we have been describing ourselves this way for the entire time I have been in higher education (13 years), and I suspect since our early beginnings at Teachers College.

I remember being so surprised by that description when I first went to an educational foundations conference. I came to educational foundations through the door of philosophy, and philosophers don't describe themselves in tragic, marginalized tones. They know they were first, with Plato and Aristotle in ancient Greece, and that they are the field from which all else has evolved. They claim to be foundational to junior fields such as sociology, psychology, even physics (metaphysics is "prior to physics"). You can accuse philosophers of arrogance, elitism, and snobbery, but you can't accuse them of having an inferiority complex. Social foundations of education seems to have an inferiority complex. Like the character Cher plays in "Moonstruck," I want to respond with, "Snap out of it!"

I want to embrace the value and importance of social foundations in helping teachers and students understand the field of education within its social, historical, and philosophical context. I want to underscore the vital role we play in helping people gain critical perspectives on educational practices so that they can begin to name what is missing or wrong about our educational systems, and they can begin to imagine how things could be otherwise. Social foundations give students and teachers a means to be able to critique the social conditions that so powerfully affect their/our lives. I wonder if social foundations' inferiority complex isn't deeply tied to the connection social foundations has to education, and the feeling that education is marginalized and viewed as unimportant and lacking in substance.

Certainly education is an important social institution in societies; it is one of the major places where our cultural wealth is passed on to the next generation; it is a key place where our young are taught what they need to know to survive as adults. At an international level we can find many examples of cultures that hold teachers in high regard and consider educating their young deeply important for the survival of their tribe or nation. However, in the United States there is some truth to the claim that education is devalued as a field of study. For many, education is not a high-priority social issue, until it is your own child who is enrolled in schools dealing with overcrowded conditions and lack of resources. Then education becomes a high priority. What if we reframe this discussion and begin by claiming our importance for education, which is vital for all of its future citizens in a democracy-always-in-the-making? Now, how does the question of "Should there be a social foundations' canon?" look?

I have also been thinking a lot about "canons" this semester, as it has been an interesting topic for our Cultural Studies Seminar. I am in a Cultural Studies of Education Program at the University of Tennessee, and every fall we have an Introduction to Cultural Studies Seminar with all the new students in our Sports Studies and Educational Studies programs who are concentrating on cultural studies. *Cultural studies* describes itself as multidisciplinary, as well as antidisciplinary. It is a "reluctant discipline" that does not want to claim a starting place or particular history, or important sources, and yet it does. It does not want to be mistaken as "anything and everything" and it does want to do rigorous theoretical work, but it does not want to work within the disciplines such as history, sociology, English/literary criticism, and philosophy, where it has to deal with a canonical text. It wants to start with the problem being researched and then choose where to go and what sources to use based on what is the best way to try to solve the problem being addressed. At the same time, it also insists that the theoretical work it does must be directly connected to practice, it must be praxis in the Paulo Freirean sense of the word.

My colleague Handel K. Wright is an internationally recognized scholar in cultural studies who earned his PhD in curriculum theory from OISE [Ontario Institute for Studies in Education], and who is himself from Sierra Leone, West Africa. He wrote an article early in his career contesting the way people were framing Birmingham, England, as "the starting place of cultural studies," much like educational foundations scholars will point to Teachers' College, Columbia University, as "the starting place of educational foundations." Yet this semester he is worried about what does count as cultural studies. He wants to avoid everything counting, so that even our own students in the cultural studies program at UT [University of Tennessee] are now finding themselves having to defend if their work counts as cultural studies work or not. Do they cite the right scholars? Do they trace their work back to Birmingham? It is ironic to watch my colleague becoming more enamored of history and sources that are important to know, as he ages. He is aware of the irony and jokes about it himself. Still, there is a serious side to this issue as well, for many have tried to pass off mediocre work as cultural studies, in America particularly, and he does not want people to associate low quality with the work he does. He holds high standards for himself and for our students as well.

I would like to suggest that we in educational foundations might want to think about following cultural studies as a model concerning the topic of canonical texts. What if we focus on trying to teach our students the kinds of questions educational foundations scholars try to answer, and then help them discover the possible sources that are out there to help them answer their questions and solve their problems? I am very uncomfortable with suggesting there should be a particular list of scholars that all students in educational foundations should read, and cite in their work. I know that list will be predominantly Euro-Western, White, and male, as those are the people who have had the time, power, and resources available to obtain an education, live a life as scholars, and have their work published, saved, and discussed over time. As a feminist scholar, I don't want to see women's work tacked on as the final chapter in readings for educational foundations courses, as I see so often. I also don't want to see a chapter right before or after women's work that is the cultural diversity chapter, where all non-Euro-Western people of color get to be squeezed. I try to select themes for my courses, and problems, and then choose a number of diverse scholars to read who have contributed to and are continuing to contribute to these themes and problems. It is a cultural studies kind of approach to educational foundations (which might explain why my work seems to fit well in UT's cultural studies program, even though I have never claimed to be a cultural studies scholar). It is rigorous, theoretical work that is directly tied to the practice of teaching/studenting, and it is political work that troubles the very discriminating roots of Euro-Western foundations of education. I am not in favor of a canon for educational foundations, but, like cultural studies, at the same time I do not want to say that "anything goes." I am in favor of a qualified relativist position that argues we are situated, fallible knowers who make decisions based on criteria and standards that are flawed and in need of continual adjusting and correcting. We need other, diverse perspectives to help us recognize our own limitations and become, as Maxine Greene says, more awake and aware of the world around us and the problems we face in education.

Eric Bredo: Thank you, Barb. Let me briefly respond, using it as a way of introducing another aspect of the problem. First, I would like to register a bit of a protest against being characterized as seeing social foundations in tragic, confused, and marginal terms. I don't think I said that. I certainly didn't mean to imply it. And it's far from the approach I (or we at Virginia) tend to take.

I did suggest that we are defenders of precarious values. We are largely focused on what is not conventionally emphasized or included. Or, if you prefer Maxine Greene's version, our job is to keep asking "how things might be otherwise." I don't see this as necessarily making us marginal or confused or tragic. But I think it does make crafting our roles somewhat more difficult than if we had a more conventionally "positive" focus. I'm also far from being a whiner and agree that we need to formulate a center that can hold rather than taking our marching orders from others. I suggested something similar in a recent article in *Educational Theory* ("How Can Philosophy of Education Be Both Viable and Good?") that responded to René Arcilla's suggestion that philosophy of education adopt a skeptical attitude. The trick, I believe, is to find a balance of a positive identity that works while maintaining openness, humility, and ability to change. Skepticism at least keeps one from behaving like the Bush team in Iraq, although I argued that one needs to make positive, normative proposals as well. Although I disagree with your characterization of my characterization of social foundations, I very much like your bringing in support for democracy as a way of casting ourselves in a positive yet not arrogant role. Of course, then we also need to be careful that we actually support democracy in practice.

Barb's points raised another issue for me that we might also want to consider in this discussion. This is to remember that this whole issue of identity trouble is widespread and not merely our own. There's a similar issue afoot in the educational research community as a whole (see the rather good *Issues in Educational Research* edited by Ellen Lagemann and Lee Shulman) and in the world as a whole (Kathleen Hall has a good chapter in the Lagemann book on "Understanding Educational Processes in an Era of Globalization"). So rather than seeing the issue of crafting an identity in divisive times as ours alone, we might note that it is virtually the same as the issue facing many cultures and societies around the world.

Noting this similarity raises an interesting question: Do we have tools designed to be helpful to others facing "postmodern" conditions that would also be helpful to ourselves? I think of many of the insights drawn from classical pragmatism, in this regard, but are there others? Can we use them in this discussion? I'm often struck that those in foundations do not use the tools of their field to analyze or interpret their own situations. Can the doctor heal him- or herself? In other words, I'd like to try to challenge us to use some of our own sophisticated theorizing to address our own issues—just as we'd like others to do. For what it is worth, my use of a populational and functional metaphor rather than an essentialist one for our field was an attempt to do this.

Barbara Thayer-Bacon: Let me clarify my response to you, Eric. When I responded to your initial writing in terms of social foundations continuing to describe itself in tragic terms as a confused and marginalized field of study that has a precarious existence, I was actually referring more to Steve Tozer's CASA essay from 1993 than your essay, although I think the tone is there in yours as well. In particular, I was referring to my students' responses to that essay, and their being surprised that educational foundations sees itself that way.

I don't want to romanticize about our past in educational foundations in general or philosophy of education in particular. I'm doubtful if educational foundations has ever really had "glory days," not like what I have seen educational psychology enjoy, and continue to enjoy today. I also don't want to position myself in contrast to educators, to consider what we can do for educators, or with educators. I am first of all an educator. I am a teacher. *And* I am a philosopher. I have been a philosopher since I was a child, way before I went through any formal training, and I have been a teacher while still a student, as a peer tutor and collaborative lab partner, etcetera. When my students walk into my class I try to help them see themselves as already educators and already philosophers, and that I am there to help them further develop their skills as philosophers and educators. I spend each semester trying to help them see how philosophy is directly involved in the decisions they must make each day as educators. I take great heart in knowing students seek out our educational foundations classes. I also take great heart in noticing that everywhere I turn it seems that I'm reading and hearing colleagues in various fields of education asking philosophical questions and turning to educational foundations to help them understand and solve their problems. This can be seen very easily at AERA [American Educational Research Association], where philosophy of education can be found going on in many of the divisions and SIGs [Special Interest Groups], not just the John Dewey Society and the Philosophical Studies SIG. It seems to be everywhere!

Joe Newman: I'd like to make a brief statement that's somewhat different from Eric's and Barbara's. What I want to talk about is a social foundations textbook that I've written, so let me tell you about the book and spend a moment or two on the difficulties I had struggling with canonical issues as I wrote this book. I didn't even name them that way when I put the book together, but now I realize, yeah, those were the problems I had: the same thing Eric described just a moment ago. A little bit about the book: Naomi [Silverman, editor at Lawrence Erlbaum Associates] and I wanted to produce a book to be used in an introductory course. Not a foundations course, but an Intro to Education or an Intro to Teaching course, which a lot of people like us wind up teaching, even though we're foundations people and we'd rather be teaching in our own specializations or we'd rather be teaching in foundations itself. There's an Intro market, and Naomi said, "Why don't you write for people like AESA members, who are asked to teach this Intro to Education or Intro to Teaching course, and bring a foundational perspective to that kind of book." So that's what I produced with her way back when—it's called *America's Teachers: An Introduction to Education*—and it has done reasonably well.

The first part of the book focuses on teaching as an occupation, teacher salaries, teacher organizations, why people want to become teachers, how happy they are, school law as applied to teaching—that kind of thing. But then the real heart of the textbook—you know, the foundational heart—is a series of chapters that I label "School and Society." There's a full chapter, for instance, on the history of American education—one of the first chapters that I wrote because I was trained as a historian of American education. There's a chapter that used to be called "Philosophies and Theories of Education," and it's now called "Theories of Education." Later I want to tell you a little story about why the title changed and why that was probably a mistake on my part. The book has a full chapter on sociology of education, a full chapter on politics of education, and a curriculum chapter, which is not really curriculum theory but curriculum from the point of view of teachers. This is a very teacher-focused textbook.

Here's what I struggled with: When I came to write the history chapter, that job was the easiest, and although I didn't have the term *canon* in mind, I really pictured historians of education—foundations people, right?— pinch hitting in an Intro course, scanning my textbook for whether they wanted to use it: "Okay, I know Newman; let's see what he's cited; let's go to the footnotes." So as I wrote, I thought, "Here's somebody I need to have in the footnotes. Here's somebody else I need to have in the footnotes." And I thought I could do this all the way through the textbook.

And here I was writing along, thinking, "Man, I'll come up with the list of heavy hitters in each discipline, and then I'll include them in the text, and the footnotes will be easy."

Not so. What I found is that even in philosophy of education, I began to struggle. And when I showed my list—it was not so much a list but the draft of my chapter—to a colleague, who is a trained philosopher of education, he said, "Oh Newman—this is primitive stuff you're doing. But okay. It's an Intro book, and I understand. You've only had one philosophy of education course, so I'll give it a pass. But you're just not doing cutting-edge philosophy at all." He said it was old-fashioned; it was too traditional. I got a mixed review, but I stuck with that chapter. When I got to sociology, it was even more difficult—and I had fewer people whom I could contact to ask, "Would you vet this for me?"

Here's what I finally decided to do—and here's my point. I'm trying to give you a sense of the difficulties I had selecting heavy hitters to include. When I got to the other chapters, I decided that if I did a good job covering the issues, and covering the topics, I probably didn't need to worry that much about the canon. If indeed there was one. Because I probably wouldn't get it right, and I could just do my best covering the issues I thought were important in sociology of education, politics of education, philosophy of education, and kind of hope and pray that the big names would turn up. So the point I've made, if I've made one at all, is that it was very difficult for me beyond my field of training to come up with anything like a prescribed "list," and certainly not a canon.

But then there's a brighter side to it: When I read Eric's work that we exchanged with our e-mail round robin, and he started talking about family resemblance and quoting Wittgenstein, I thought, yeah. There may be a common pool—I think he called it a gene pool or something—a family resemblance among us that might make it possible to come up with a "greatest hits" list; maybe it is possible. And then I really did get encouraged when I saw Eric's list this morning, because he and I come from the same academic tradition—although he's a philosopher and I'm a historian—and we both have gray hair. You know, there's a generational thing here, too. Eric and I are close enough so that we really did at one point in our training and in our professional development dip into that common pool enough to say we're both foundations people. Another thing I want to say: Going beyond my own field, if I had to recommend some readings in foundations—not in history of ed, not in sociology, not in philosophy—and a grad student said, "Give me something canonical to read in foundations," let me tell you what I'd do. I'd go back to some of the original Teachers College, Columbia University, professors, who named the field and taught some of the original foundations courses in the 1930s. I'm going to talk about George Counts, for instance, tomorrow night in my presidential address. Eric included on his list Harold Rugg, who was one of the Teachers College professors of foundations. Yeah, I'd say read some Rugg, read some Counts ... William Heard Kilpatrick of Teachers College was an excellent early philosopher of education. I'd put him on the list. And these are only representative examples, you understand. I'd say go back to that Teachers College group and look at what they took to be foundations in the early '30s when they developed the program, when they put together that academic division and the Teachers College program. Then, I'd say if you want some interpretive work by somebody who's alive, go to Steve Tozer's work. Steve has written a very thoughtful series of essays on the history of foundations. I wish I had written some of that stuff. For someone who's alive and walking among us today, I would say go to Steve Tozer's interpretive work, but also go back to the original source. Don't stop with Steve, go back and read Counts, and Rugg, and Kilpatrick. So that's my point. Our task is difficult, but I think it can be done by thoughtfully identifying a common pool. And I'll leave that to others here.

In conclusion, let me finish the Intro textbook story I started earlier. When I revised my book for a fourth edition, the publisher pressured me to cut some pages, so I went to some of the material my philosopher friends had called too traditional, too old-fashioned: the section on philosophy of education. I cut out the first part of the chapter—the introduction to the philosophies of idealism, realism, pragmatism, and existentialism—and the references to such thinkers as Plato, Aristotle, James, and Sartre. Well, when the revised edition came out, I got letters, e-mails, and phone calls from philosophers of education who had been using my book. They were upset because I had cut out the material that was closest to their hearts—even though some of them had branded the material old hat and old-fashioned! Believe me, I plan to restore that section in the fifth edition. So my conclusion is that we can probably define the canon of an academic field as the sources that people miss most when they're omitted in an introductory or general textbook.

Wendy Kohli: I really like the phrase, "defenders of precarious values." I think that's a great description of what we do. I also like the idea of the "partial and changing list" and the "contextual judgments." And that's what I want to focus on. Going back to the questions of what is *social foundations*, I've never actually taught a course called Social Foundations in 22 years of teaching. I think every context is really different. So to say, well, what would we use, especially texts, I would have to say, "it depends." Not just on the school you're in, but also what the curriculum of that school is. Are you teaching graduate courses? Are you teaching undergraduate preservice? For example, I've only taught graduate-level, master's preservice and in-service teachers. For me, choosing the books for a course on contemporary issues of education—which could be a social foundations course or it could be something else, depending on how somebody conceptualizes it—you have to look at what the purpose of that course is in the curriculum for that particular teacher preparation program. Is it supposed to serve the history and philosophy requirement, or is it, as in Fairfield University, an addition to philosophical foundations, where people take two foundations courses? Choosing what I teach in those courses is a different process than what I might do if my students only took one foundations course. In some places, that one course has been transformed into foundations of multicultural education.

So I think the whole issue of context is really important, as is the level at which you're trying to reach students. For me, I never—no offense to Steve, or to Joe, or to anyone who's written a textbook—I never use textbooks in graduate courses. It's a principle of mine because I want them to read texts, full books, with the original authors if possible. That doesn't mean that I don't gain from textbooks, but I really want them to have to grapple with the full texts. Of course, this leads to bigger problems, because then I must decide which ones to choose for a 14-week course. And can I really do justice to them? So it doesn't get rid of the problem. I'm just pointing out the dilemma for me in choosing readings.

I also want to think of what values and content we are defending in our efforts here. The purpose of an Introduction to Education course for undergraduates is a very different kind of course from a graduate level philosophical foundations course. The one I teach at Fairfield is a requirement for all master's programs in the Graduate School of Education, which includes school psychologists, school counselors, and media specialists, as well as teachers. Which is why I have to think of my clientele, too. I need to ask, what I am hoping to get from this, and what am I hoping they will get? What's the point of the course? I don't have a canon with regard to specific authors or texts. But I do organize around specific subjects and themes. In revising the course one semester, I ended up with almost every book except Dewey written by a woman philosopher of education. The students said, "Hmm, this is interesting." It just wasn't "the usual suspects." But we ended up covering the usual subjects through perennial questions and themes. It encourages students to try and read something new that's out there. Of course, I also point them to the more "canonical" texts as well. At the same time, I *always* have them read Dewey. I always have them read Dewey—for lots of reasons, including I want them to see that what's happening in the present is not new: that in education, there is nothing new under the sun. People build on each other. But when I teach Dewey, I also want to include Jane Addams, in order to talk about the Progressive context and ask, Why does Dewey emerge as *the* one who was put forward as the primary progressive educator when in fact there was a collective of people? That's part of what the canon does—it reinforces a very partial picture and reifies reality.

In the philosophical foundations, after realizing that I didn't just have K–12 teachers in my class, I needed a text that dealt with psychologically oriented issues, too. I found Howard Gardner to be a useful bridge—he thinks philosophically as well as psychologically, with practical implications. Now I know that my colleagues in PES [Philosophy of Education Society] would exclaim, "You use Howard Gardner in a philosophy of education class?" But it works for my context, in that particular group of students. So, I think we have to use our professional and intellectual judgment in our situations and generate a really big list. But I still don't know about that list!

Barbara Thayer-Bacon: It's interesting in hearing you talk about your context … I started in a teacher education program at Bowling Green. It was one of the biggest teacher education programs in the country. I think they graduate over 400 teachers each year. And I started with an Intro to Education course with 190 students. And the course was supposed to decide whether they wanted to be teachers or not. In my interview, I said, "Well, this is totally contrary to my philosophy of education. I don't think you want to hire me to teach 190 people in a lecture hall." And they said, "Well, we know that the lecture hall isn't working, so that's great. Please change it." So I got the job of changing it. For 6 years I taught that course. And I also taught the social foundations course that they took as juniors and seniors. I struggled at first with realizing, feeling very obligated to all of this history and sociology and philosophy, and how to fit all of this into one course. And feeling apologetic about using my philosophy … and at some point I took ownership of it. And decided, no, I have a PhD in philosophy of education, and they hired me to teach here at this program, and it's okay to use my philosophy of education. I designed an Intro to Education course as a philosopher would, looking at the questions of what is education, and what is the role of the teacher, what is the role of the student, and what is curriculum, and what are methodologies and ways that we teach it? I took the way of philosophy of education as the way to set up the whole course. Then I shifted into the social foundations stuff.

At the next level, I ended up writing my own text. Because I couldn't find my own example of a philosophy of education text that I thought modeled for teachers who have no background in philosophy at all why philosophy even matters to them. And why they should even study this and think about this. So I wrote *Philosophy Applied to Education: Nurturing a Democratic Community in the Classroom*, as a way to set a model for them that it does matter. And you're dealing with philosophical questions all the time. That meant not using Steve Tozer's book, not using other books, and at some point as I was dealing with curriculum, it just kept getting larger and larger and larger as I kept trying to make sure that I was covering all these different things.

I came face to face with the fact that there was no way I could possibly do it and do it well. And so Sir Alfred North Whitehead's philosophy came crashing in on me: Do a few things, and do them well. And that's what I try to do. I try to do a few things, and I try to do them well. And I trust my students. That's my Montessori background as well. I trust my students that if I teach them how to do a few things well, they're going to take that and they're going to go off in their own directions with that. My social foundations course was also supposed to take care of Bowling Green's multicultural education requirement. Fifty percent of my curriculum was supposed to be in some multicultural perspective. So that shaped how I taught that course, and it has ended up shaping my research in a lot of ways. But I tried to put the choices back in the student's laps, and allow students the opportunity to choose within the themes and within the issues and topics what they were interested in. And they got to build their own reading background from that, instead of me feeling like I had to make all those choices.

Now when I went on sabbatical, it forced me ... I had the time to actually re-look at what I was doing. And I made a political decision when I was on sabbatical. I had as a student, as an undergrad, and as a graduate student, never read any work by women. Or minority scholars. As I looked at my class, I felt like it was the same kind of deal. By the time I finished all these canonical voices that I felt like students should know, these voices of women and scholars of color were tucked in at the end. And if you look at most social foundations texts, there's a chapter on multicultural education and there's a chapter on feminist theory. And they're at the end. And so I made a political decision based on Jane Roland Martin's looking at how we need to redefine education and include women's voices and include different cultural perspectives all the way back to the beginning. And I had to really think, how am I going to teach a classical philosophy of education course with Plato and Aristotle and Locke and Rousseau, the folks you named. And up through Dewey and James, and get women's voices in there.

So I use Jane Roland Martin's *Reclaiming a Conversation*. And we read Plato. And then we read what Jane has to say about Plato. And we read Susan Okin's *Women in Western Political Thought* about Greek society, so the feminist perspective comes in right from the start, and is right in there as the critical voice all the way through. Martin and Okin help me with Plato, they help me with Aristotle, they help me with Locke, they help me with Rousseau. I'm one of those students that when I was taught to read Rousseau, we didn't read the chapter on Sophie and Sophie's education. It's like Jane describes. I realized, wow, I need to make sure this doesn't happen with my students, and that they see the political side of what goes on in choosing what voices are heard and which ones aren't heard. And that that's all the way through the course. So I guess without realizing it I took a sort of cultural studies view of my teaching and the curriculum I was using. When I get to Dewey now, we read Charlene Haddock Seigfried's book *Pragmatism and Feminism*, and we get those women's voices in there and all those stories about women in progressive education. Those voices have disappeared, and I didn't know about those voices until I read her text. And so it's been a recovery of work for me as well. But that's how I deal with the social foundations. And how I as a feminist scholar and as a cultural studies scholar wrestle with it. I see it as a political issue.

Dan Butin: Can I follow up with two questions then? Because I'm very sympathetic to the idea of following specific themes and issues either from a disciplinary perspective or from an individual's theoretical perspective. But what I'm wondering—Barbara, you brought up this idea of cultural studies—is if approaching social foundations in this manner leaves us open to the problem of an "anything goes" mentality. Put otherwise, do we allow— Eric, to use your notion of tools—do we allow people to use tools that we or other so-called social foundations scholars would say, "You know, that's not really a foundational perspective"? And second, to push the political point slightly more, if we don't define our boundaries to one extent or another, won't others define it for us? I've seen several foundations books out there that are written by non-foundations people. They're very popular, but they don't seem to be talking about foundations the way we seem to be talking about foundations.

Barbara Thayer-Bacon: Fear of "anything goes," I'm not worried about that. For me, I'm much more worried about the voices that haven't been heard, that haven't been in the conversation, and making sure they get in the conversation. So I see that as sort of a fear of relativism, and as a philosopher of education a few years ago I decided to come out as a qualified relativist. I decided to embrace that concept and work for how can we think about relativism in a much more nuanced way. We had absolutism being softened so that it didn't have this heavy universalism. In my field, Harry Siegel has worked really hard to soften this concept of absolutism, but he still wants to hang onto it, due to the fear of relativism. And so I decided to work at it from the other side, and think about qualified relativism. That's the idea that we need to get as many people involved as we can in this conversation and that's how we enlarge our views and enlarge our perspectives. And so I'm not worried about that here.

Steve Tozer (from the audience): Just a couple of things. One is that something got assumed in the discussion that I think needs to be made much more explicit. You talk about the canon as a tool, and what are the purposes to be served. And when you talk about context, you say something like, "Our most shared value is the appreciation of the excluded." However, nobody really talks about what are the fundamental purposes to be served. And I think Wendy's right that you can't give an answer to that apart from context, so context is critical. So, for me, already when you try to get some agreement on that, which is a necessary step before I think you can make much progress on the concept of a canon, already the question is, "What are the purposes to be served by our teaching of social foundations courses?" That right there generates the kind of discussion that I think is more foundational than the canon, so it would be interesting to have a few comments on that.

I also have an anecdote to share with you. I spent eight hours with R. Freeman Butts [the only still-living member of the Teachers' College group of the 1930s and '40s] last February, in interviews about social foundations. And I asked Butts to reflect for me on this difference that he had with disciplinarity … with the single disciplinary history of education rather than the multidisciplinary sociological, philosophical, and historical perspective on education. I knew that Butts was multidisciplinary, so I asked him what he thought about that. And he said, "Well, I think I have a different answer now. I don't think it's the discipline that matters so much one way or another. What I think matters is whether you're serving democratic ideals or not." He was 90. That struck me as pretty damned profound. What's the fundamental purpose to be served here?

Eric Bredo: I think that's a very good point. One other way of thinking about social foundations is it's basically about making school more ethical. And if you think of ethics and ethical conduct as a species of mutually co-operative behavior, it involves the question of how you can get all the interests, all the goals that are involved, on the table, in the discussion, so that you can actually try to harmonize them. And that clearly means that issues that are involved but that commonly don't get on the table have to be included in the discussion. It means you have to actually establish some kind of mutuality so it isn't just, "Hey I've got this view; you've got that view." You actually have to come together to see some common way. I think that's part of what we attempt to do that I see as closely related to Butts's point. I am also struck with Emerson's metaphor of humanity as once being a single organism whose limbs got chopped off and now going off in separate directions. Maybe we actually need to help one another rather than simply acting as separate, unrelated limbs. I'm also struck at the resistance to the notion that we have a common humanity, as though that denies difference, which to me is kind of silly.

Audience Member: I don't know if it's a question, maybe it's a comment. I really agree with Whitehead. I think that this notion of doing small things and doing them well is a profound thing that we need to do. And whether we frame it in terms of questions, or themes, or the context ... I stick to ancient text sources and then include my own ideas and that's it. Because what we're fighting for I think in foundations courses is to undo a lot of what's being done in the public schools with this superficial kind of fragmented knowledge that is based on lists and names, and we need to get students to thinking deeply about issues and take time on those issues, so that's my thinking about this. I think that we shouldn't worry too much individually. I agree that all of us have this bias. That if we put it on the table, and make students aware that this is our particular bias, not someone else's, and they're welcome to disagree with it, we don't have to necessarily worry about covering everything.

Wendy Kohli: Right. Because that's the other thing. Covering the material is what we're all trying to get them *not* to worry about. And yet, we find ourselves in the same situation. This makes me think we need another panel for next year. If we take the risk of doing a roundtable of some kind, we could bring our syllabi and talk about how we construct our courses, and why we make the choices that we do. We could talk about the different contexts in which we teach and examine the purposes of our respective courses in those contexts. In so doing, we could explore how this relates to the general purposes we assume about foundations-like courses. This could be a really nitty-gritty, yet theoretical, conversation about what is it that we do. We don't talk about our teaching very much. Every time I do a syllabus, I'm figuring out what is social foundations or what is philosophical foundations, because I'm deciding which books are worthy. I've started using fewer books—four or five—because I've found six felt too much like "covering the material." With four I get to the key questions, and then refer students to other texts that they can explore more deeply on their own.

Audience Member: The preliminary question that we should use is, "How do we defend ourselves in the field of education?" Because what is education supposed to be? I tease my colleagues all the time, "What justifies your presence on the whole campus, in the program?" Most folks really don't care about foundations. Foundations can literally be taught by a school drop-out. [The key issue is,] what's the relationship between the body of knowledge in foundations of education and the preparation of teachers? It's not about what constitutes the canon. That's secondary. Nobody asks for the canon in elementary education. Nobody asks for the canon in special education. Nobody asks for the canon in whatever. Why are we pinpointed?

Eric Bredo: I think those are very good questions. I guess my response to the first question about our function is that it is probably hard to articulate it in terms of the defense of precarious values. But there's another way I think about it that I also use at times, which is that we're trying to counteract fragmentation and lifelessness in the educational system. In my institution, the gifted teachers get trained at one end of the school, and they get one set of theories. The special education teachers then get trained at the other end of the school and they get another set of theories. The administrators are trained downstairs and the teachers are trained separately upstairs. Meanwhile, the counselors are in some other place. By and large these people never talk to each other or have a class in common.

That's only one set of fragments caused by the division of labor in our school. There is, of course, a whole other set of fragments caused by class, race, gender, and other divisions outside of the school. Part of our job is to try to weave these intellectual and social divisions together so that people can see the connections between different aspects of education that occur in practice but tend to be overlooked or institutionally separated. Second, there's also the issue of deadness, or goal displacement, when means become ends in themselves—when schools become simply factories for producing students who can pass tests. Part of our job is to address these issues and help point the way to forms of education that can serve a wide public interest in a lively fashion.

Now in terms of who's judging us, that's a very interesting question. We had the legislature pressing on the University of Virginia a few years back, saying, "You guys, you have to develop measures of our output." In response, the provost and the president came down and had our central evaluation people sending questionnaires to everybody: "What are your goals? Define them in triplicate. What are your measures of attainment?" And so forth. So they wanted us to play out this ritual of rationality, as John Meyer terms it. Our program works more like a craft guild than a factory, with different goals and different sets of courses for every student. We seek to find the unique ways each individual can contribute to the field, rather than assuming they will all approach it in the same way or all adopt the same roles. So rather than playing the game, we noted that we have some incredibly concise, articulate goals. Only they're not about do you know fact one, two, or three. They're about getting our students to be competent professionals who contribute to the field, who are committed to helping the field advance, who help it better serve its public interests. We test this by checking on our graduates and getting together and seeing how they're doing, how they're prospering, and how they're contributing. So we tried to reframe the issue in a different way that reflected our actual aims rather than an artificial and invented set of defensive ones, and these actual aims are broader than whether all of our students know x, y, or z. In the end they know a lot, of course, but it is not standardized in this way.

Wendy Kohli: I really applaud these comments because I do think that this is the crucial thing. How do we reinforce our relevance to ourselves and to our peers in education? There's a general sense that *anybody* can teach foundations. It's historically true in places I've worked: If you have some general approach to education, you can do a foundations course. When this happens, we are forced to defend (falsely?) disciplinary boundaries, to say, "No, you didn't get a degree in Philosophy of Ed, so, you can't teach that course." I really hate to go down that road, but sometimes it's necessary. Once again, it depends very much on the particular context. We need to be reminded of, and remind others about, why we're here, about our unique and important role, and how invigorating we can be to/for students. I disagree with Eric when he says that students don't see us as the group that brings liveliness to the classroom. I think my students do, once they get to class and experience me as a teacher. I know many of my students dread the required philosophical foundations course. Yet many people have told me after truly enjoying the course that "I never thought I'd like this course. I hated that so I put it till the end when I really should have been placing it early in the program." It's understandable; they're in a culture that devalues what we do. They think it's not going to be relevant. They're thinking, "How will this have any relation to my professional work?" So we have a big job to do. A big job within our own institutions, not to mention the external political pressures. The issue of NCATE is interesting too. I used to be on the Board of Examiners representing foundations associations. It was an opportunity for me to be kind of a watchdog, and to ask, "Where [in the program] are these institutions doing foundations?" and making sure that it was put forward as important for them to do. NCATE provides us with an interesting opportunity to help our non-foundations colleagues conceptualize what we do in preparing educational professionals. I think, paradoxically, the accreditation movement has opened a way to legitimize social foundations.

Audience Member: I think what happened is there are people who are not professionally prepared and whose area is not, for example, multicultural education, who are actually teaching it. In some courses, for example, Blackness qualifies you. Or one's non-otherness. But who's the "other"? [A standard response is] "Once you're not white," or "If you're a female." But that doesn't qualify anyone to teach anything. Someone who is disabled does not automatically qualify. But that's the practice.

Steve Tozer: Some of you know that the Council of Social Foundations of Education is in a sense the political arm for the Philosophy of Education Society, the American Association of History Society, and so on, and all of those groups pay dues to the Council of Social Foundations to have a voice on the table as an educator. So that in fact at least at that one major accrediting agency site we don't lose a voice. For the foundations are constantly under the threat of marginalization. We in the Social Foundations Council of Education don't think that that's enough, what we're doing. And even our ruling entity is right now threatened because we don't have enough membership dues to pay the fee to actually keep [a place] at the table. So it becomes in a sense a kind of moment of marginalization …. however, having said that, I just want to say that we have, many of us here have engaged in episodes of trying to say, "What is it that Social Foundations of Education distinctly brings to the professional preparation of teachers?"

This is not about liberal arts initiative here. This is about something that, if we *cannot* make clear to our colleagues what our distinctive contribution is to the professional preparation of teachers and the ongoing development to their practice then we have a very difficult time defending our place. In a sense, I just want to point out that that is partly a political and partly an intellectual argument. And I don't think that those are separable. And I think that the issue of the canon here started out not so much as a political discussion but as an intellectual discussion. A young scholar in the field is saying, "Look. What's the shape of the field in terms of the acknowledged texts of the field? To what extent is their consensus about the acknowledged texts?" Which is a perfectly legitimate intellectual question to ask. And what I don't want is for the politics of the field, the important politics of your question, to be undermining the legitimacy of that question, either. These two things do go hand in hand, and it is right and good that they end up being discussed in the same session. At the same time, this remains a legitimate pursuit among a community of scholars: What are we teaching? Why are we teaching it? What is the range of materials that we use to teach it, and how do we use those materials?

Dan Butin: I asked the question knowing full well that we're going to get into these political issues. But you are exactly right, we have to be able to articulate [what it is that we offer]—for example, I was speaking recently to a student who took Educational Psychology and my class at the same time, and at the end of the semester he could articulate what he got out of Ed Psych. He had a much harder time articulating what he got out of my class toward his teaching practice.

Steve Tozer: That brings me to Wendy's point that there's a culture as such that students have this condition that tends to be negative going in it. Second, many empirical studies over the years have shown that teachers themselves claim that among the least valuable courses they took were among their social foundations courses. But it's also in part that over 50% of people teaching social foundations are not trained in social foundations. So if you have the majority of people teaching social foundations who are not trained in social foundations, and they resort to watered-down textbooks that don't represent the tradition of social foundations, then, well, you're going to get that very outcome. So again, the issues remain political and intellectual at the same time.

Audience Member: Who'd allow somebody to teach about school finance that knew nothing about school finance?

Steve Tozer: When there is a foundations person on the board of examiners who raises that issue, you get an indication of the weakness of the institution. When there is not a foundations person to raise that issue, it may not be clear about why a certain person was not qualified to teach foundations. "That person has a PhD" [is the presumption]. So this is one of the values of foundations people participating in that discourse at the ground level. Because unless somebody at the foundations level says to the unit board, "This is a weakness in this school. Those people aren't qualified," then the unit accreditation board isn't going to say anything that they won't know. However, it takes somebody knowledgeable about foundations to see that that curriculum person really doesn't have the background. So that's the shortest answer I can give.

Audience Member: I wonder if one answer to that one question of our value *is* the canon. [For example], it's a fact that they won't graduate [from my institution] without having read Dewey's *School and Society* in their curriculum. That text is not taught in elementary education. For elementary education people, Dewey would never be read. And yet they find it hard to disagree that Dewey should be read. And they would find it difficult to disagree that Rousseau should also be read. So I think that's at least a partial answer. But that is not an answer that goes as far as I hear you all taking it, that the canon is anything, or many things, or a lot of things. I do think that we have to say, "No, well, the canon is *this*." And I do think we're better off that way.

Eric Bredo: Great response. And this brings us back to the canonical issue again. As Wendy suggests, some things may involve great overlap. Maybe a lot of people love a certain text or think it is vital, whereas others are shared by fewer, placing them more on the periphery. But you don't have to draw absolute lines. You can have choices. More or less constrained choices .... The approach outlined earlier [a population metaphor where communities have something in common because they sample concepts or materials from a common pool] allows for degrees and areas of overlap, rather than requiring absolute sameness or difference. It is not hostile to the notion that some materials may be of crucial importance because they are used by almost everyone, whereas others may be *more* marginal to the field as a whole, although valuable for certain specific purposes or to certain people. A curriculum could then be put together emphasizing different sampling rates from different parts of the "pool." For instance, student choice might be constrained more in some areas than in others. Some things might be required reading for everyone, some might involve choice among three or four good works, and some might have even freer choice among alternatives. This allows for relative degrees of constraint or centrality, giving us greater flexibility.

Now that I think about it, this approach may also give us a way of handling the [evaluation] issue, raised earlier. One way to handle this, which is somewhat different from the approach I suggested earlier, is to evaluate a student's competence in using different sets of concepts or different spheres of knowledge, with different degrees of choice within such sets. For instance, one might be required to be familiar with three out of four really central works but only two out of 20 more peripheral ones. In each case one would have choice, in, say, selection of questions to answer for an examination, but some choices would be more constrained than others. This would, again, leave room for both individuality and commonality.

Finally, let me return yet one more time to the issue of how we conceive of our function. I began by suggesting that we are defenders of precarious values. Later, I suggested that our job is to help relate the social and intellectual fragments into which education tends to be divided so we can have a more cooperative and continuous form of education. Let me now suggest a third take on the issue, which is that it is our job to offer "perspective." This is similar to both of my earlier suggestions in that people with perspective do not focus only on a single core or center of attention. They consider the fringe and what is excluded. They also consider how things that are chopped up into functional or social pieces are in fact related, if only indirectly, even though this is not evident to those in each role or group. I sometimes call social foundations "policy studies with a memory." That's part of it surely, as historians like my friend Joe Newman would emphasize. There's also social and cultural and intellectual perspective (not that these are mutually exclusive). But the point is that another way to understand and promote our function is to say that we attempt to offer perspective on issues that others treat in more narrowly focused ways. And the reason perspective is important is evident any time one sees a person persevering in solving the wrong problem at the wrong time.

Joe Newman: Let me ask the gentleman who just raised the question: Would you push hard for Dewey, or would you push hard for that particular work by Dewey? Was that just an example to make a point?

Audience Member: I don't know if it's especially necessary for that text, although I think that text works well. I guess that I think that that text lets me answer all of the objections that anybody would care to ask about foundations classes. It lets me answer the elementary educators who may be dubious about the role of foundations. It lets me say, "Look, you want to talk about hands-on education. You want to talk about stations, and learning centers. You want to talk about all of those things, but you are not reading Dewey!" And now this to me is a little bit of a miracle, why you would not read Dewey and get into alternate approaches for elementary education anymore. But meanwhile you get to a child-centered curriculum, which speaks as much to secondary students as it does to elementary students. Although it sort of blows the mind of the elementary teacher that they have to know a whole continuum, they have to know the end and the place where we're going before they know what they should be doing. And all of the agenda in between. It gives us a whole range of broader issues to talk about. And I think my course becomes an interest to students and perfectly defensible to all of my peers. I think that it becomes virtually impossible for them to argue against my course, because that's where that really great discussion happens. Now I have to tell you I was sitting here thinking that I had gone to the wrong school or something. I'm in the sixth week of talking about Plato's *Republic*, and we've got about three more to go. And so this gives us a little chance to see where my bias is, and I can defend the use of that text in that kind of depth in the same way.

Joe Newman: I think it would be impossible for a group like us to ever reach agreement on a prescribed way of doing this. To make ourselves politically defensible, more politically defensible, I still fall back on Eric's original position that we have to identify a common pool that we're drawing from. Let me tell you why I defend that so strongly, and why I think you're on target in saying, "You know, we have to teach *something*." And in your case it sounds like it's philosophy: It's Dewey, it's Plato. A colleague of mine in the early eighties, when I first came on the academic scene, lost her job at a major state university because she insisted—and she was a trained foundations person—on using *Zen and the Art of Motorcycle Maintenance* as her only textbook. We would pull her aside and joke with her; she used to come to this conference. We'd say, "You know, that's a little too far out." We all had long hair; we were all hippies then. But using that book alone struck us as a little too far removed. We didn't use [the word] *canon*, but [we asked], "Are you sure you can raise all those important issues through that book?" Somewhere between "You have to do Dewey, and you have to do Plato, and you have to look at this list" and letting professors teach anything and everything, there has to be a middle ground. I don't think it's defensible to teach a whole foundations course using just that book [*Zen*], although it is a neat book. Doing that cost someone a career. That's an academic issue, and it's an issue of job defense and political defense.

Barbara Thayer-Bacon: I just want to say that Conrad Pritcher was one of my senior colleagues at Bowling Green, and he used that text. And it was one of the things that drew me to Bowling Green, that made me curious and interested in Bowling Green, in how he was doing that and why he was doing that. I think that a really important thing for us to keep in mind as we do social foundations is that we offer teachers and students a chance to understand the field of education within a social, historical, and political context. And that gives them a chance to find a way to critique what's going on in the field of education and have the chance to actually talk about issues. I know that someone said here that students never get the chance to talk to each other because they're stuck in their fields. So you've got special education, and you've got elementary education and secondary education, and I know that our social foundations courses are often the one place where they get to come together. And my students will often say that even at the doctoral level that's still happening: The doctoral level social foundations course I'm teaching right now has in it instructional technology people, ESL [English as a second language] people, it has elementary and secondary education PhD students, as well as cultural studies students, this whole amazing mix of people. And that is an important conversation that's going on across all of those discipline boundaries. But it also is a place where you can gain some sense of the context of education. So you know what's been going on historically in education, and you know the philosophical arguments that have been going on and the sociological views that have been argued over the years. And it allows them to have a chance, a way to critique their current situation that I think is vital.

Dan Butin: Yes, it seems to me you can't be monofocal—at least the way I construct my course is that I have a unit on philosophy and history of education, a unit on sociology of education, a unit on anthropology of education, and a unit on the politics of education. So my students see that anthropological questions are different from philosophical questions, which are different from sociological questions. And it seems to me that you can't teach a social foundations course simply from a philosophical perspective, or simply from a feminist perspective. It seems that inherent in the discipline is the multidisplinarity of it. So for the sake of argument, can we sit down and make a maxim that social foundations has to have at least two disciplinary social perspectives in it?

Audience Member: For me, the point of social foundations is to teach skills on interdisciplinary balance. And the keyword there is discipline, and that means history, sociology, and philosophy .... Oftentimes, as historians of education, we talk about the history of education and the skill of historical analysis. The skill of historical analysis and the skill of sociological analysis are really critical and to me really distinct to what we do. And I often feel that to advocate that kind of position is to argue to not advocate a multicultural education. That cultural studies and multicultural education talk about diversity, and we're talking about skills. And that's different. And I really argue against that. I think that to be able to center social foundations about how to develop those skills and how to spread social foundations across the diversity and across the issues that come into education. But in a way they're probably going to have the skills anyway. But I'd just really advocate that.

Eric Bredo: Just briefly, social foundations came about at [Columbia's] Teachers College [TC] because the disciplines were wandering off by themselves becoming isolated and with opposing interests. Those at TC wanted to apply varied disciplinary tools to solving common social problems, such as those emerging from industrialism at home and totalitarianism overseas. This way of utilizing the disciplines makes us think about why we have them in the first place. What are they for, anyway? Certainly, they involve specialists getting together to work on problems they are interested in. But they also involve the attempt to develop intellectual tools and results that address human problems. So the question is, how do we bring that back together again?

In our group at UVA [University of Virginia] we've got a historian, an anthropologist, a sociologist, a philosopher, and so forth, and the commonality we experience is really great despite being serious about our respective disciplines. What we all do in common is, as I've suggested earlier, attempt to bring perspective to common ways of conceiving things in education. So our anthropologist (Diane Hoffman) might show how for a given society or culture, "No, we don't do that this way here." And acting as the philosopher I might say, "Well, there are other ways to think about it." And our historian (Jennings Wagoner) might note how "It wasn't always like that." So in fact we have a rather common moral purpose that works across the disciplines very well. There is skill involved in doing this sort of thing using any discipline. But the centrally important skills are rather broad, and can be pursued competently in many different ways. Just think of anyone that you respect in your own field and consider what they can do well as opposed to what you can do well and I think you will see that here, again, an essentialist approach is both unrealistic and unnecessary.

Wendy Kohli: But this gets at a different level of the question. I think that part of one of our conversations over e-mail focused on what a PhD program needed to do to train social foundations scholars. That's a different issue from what do we do in our teacher education program as social foundations faculty. And I think this is where it gets a little confusing when talking about a canon. There are very few PhD programs left in social foundations. They've become more diffuse: cultural studies, educational policy, multicultural education, etcetera. So we've all come from different sources to begin with. I agree with your point in terms of disciplinary expertise, but not everybody teaching social foundations has a "legitimate" PhD in social foundations of one form or another. Some of us might've been trained more as sociologists. Or maybe somebody had one course in philosophy of ed, but is mostly a historian. Some of us might even have come out of a curriculum theory program and are teaching foundations. It's difficult to say, in general, that those without disciplinary training are less well trained as social foundations teachers. Once again, it depends.

Audience Member: It's not the canon, or the teachers. I think that's what we've admitted. But is there a canon for people going to doctorate program to teach social foundations? I cannot imagine somebody getting a doctorate in philosophy of education if they haven't read Plato. If they haven't read Dewey. So, there is a pool for the undergraduate. And each of the disciplines in the foundations drift into that pool. How that particular teacher wants to use it in his or her course is up to him or her. But overall, this thing that we call foundations—each one of those subdivisions has to have a canon. I don't understand how you could be trained in any of those disciplines without some standard works that you have to look at.

Eric Bredo: I guess what I was arguing is there may be areas of huge overlap, where basically there is that chance. Where basically you say, "Well you really ought to have this because everybody uses this." There are also areas of looser overlap. But I think there are 56,000 ways to do the sociology or philosophy of education. I really think everybody has a unique way of doing it. So our job is not to fit everyone into the same round hole but rather to work back and forth between each unique student and a varied and changing field, to see how what the student can offer can contribute to the field, possibly changing it in new directions. After all, neither the field nor the student is a fixed essence. Both are plural and changing.

Audience Member: It's not *how* they're a sociologist or philosopher of education, but how they got there. I might be wrong, but I don't know any that didn't read Plato. Now there might be some ...

Joe Newman: I'm sure there are some.

Dan Butin: So you brought us back to the beginning, to "Is there a social foundations canon?" So obviously, the answer is ... no. Yes? No?! Thank you very much for coming.

Part II

MODELS OF SOCIAL
FOUNDATIONS PRACTICE

Making Educational Research Real: Students as Researchers and Creators of Community-Based Oral Histories

Eugene F. Provenzo, Jr.

From a teaching perspective, the main purpose of the social foundations of education is to assist students in understanding the connections between the educational system and the larger social, political and cultural forces at work in American culture. Underlying the field is an assumption of the importance of *praxis*—that is, the integration of theory and practice.

In this chapter, I discuss my experience, as a professor in the social foundations of education, working with students studying education who create oral histories of their local communities. I wish to suggest that such an approach not only makes research more meaningful by connecting theory to practice, but also represents a model of action research in which students become more politically and socially aware of the communities in which they live. In doing so, I believe the abstract and theoretical reality of the university curriculum can be grounded in the historical experience of local communities—thus achieving *praxis*.

ACTION RESEARCH AND THE IDEA OF STUDENT AS RESEARCHER

The idea of students as oral history researchers is consistent with the activist tradition of the founding leaders in the field of the Social foundations of education, such as William Heard Kilpatrick and George S. Counts. It also resonates with the tradition of action research, which came out of the work of the social psychologist Kurt Lewin (1946), and the philosopher Donald Schön's belief that professionals such as teachers need to be "reflective practitioners."

Action research in education, and more specifically teachers as researchers, can be traced back to the period around the Second World War, and the work of Stephen Corey at Teachers' College, Columbia University. Working through the Horace Mann-Lincoln Institute, Corey and his collaborators maintained that "every teacher is a potential researcher" and that engaging in group research was "a must for good teaching" (McFarland & Stansell, 1993, p. 15). Action research in Education went into decline during the late 1950s, as policy makers began to depend on "experts" to create new knowledge and curriculums (Kincheloe, 1991, p. 19; McFarland & Stansell, 1993, pp. 14–16).

Action research was reintroduced during the 1970s, and by the late 1980s had "aligned itself with the attempt to redefine teacher professionalism" (Kincheloe, 1991, p. 19). In this context, teacher researchers became involved in a self-reflective form of analysis based on their experiences and observations in the classroom. Underlying the idea of teachers achieving praxis through action research is the idea of the teacher as "reflective practitioner." As defined by Donald Schön in his book *The Reflective Practitioner* (1983), professionals such as teachers must look beyond prescriptions and formulas to guide their instruction. According to him, "In real-world practice, problems do not present themselves to practitioners as givens. They must be constructed from the materials of problematic situations which are puzzling, troubling and uncertain" (p. 40). Historical research—and the social foundations of education in general—have the potential to contextualize the actual work and practice of teachers in the classroom.

Historical and social/cultural knowledge extends the types of questions teachers have about their work. Thus the question "What specifically am I doing in my classroom?" becomes "What historical forces (race relations, gender discrimination, economics, etc.) shape what I do in the classroom?" "What does it mean that I chose to do it this way?" becomes "What hegemonic forces or traditions in the culture shape or direct how I present my curriculum?" "How are students responding?" becomes "What economic, cultural and political forces shape how my students perceive schooling and the process of instruction?" and "To what extent is their response to me based on my own race, culture or economic standing?"

HISTORICAL RESEARCH AND STUDENTS AS RESEARCHERS

I feel strongly that historical research is one of the most important areas for raising the critical consciousness of students. As someone primarily trained at both the undergraduate and graduate level in history, I find its uses in the education of teachers and other professionals disappointing. Historical research in most universities is something done by professional historians. Undergraduate and graduate students, except those pursuing a doctorate or writing a master's thesis, rarely engage in meaningful historical research. Instead, they read textbooks, review monographs, and write book reviews and reviews of literature based on other people's research. By constructing historical knowledge in this way, I believe many academic historians have often made history dull, insulating it from the real world and, in turn, the testing of their findings and theories in practice—that is, praxis.

Such an approach is essentially undemocratic and uncritical. Like Joe Kincheloe, I believe that historical knowledge is the foundation on which much of our knowledge from other disciplines is based:

> Before ethnography, phenomenology, semiotics, and hermeneutics, history resides. It is history that paints the setting which gives meaning to the details of ethnography, phenomenology, semiotics, and hermeneutics. In Critical constructivist research none of the qualitative methods stand alone—they are all employed in relation to one another. The methods of emancipatory pedagogy are always historical, as memories of the struggles of our ancestors are recovered and put to use in the present. (Kincheloe, 1991, p. 185)

Kincheloe's arguments resonate clearly with the experience I have had in conducting oral history projects with graduate and undergraduate teacher educators at the University of Miami over the past 25 years. In the following sections, I discuss my experience in working on several of these projects and how they can contribute to an historical model of the student as researcher.

ORAL HISTORY AND STUDENT RESEARCHERS

My work on oral history projects with student researchers has been an ongoing part of my teaching and research at the University of Miami. It is not something I do every semester or with every class. These projects are time-consuming and often exhausting. Many times, projects are the outcome of a crisis in the community. During the Mariel Boat Lift in 1981, for example, students and I collected interviews with newly arrived refugees. Likewise in 1992, following Hurricane Andrew, I undertook a large oral history project with students dealing with the impact of the storm and the recovery efforts of the community.

Often these oral history projects have been a direct outgrowth of the interest of students. When I first came to the university, for example, I found myself teaching a social theory course to a group of graduate students primarily interested in reading instruction. Students in the class indicated an interest in conducting oral history interviews with leading figures who had contributed to the field of reading research or children's literature and who were from Florida or who had retired in the area. Over a dozen interviews were eventually conducted with people such as the science writer Hebert Zim, the children's writer Marianne Prieto, and reading specialists such as William McCall, Emmett Albert Betts, Albert J. Harris, and George Daniel Spache. Several of these interviews were eventually published in a regional journal, *The Florida Reading Quarterly* (Provenzo & Carneal, 1980; Provenzo & Moller, 1980; Roland & Provenzo, 1982).

Significantly, the topics for these projects arose directly out of the interests of the students. They were subjects they wanted to pursue in relation to their own professional work and development. My initial approach involved having students read about oral history methodology and then have them begin to discuss, as a class, the development of interview schedules. As an instructor, I used a previously developed interview schedule drawn from another project about early memories of going to school. Students watched and critiqued me interview several of their classmates. When the interview was over, we would discuss how I approached the interview, what was good and bad about it, possible additional questions that could have been asked, and so on.

Students would then have to prepare their own interview schedules. Dividing into groups, they interviewed one another. Using me as an expert guide, students would discuss their interview techniques, debate with each other about the effectiveness of certain questions and approaches, get comfortable with using a tape recorder, and, in general, improve their skills as oral historians.

Next, each student researched the person they were going to interview and developed an interview schedule. This was extensively discussed and critiqued by me and eventually brought back to class for review by the group. The interviews were conducted with me present, but only as an observer. On rare occasions I would participate in the interview when students got overly nervous, or got too far off the assigned topic. In general, I found students were more comfortable having me at the interview because the project focused on leaders in their field—people who often intimidated them. By being there, I seemed to provide them with greater confidence and security.

When the interviews were completed, students transcribed them and then were given the option of submitting them to a journal for publication. This involved collaboration between the student and me. Many students simply opted to have their interviews archived in the university research collection and the project ended there. As mentioned earlier, a number of the interviews, however, were eventually published.

A second oral history project involved working with several classes of master's level Cuban exile teachers who were part of a federally funded training program at the university. Essentially, these teachers had received most of their training in Cuba and had been teaching in the Dade County Public Schools for a number of years. Almost all were seeking advanced graduate credit and permanent certification.

Students voluntarily elected to conduct research on the experience of exile teachers in Cuba who had come to the United States following the Communist revolution under Castro. A few students in the two classes where this research was conducted opted out of the project because they were concerned about political repercussions. They were given alternative assignments. For the remaining group of approximately 75 students (two classes conducted over two semesters), the project proceeded.

The project was unique in that all of the students conducting the interviews had themselves been teachers in Cuba. The students' interest in the study was intensified by the fact that they were collecting historical data closely related to their own personal experiences. Questions addressing the ability of the students to be objective in their interviews were discussed at considerable length. Model interviews were conducted by me with students in the class while the rest of class observed. As in the previously described reading project, students discussed and critiqued these interviews. Students then conducted their own practice interviews. Both the instructor and the members of the class critiqued the content and quality of the interviews.

This method for training students, while tentative and experimental in nature, proved to be highly successful. After receiving further instruction, students were sent out into the community to conduct interviews of their own. They were then responsible for the transcription and editing of their interviews under the supervision of the instructor. Tape recordings of the interviews were carefully checked against the typed transcripts. Approximately half of the interviews were conducted in Spanish and were translated for purposes of the study.

Certain problems and advantages resulted as a consequence of having students collect the data for the study. On the positive side, students had contacts with exile teachers within the Miami Cuban community that were much more extensive than those available to a researcher who was not a member of that community. Having shared similar experiences, many students proved to be particularly effective in drawing information from the individuals being interviewed. The interviews were strictly anonymous, because many of those being interviewed still had relatives in Cuba. The candidness and willingness of the former Cuban teachers to discuss their experiences would probably not have been possible without actual members of the Cuban community conducting the interviews. Using students as interviewers also made it possible to conduct many more interviews than would have been possible if only one or two researchers had conducted the fieldwork.

Limitations were imposed by the abilities of different students. The interviews were eventually used as the basis for an article in the journal *Cuban Studies/Estudios Cubanos* entitled "Exiled Teachers and the Cuban Revolution," which was coauthored with a well-known and respected elementary school teacher in the Cuban exile community. (Provenzo & Garcia, 1983) Students in the class elected not to be listed on the article, because they were afraid it might compromise the confidentiality of their informants. Approximately a third of the interviews could not be used in the journal article because of their poor quality. Most of the problems involved students not being skilled enough in their probes and follow-up questions.

Overall, the interviews were highly informative and revealing. Following the nationalization of the schools in 1961, for example, one exiled teacher explained how she felt that she could no longer trust the students whom she taught:

> Most of them were our enemies and were spies. They watched the teachers all the time and the way we behaved about the revolution. In each classroom the principal had some student whose job was to watch the teachers. (Provenzo & Garcia, 1983, p. 9)

Another exiled elementary teacher described:

> Students did not act with the same discipline that they had before. Some of them felt very powerful, either because their families were strong supporters of the government or because they themselves had some reputation as revolutionaries. Of course, they had a new weapon to intimidate everybody in the school, even classmates, that was to accuse them of being counterrevolutionaries. (Provenzo & Garcia, 1983, p. 9)

The research on which I collaborated with students dealing with exiled teachers and the Cuban revolution was important in making me aware as a scholar and teacher of another side of Castro's revolution. My students, and the people whom they interviewed, were not elites, but middle- and lower middle-class intellectual workers. Their experiences brought to me a different understanding of the revolution than I had obtained from the work of people such as Jonathan Kozol in his book *Children of the Revolution* (Kozol, 1978).

The stories I heard from my students and the research they collected did not address the revolution and the struggle for social justice and literacy under Castro. Instead, they described the experiences of people who failed to be reborn as part of the new educational and social system under Castro. What I became aware of with my students was the extent to which Castro's revolution depended on the elimination of the traditional teaching population, curriculums, and books, and on rejection of old models and ways of looking at the world. In the end, the research suggested to me that in Castro's Cuba, the implementation of revolutionary models of educational practice was directly linked to changes in teacher behavior. The research brought a clearer understanding of the extent to which education functions as social reproduction. I came away with the additional insight that in almost every post-revolutionary culture, teachers, ministers, and university professors are often the first replaced, some of the first to go into exile.

HURRICANE ANDREW
AND THE SOUTH FLORIDA COMMUNITY

The most recent oral history project that I have engaged in with my students is one that I have recently completed for publication with my wife Asterie Baker Provenzo entitled *In the Eye of Hurricane Andrew*, and is a collaboration on the part of Asterie and myself with a total of 43 undergraduate and graduate students in the School of Education at the University of Miami.

The book deals with the impact of Hurricane Andrew on the South Florida community. Describing the storm and its impact to someone who has not gone through this type of natural disaster is difficult. Hurricane Andrew struck South Florida early Monday morning, August 24, 1992. Winds were recorded at the National Hurricane Center, five blocks from our home, at 164 miles per hour—at which point the wind gauge broke. Going through the storm was the most frightening and exhausting thing I have ever experienced.

Immediately following the storm, 1.4 million homes were left without electricity. Fifty-two people were dead (*Orlando Sun-Sentinel*, 1992). More than 107,800 private homes were damaged or destroyed; 49,000 of those were uninhabitable. More than 1,600 public housing units were also damaged or destroyed ("Andrew, Recovery by the Numbers," 1994, p. 18A). As a result, 250,000 people were left homeless. Damages were estimated at between $20 and $30 billion. From a financial point of view, Hurricane Andrew was the most costly natural disaster in modern American history. From a psychological and social point of view, the storm was similarly unprecedented.

Almost immediately after the storm, I began informally interviewing people. For me, it was a way of coping, of trying to understand the enormity of what had happened. I also realized that it was an extraordinary opportunity—a moment to witness history. The project continued as a collaborative effort with my graduate students and undergraduate honors students at the University of Miami during the 1992–1993 school year. Nearly everyone who conducted interviews had lived through the immediate terror of the storm. Andrew had dramatically changed almost all of their lives. For them, too, this project seemed to be a way of coping.

Basically, I employed the same type of training techniques that I had used with students in earlier oral history projects. One student opted out of the project for personal reasons and was given an alternative assignment. All of my undergraduate honors students in my Introduction to Education course participated in the project, during both semesters of the 1992–1993 school year. Essentially, each student conducted two interviews with subjects he or she selected. Often students spoke to relatives or friends. Many of the interviews were with specially selected individuals such as Bryan Norcross, a local TV weather reporter who played a prominent role in the storm, or Bob Sheets, then the director of the National Hurricane Center.

The selection of the people to be interviewed and the construction of an interview schedule were a significant part of our weekly class sessions. Interview schedules were drafted, compared, and critiqued—all of this taking place while many of the students were actually in the rebuilding process and still very close to the terror of the storm and the massive destruction it had caused to the community.

Originally, I had simply intended to put together a collected set of interviews. Each student's transcripts would be published privately, reproduced and distributed among researchers and interested parties, and would be filed in the University Archive as a permanent record. As the interviews began to come in, a number of things became evident. The first was that the data were much richer and told a much more comprehensive story than was originally anticipated. In addition, it was clear that although many of the interviews could stand by themselves, they needed to be grouped, analyzed, and compared as a collected body of work.

During the fall semester following the hurricane, extensive discussion was undertaken with students concerning the meaning of the interviews and their relationship to one another. Over the Christmas break I began to draft a larger chronology or framework using not only the interviews but also newspaper accounts, magazine articles, and government reports. These sources, in particular the articles describing the storm and its aftermath in *The Miami Herald*, eventually provided an invaluable resource for putting the interviews in context.

Work continued on the project in the spring. With the permission of my students, I decided to use the interviews to create a full-scale history of the storm and the rebuilding process from the perspective of the community. Simultaneously with this project, a colleague Sandra H. Fradd and I worked on a book length study of the impact of Hurricane Andrew on children and the public schools, entitled *Hurricane Andrew, the Public Schools, and the Rebuilding of Community* (Provenzo & Fradd, 1995).

In the Eye of Hurricane Andrew (Provenzo & Provenzo, 2002) was published by the University of Florida Press in the fall of 2002 for the 10th anniversary of the storm. We consider this book a collective and shared history.

We list all of the students who participated in the project as coauthors and members of the Hurricane Andrew Oral History Research Project. A portion of the royalties for the book has been set aside to fund future research projects in the School of Education at the University of Miami.

In many respects, doing the project with my students was more difficult than if I had conducted the interviews by myself. I am convinced, however, that doing the interviews by myself would not have produced results as rich or representative of different perspectives in the community. Students came up with remarkable subjects—people I would not have known or had access to. One of my African American students, for example, went down to the Black neighborhood in Richmond Heights and recorded the following comment from an older member of the community:

> The black people in Richmond Heights were real good to one another during this time. You know the white man didn't help us. It was the people down there that got out and walked from door to door letting us know where to get food and stuff. The churches down there was real good about helping folk out. They fed us, provided shelter if you needed it, and gave you clothes if you didn't have any. (interview with Roberta Smith, conducted by Tresca L. Whitehead-Jenkins, Coconut Grove, FL, 18 April 1993)

Comments such as this probably would not have been shared with me as an outsider.

It could be argued that the process of creating an oral history of the hurricane with student researchers was out of the normal range of a graduate course on teachers and American society or an introductory undergraduate honors School and Society course. Hurricane Andrew, however, represented a critical turning point in the history of the South Florida community. Although rapidly forgotten on the national level, its impact will be felt in this community for decades to come. It was important to try to understand the role of the storm in shaping the community, and to reflect on the structural and social inequities that it brought to light. Why did it take longer for poorer areas of the county to recover than more well-to-do areas? What role did teachers, firefighters, and police play in rebuilding the community? Who were the real leaders in the community in the days, weeks, and months following the storm? These were all questions that students began to ask, and eventually answered, as our interviews and their analysis progressed.

By having students collect data from the Miami community—specifically about the experience of surviving Hurricane Andrew—historical information was no longer abstracted but became real and, in a Piagetian sense, "concrete." Students were able to see historical events connected to real people and actual places. In doing so, I would like to think that my students became more aware of their own place in history, and even the importance of their roles as witnesses to one of the most important events in South Florida history.

Such insights and experiences are not easily gained in traditional college and university settings. Although demanding, projects like the one just described are rewarding for both teacher and student. Parallels can be drawn to education students doing case studies, observations, and interviews in actual schools. It is here that the reality of what we describe in our classroom lectures and discussions comes to light. Likewise, it is in the social context of community studies like the one described here that social history becomes real.

CONCLUSION

Joe Kincheloe maintains that the idea of teachers as researchers is an old idea made new, which "when reconceptualized in conjunction with a reasonable system of meaning may provide a starting point for a democratic reorganization of the way schools work" (Kincheloe, 1991, p. viii). My experience in doing social and historical research with students confirms this notion. Social and historical research carefully pursued by teachers or teachers in training has the potential to make them critically conscious and reflective about social issues and forces in the local communities in which they live and work in ways that are not as evident when instruction is limited to more traditional methods. When using this model of teaching and research, I am convinced, for example, that questions of social justice, race, gender, class, and equality become more evident.

Expanding the model of teacher as researcher, and in turn the student as researcher, to include social, cultural, political, and historical dimensions is a process that I believe is inevitably empowering—not only for the student, but also for the university instructor and for the profession of education at large. In the use of methods and techniques like the ones outlined here, I believe we will find a greater potential to use the schools to build an improved social order than in the more common models of technical reform that have dominated education in recent years.

Such models are, however, threatening. They attack elite social science and historical knowledge. They raise questions that are not the exclusive domain of specialized academics. As an interdisciplinary scholar, I have always wondered at the opposition I have confronted over "breaking ranks" and working across fields. Working with students on the types of projects I have outlined here has made me increasingly aware of the threatening nature of this type of work.

Undertaking research and teaching models such as I have described is difficult. The model of student as researcher and oral historian suggests a radically new role for the foundations of education, not only within our colleges and universities, but within our educational system and the culture as whole. Most importantly, it also suggests the opportunity to achieve praxis—one that makes history relevant to the work of teachers, and teachers into historical researchers critically exploring and interpreting the realities of the communities in which they live and work.

Note. The oral histories described in this chapter, which were created for the Hurricane Andrew project, are available as audio files and as printed transcripts at the following Internet address: http://digital.library.miami.edu/andrew

REFERENCES

Andrew, recovery by numbers. (1994, 24 August). *The Miami Herald,* p. 18a.

Kincheloe, J. (1991). *Teachers as researchers: Qualitative inquiry as a path to empowerment.* London: Falmer Press.

Kozol, J.(1978). *Children of the revolution.* New York: Delacorte Press.

Lewin, K. (1946). Action research and minority problems. *Journal of Social Issues, 2,* 34–36.

McFarland, K. P., & Stansell, J. C. (1993). Historical perspectives. In L. Patterson, C. Minnick Santa, K. G. Short, & K. Smith (Eds.), *Teachers are researchers: Reflection and action* (p. 15). Newark, DE: International Reading Association.

Orlando Sun-Sentinel. (1992, 24 August). Andrew! Savagery from the sea, p. 5. Orlando, FL.

Provenzo, E. F., Jr., & Carneal, A. S. (1980). Oral history interview: Albert J. Harris. *The Florida Reading Quarterly, 17*(2), 18–19.

Provenzo, E. F., Jr., & Fradd, S. (1995). *Hurricane Andrew, the public schools, and the rebuilding of community.* New York: State University of New York Press.

Provenzo, E. F., Jr., & Garcia, C. (1983). Exiled teachers and the Cuban revolution. *Cuban Studies/Estudios Cubanos, 13*(1), 1–15.

Provenzo, E. F., Jr., & Moller, B. (1980). Oral history interview: Dr. George Daniel Spache. *The Florida Reading Quarterly, 16*(2), 33–34.

Provenzo, E. F., Jr., & Provenzo, A. B. (2002). *In the eye of Hurricane Andrew.* Tallahassee: University Press of Florida.

Roland, J., & Provenzo, E. F., Jr. (1982). An oral history interview of Dr. Emmett Albert Betts. *Florida Reading Quarterly, 19*(2), 5–8.

Schön, D. (1983). *The reflective practitioner: How professionals think in action.* New York: Basic Books.

Chapter 4

Social Foundations as Pedagogies of Responsibility and Eco-Ethical Commitment

Rebecca A. Martusewicz
Jeff Edmundson

The approach to teacher education that we address here begins from a fundamental commitment to the recognition that we live together on this planet among all kinds of living creatures, human and nonhuman, in a fragile but essential interdependence. To push this further, to be human is to live engaged in a vast and complex system of life, and human well-being depends on learning how to protect it. As Wendell Berry (1995) said, "In taking care of fellow creatures, we acknowledge that they belong to an order and a harmony of which we ourselves are parts. To answer to the perpetual crisis of our presence in this abounding and dangerous world, we have only the perpetual obligation of care" (p. 77). To behave otherwise is suicidal.

To become educated as humans means that we must learn how to engage with others to consider questions of how to live on this planet, how to live just and sustainable lives without destroying the immensely diverse system that makes life possible. We argue in this chapter that teachers using a pedagogy of responsibility recognize these relationships as critical to both human and non-human well being. Their work is aimed at fostering the necessary interconnectedness and interdependency between individuals, groups, species and the environment. Although other critically oriented, social justice perspectives on teacher education may

71

pay lip service to environmental concerns, adding it onto the list of race, class, and gender injustices to be studied, we see these approaches as limited by individualism and by an anthropocentric concentration on human culture as separate from and even dominant over the rest of the living world.

In contrast, we believe that diversity must be understood as a motivating factor in all life systems, and not just a matter of cultural politics. If diversity is the generative force in biological as well as cultural systems, it must be protected via the development of both democratic and sustainable communities. And this is where a pedagogy of responsibility begins, with the development of attitudes, languages, and practices—in short, the engagement of ethical responsibilities oriented toward the protection of life systems supporting diverse human cultures. We see this approach as "just good teaching" in a way that goes much deeper than conventional or critical approaches to teacher education.

Thus, this chapter lays out the fundamental principles and practices underlying what we call a cultural ecological perspective necessary to the development of eco-ethical consciousness in teachers. Although we describe the educational practices and relationships as a "pedagogy of responsibility," such an approach is part of a larger movement toward what C. A. Bowers called ecojustice (2001).

Our intent here is to focus specifically on how a pedagogy of responsibility grows out of principles of ecojustice, and is required if we are to address the rising tide of ecological destruction and related cultural domination. Teacher educators must, we believe, begin to recognize the limits of social justice approaches that do not address our interdependence as humans with threatened natural systems. Offering an alternative lens from which to see, a cultural ecological approach asks teachers and teacher educators to attend to this interdependence and to examine the cultural assumptions they unconsciously carry into the classroom.

AN ECOJUSTICE FRAMEWORK

The ecojustice perspective we introduce offers an ethical and political framework that encompasses, deepens, and even critiques social justice thinking, beginning from the recognition that human cultures are nested within and dependent on larger life systems. Ecojustice is framed by at least six interrelated interests/issues that should be taken up by educators:

1. The understanding of local and global ecosystems as essential to human life, as well as the recognition of the deep cultural assumptions underlying modern thinking that undermine those systems.

2. The recognition and elimination of environmental racism, such as the dumping of toxins in the communities of economically and socially marginalized peoples.

3. The recognition of how Western patterns of hyperconsumption reproduce the exploitation of the Southern hemisphere by the North for resources both natural and human.

4. The recognition and protection of the commons, that is, the intergenerational practices and relationships of nonmonetized mutual aid (relationships that do not require the exchange of money as the primary motivation for the relationship), among people and with the land and waters, leading to healthy communities, and the related recognition of the ways that industrializing forces undermine these relations and practices.

5. The recognition, protection, and establishment of earth democracies—that is, the decision-making practices established to ensure the renewal of water, soil, air, plant life, and other living creatures in natural systems, and necessary to socially just communities. Earth democracies exist as spirituality and wisdom in many traditional and indigenous cultures creating sustainable communities in balance with natural systems.

6. The recognition and emphasis on which local knowledges and practices lead to the requisite responsibility in communities for leaving the future generations a viable and healthy environment.

With these broad categories and goals in mind, *a cultural–ecological approach* to teacher education seeks to examine the ways that specific cultural ways of knowing impact natural systems and thus our ability to sustain our communities into the future. What are the specific patterns of belief and behavior, and more specifically the moral codes that are imbedded in the symbolic patterns of a culture that create the relationships and attitudes toward each other and toward the larger community of life in a given culture? Thus, this approach is interested in uncovering the linguistic codes and deep cultural patterns that are exchanged and reproduced in day-to-day life and that create the particularly destructive relationships among humans and with the more than human community.

ECO-ETHICAL CONSCIOUSNESS

If ecojustice is the framework, and a cultural–ecological perspective is the way of analyzing, then the corresponding mode of being and living is eco-ethical consciousness. We define eco-ethical consciousness as the awareness of and ability to respond carefully to the fundamental interdependence among all forms of life on the planet. This way of thinking requires what Susan Griffin (1996) called "a collaborative intelligence," the recognition that human intelligence is part of a vast and complex system of reciprocal relations where the sense-making processes that lead to human cultural forms cannot be separated from the patterns of communication within the natural world, and indeed is highly engaged with such patterns at every moment. In this perspective all life, including human life, is seen as highly dependent on a balance of well-being within this web of interconnected patterns (Bateson, 1972).

Intelligence and responsibility in this sense is defined by the constant willingness to read these patterns, and to understand the ways that our actions as humans impact and are impacted by the world around us. As C. A. Bowers (1999) put it, "A form of cultural intelligence that ignores how toxins introduced into the environment disrupt the reproductive patterns of different forms of life jeopardizes its immediate members as well as future generations" (p. 169).

Although we have become quite adept in the social foundations of education at examining the political, economic, and cultural relations and structures leading to the marginalization of people, the ethical perspectives guiding this discourse are often limited by the same cultural assumptions underlying a technoindustrial or modernist mind-set. Educators interested in social justice look primarily at race, class, and gender issues, as these interfere with economic and social opportunities or access, and seldom acknowledge our interdependence with a more than human world as more than an add-on category. Diversity is generally limited to notions of multiculturalism that range from acknowledgments of differences in foods and holidays, to Marxist-oriented analyses of unequal distributions of resources in a social system stratified around the devaluation of people. Although we agree that the capitalist economic system leads to suffering, we insist that the analysis must go further than human suffering, and the sources must go beyond economic structures, to an understanding of culture.

As Bowers taught us, Western cultures dominated by market ideology and classical liberal conceptions of democracy are based on a technoindustrial model founded on a powerful symbolic system. Drawing on the early work of sociologists of knowledge, Berger and Luckmann (1966) and Lakoff and Johnson (1980), Bowers analyzed the ways that language as a metaphorical system shapes our understanding of and practices in the natural world. He used the notion of root metaphors as the deepest assumptions that structure our worldview. Root metaphors of technoindustrial societies (see the appendix) include mechanism, individualism, anthropocentrism, science as the only valid way to know, and linear conceptions of progress. More than abstract concepts, they are the energy source of our day to day interactions. As generative ideas, they socialize members of the culture for a hyperconsumeristic lifestyle based on material definitions of success and wealth, mechanistic conceptions of life processes, and hyperseparated relationships with the natural world. The universalizing tendencies in the conceptions of science and knowledge reproduce colonizing assumptions that lead to deficit definitions of non-Western or so-called "undeveloped" cultures. Moreover, cultural patterns of belief and behavior, immersed as they are in hierarchized systems of value, contribute to globalizing economic processes that are causing massive loss of biological, linguistic, and cultural diversity across the planet. Although we understand that the link between cultural assumptions—or worldviews—and actual behavior is not deterministic, worldviews tend to define the range of behavioral options that are available to people.

As members of this culture, we are the products of a centuries-old way of thinking about what it means to be human that requires that we see ourselves as atomized selfish individuals programmed with a primarily competitive orientation with the world. We set ourselves apart from and above other life forms (and as history demonstrates, this includes defining some humans as not human or as less valuable in order to legitimate their domination or destruction; Plumwood, 1993). Such a perspective presumes that because we are the creatures who reason, the world belongs to us, and is there for our individual use, pleasure, and accumulation. This is the very mindset that creates war, poverty, patriarchy, genocides, and mass species extinctions (Bateson, 1972; Capra, 1996; Quinn, 1992). It is hardly just or democratic.

Examples of the ways that these metaphors find their way into teacher education programs and on to public school teaching abound, even among the most well intentioned and seemingly well informed. At a recent forum attended by one of the authors, local environmental and community groups, public school educators, and university professors discussed the ways that their work engaged important community and ecological issues. A high school teacher reported that she was teaching her students to think critically about the importance of watersheds. To great enthusiasm from the participants she discussed classroom methods for teaching students to see "wetlands as a living machine." When one of us, Rebecca, asked her undergraduate students to think about what is hidden by such a metaphor, it took them quite a while to come up with anything. Finally, one student said, "Do you mean that it sounds like humans have somehow made the watershed, instead of it being a living body with integrity of its own outside of our uses?" Mechanistic metaphors are so common that we barely stop to think of their implications for our relationships to the natural world.

THE NEED FOR RETHINKING TEACHER EDUCATION

As an example of how this plays out in teacher education, one of us recently observed a colleague known for his passion for social justice. "Technological progress," he said, "specifically schools wired for the Internet, offers new opportunities for marginalized students. They have access to information they could not have access to previously." Another colleague was teaching a lesson on constructivist math. After introducing the concept of having students construct different pathways to get answers, she emphasized that the point was to have students "think for themselves." She went on to point out the social justice implication: that students could find success in different ways rather than having to follow a rigid protocol.

Indeed, it is now common for teacher education programs to focus on social justice across the curriculum. It is widely understood that schools will tend to reproduce the divisions of race, class, and gender unless teachers are explicitly taught to challenge oppressive assumptions and behaviors. Our objection to the first colleague described here is not to his social justice focus per se, but to what he misses: the reproduction of ecologically damaging assumptions. Specifically, he assumes that technological progress—in this case, information technology—is a positive development. As a result, he is essentially telling students to ignore the tremendous environmental and social destruction created by technology, from the rapidly growing toxic waste to the fragmented communities and loss of tradition. Similarly, our objection to the constructivist instructor is to her reproduction of the hidden assumption of individualism. By simply encouraging students to think for themselves, she encourages them to see themselves as individuals outside of society, rather than to see their ideas as rooted in the culture in which they participate. Unconstrained individualism, however, is a basic source of our abuse of the environment; among the results are massive overconsumption and an undermining of community. Moreover, constructivist perspectives often rely on the notion that social transformation emanating from emancipated individuals ought to be the primary purpose of education, yet such points of view disregard the great need for preservation of practices and ways of thinking that will help us to conserve the natural world for future generations. We have more to say about this later, when we discuss the limitations of critical pedagogy, specifically with Freire's ideas.

We are not questioning the competence of these instructors. Rather, we are emphasizing the kind of socialization they have undergone from within a particular cultural framework, and the need to become aware of the ways that specific patterns of belief and behavior are reproduced among educators and passed on to their students. Not long ago, few faculty in schools of education were aware of the ways they reproduced gender stratification when they called more on men than on women, or used gender-specific pronouns to refer to humans more generally. As teacher educators gained more awareness, they challenged their behavior and their language and began to teach prospective and practicing teachers how to uncover hidden assumptions in the symbolic patterns that they live in and exchange daily. In the same manner, we contend that faculty in schools of education must learn to challenge the assumptions that underlie the ecological crisis and the ways these link to social and cultural marginalization as well.

Teacher education must take into account that both social and ecological justice are dependent on the recognition and development of responsible ways of thinking and living found in the intersection of diversity, strong democracy, and sustainability. These ways of thinking take into account and promote the necessary reciprocity between human and nonhuman communities, and look to decision-making processes that consider the community of life as integral to human survival. Vandana Shiva (2002) called this interlocking relationship Earth Democracy. Across the world, traditional cultures based on centuries-old understanding of how to live sustainably offer diverse wisdoms that we ought to be learning from. Instead, they are being threatened by processes of monoculturalization that result from the globalization of Western ways of thinking (Appfel-Marglin & PRATEC, 1998; Norberg-Hodge, 1991; Shiva, 1993, 2002).

The forms of responsibility that can result from cultural ecological approaches to education are necessary to reverse the destructive results of Western modernist perspectives based on hierarchized relationships and assumptions that lead to all sorts of interlocking oppressions, within both cultural settings and the larger ecosystem. These hierarchized relationships, built within a culture's language systems, devalue both human and nonhuman lives, leading to the exploitation and domination of nature and human cultures living within natural systems.

Educators, we argue, must begin to understand and teach about the ways that human cultures are nested within and impact larger life systems. Our very survival depends on ways of living that take into account our interdependence with diverse species as well as diverse ways of knowing. Clearly, some ways of enacting human life on the planet are more sustainable and healthy than others. Engagement with our students about what it means to live responsibly begins here at the intersection of diversity, democracy, and ecology.

A DEFINITION OF PEDAGOGY

Pedagogy is often defined simply as the "how" of teaching, but it cannot be reduced to method, and arguably is not always constitutive of the "good society" (Martusewicz, 2001). Pedagogy is always relational. Framed by particular interests (conscious or unconscious), it can take place in any context, and is generative of an unpredictable array of different possibilities. In this sense, pedagogical relations are both framed by and can lead to an infinite range of identities, knowledges, and practices.

Even in so-called "banking" approaches to pedagogy, the teacher teaches and the students struggle to understand, but what they "get" is always mediated by their unique cultural, linguistic, historical, and familial traditions and meanings, all the "stuff" that they bring to each encounter and relation. As such, every student's interpretation or translation of a given lesson will be a different interpretation, even if the difference is barely discernible or deemed unimportant. And if the teacher is interested in encouraging open discussion, the differences in interpretation can be vast. Just think about a conversation about, say, gay and lesbian lifestyles, or what a community should do about urban sprawl. All sorts of interests, meanings, and prior understandings will influence what students say or think. Such differences generated out of pedagogical relations are important, for sure; necessary and inevitable, they teach us a lot about the problematic relation between diversity and democracy in any social relation.

But differences created within pedagogy are not all desirable or sufficient to sustain well-being among humans or in the world more generally, and thus pedagogy (as a concept and as a practice) should be considered separately from education. What makes a pedagogical relationship constitutive of education, we argue, is ethics—the willingness and commitment to confront the question of how we ought to live together on this planet, what it means to be mindful of and engaged with the well-being of others, both human and more than human. Complicated and unanswerable in any final way as that is, this is where ethics and responsibility intersect with teaching and learning to create pedagogies of responsibility.

Certainly, then, being conscious and intentional about what one believes and wants to accomplish via this relationship is essential. Underlying any conscious approach to pedagogy is a conception of how people learn, a conception of whether and how the status quo is to be challenged or reproduced, and a conception of knowledge, or what it means to know.

Ladson-Billings (1994) drew a definition from Giroux and Simon that emphasized the broader epistemological and moral aspects: "Pedagogy refers to a deliberate attempt to influence how and what knowledge and identities are produced within and among particular sets of social relations. It can be understood as a practice through which people are incited to acquire a particular 'moral character'" (p. 14). With the addition of an understanding of ethics as related to both culture and natural systems, we restate this: Pedagogy, when it becomes educational, is the enactment of an ethical stance, defining what knowledge and identities should be reproduced within and among particular sets of cultural relations. Rooted in particular traditions and encoded by specific metaphors, it is oriented toward the enactment of specific beliefs and behaviors oriented toward the well being of the community of life.

A PEDAGOGY OF RESPONSIBILITY
VERSUS A PEDAGOGY OF LIBERATION

Gloria Ladson-Billings noted that one response to her description of "culturally relevant" teaching is to comment "but that's just good teaching" (Ladson-Billings, 1995). Similarly, we argue that the pedagogy necessary for eco-ethical consciousness is at its heart "just good teaching." But first, we need to emphasize that "good teaching" is a culturally constructed concept, not a universal prescription of best practices. Definitions of good teaching will vary widely not just between Western and non-Western cultures, but within Western societies. For some in the West, good teaching is that which teaches students to be obedient consumers of the status quo, while against-the-grain teaching such as Ladson-Billings's culturally relevant teaching challenges that status quo. To push this even further, good teaching within an ecojustice framework has as its goal examining when to challenge not just the economic but cultural and ecological status quo, and when conserving particular traditions, practices, and beliefs is necessary to revitalize a sustainable community.

Despite our agreement on the importance of good teaching, there is an essential difference between Ladson-Billings's concept of good teaching and our concept. At the heart of Ladson-Billings's work is a Freirean conception of a critical pedagogy or a "pedagogy of liberation." We offer a different underlying conception: A pedagogy of responsibility first asks "what are my just obligations to this community?" before asking, "what are my oppressions (or my students' oppressions) from which to be liberated?" This formulation is not intended to ignore oppression nor to celebrate all obligations, but to refocus against-the-grain pedagogy from unchecked liberationism to an emphasis on the obligations, wisdom, and practices (many of which currently exist within both traditional cultures and industrialized cultures) that are necessary for a just and ecologically sustainable society. Thus, a pedagogy of responsibility exists in the tension between two necessary ethical questions: What do we need to conserve, and what needs to be transformed?

Although a pedagogy of responsibility finds value in the Freirean practices of teachers examining their own lives within communities, and of challenging oppressive social structures, it challenges the underlying modernist assumptions: of progress as positive and tradition as oppressive, of individualism, and of anthropocentrism.

Rather than being predisposed to see tradition as oppressive, a pedagogy of responsibility asks what the consequences of the tradition are for the community, and what would be lost if the tradition was changed. Rather than leaving the source of authority in the students' (or teachers') limited experience, a pedagogy of responsibility suggests that an important and too often ignored step is to look for sources of moral judgment in one's community of experience. What traditions and relationships exist in the community that are nonoppressive and support a community's responsibility to its members? And what could we learn from those who engage such practices of mutual aid and responsibility?

In Detroit, for example, grass-roots activists organized through the Boggs Center and an organization called CPR-Detroit work with people in neighborhoods to use intergenerational knowledge to revitalize relations of mutual aid and subsistence. Their work is important in a context where job loss, White flight, and urban blight is the result of corporate abandonment of the city by the Big Three automakers. In Detroit, a hyperconsumerist lifestyle is impossible for most residents remaining in the city because jobs and a living wage are rare. These organizations help people forced into subsistence levels by valuing and supporting the ways that neighbors use the wisdom and practices passed down through families to help each other. People in these neighborhoods provide aid and care to each other, sharing knowledge about argriculture, food preparation, health and child care, or home repair through storytelling and unpaid exchange of work. While working with a group called CPR-Detroit (Committee for the Political Resurrection of Detroit) to clean up a brownfield, one of us, Rebecca witnessed such nonmonetized exchanges firsthand: women checking on sick elderly neighbors, men working together to fix a roof, or neighbors coming together with their children to till and plant a garden where they could share food. As we worked together to create a playground in that abandoned factory brownfield, a woman brought us a pot of coffee, and people from the neighborhood exchanged stories about all kinds of things, teaching each other about community, about taking responsibility and caring for each other. There was incredible warmth and love expressed in those exchanges. Children shoveled rock and old concrete into wheelbarrows, and elders told stories about their families' lives in the South or about an earlier time in Detroit when Malcolm X or the Reverend Martin Luther King spoke at a nearby church. As we planned to create a neighborhood garden, grandparents and parents spoke with young children about what it means to be good to each other, and neighbors taught each other better ways to turn the soil or build a fence.

In raising the question of tradition, we are not harkening back to a "golden age" in Detroit's history, or in our past as a nation. These are current practices, where shared relationships and knowledges around the creation of community take the place of mall shopping and other money-dependent activities taken for granted in the nearby White suburbs. In an age when paid work is being outsourced, life is regenerated in a constant intergenerational pedagogical exchange that relies on intimate connection to both people and place. This is what we mean by a pedagogy of responsibility, and it is found in what may seem to be unlikely places.

A pedagogy of responsibility also needs to challenge the tendencies in Freirean pedagogy to reproduce the notions of universalism, anthropocentrism, and individualism central to modernity. The desire expressed recently by Moacir Gadotti, director of the Freire Institute of Brazil, to use Freire's final work to bring to Brazilian peasants a "planetary citizenship" is clearly based on the assumption that Western ideas are universal models for healthy communities. Such objectives also continue the role of the intellectual or the teacher in the Freirean model as that of "emancipator," a distinctly paternalistic approach to education.

Further, Freirean pedagogy is anthropocentric. Although it may challenge the capitalist tendencies to exploit nature, it puts in the background the needs of the biotic community, thus tending to discount its importance in favor of the self-reflective critical individual. In fact, until just months before he died, Freire ignored ecological concerns altogether, an oversight Gadotti and the Freire Institute are now seeking to resolve via a universalizing approach already mentioned. Such thinking discounts what Gregory Bateson called an ecology of mind, where human consciousness is understood to be nested within and dependent on a larger system of differentiation and communication in the natural world. Although a pedagogy of responsibility decenters and then refocuses humans as part of a complex web of life, the Freirean framework retains the enlightenment emphasis on the individual as the basic social unit.

When progressive pedagogy from Dewey to Freire encourages students to reflect critically, or "think for themselves," it encourages them to see themselves as the creator of ideas and as the source of moral authority. Not only does this stance hide the true cultural roots of any person's thinking, it serves to further distance them from the belief that we have an obligation to the communities in which we live.

In Freirean work in the West, the focus on liberation can lead quickly to glorifying the subjective, as in Ellsworth's (1989) critique of repressive tendencies in critical pedagogy, which ends up as an enthusiastic paean to liberation from traditions of all kinds, or in McLaren's work (e.g., 1995), where he encourages students to question everything, thus developing a "pedagogical negativism." Or consider the recent work of Giroux and Lankshear, who have seen liberatory potential in "boundary crossing," or decentering modern identity and authority structures by crossing cultural borders (e.g., Giroux, 1996; Lankshear, 1996).

By emphasizing the breaking of bonds, the notion of decentering both puts a premium on deauthorizing traditions (the practices that socialize and constitute identity) of all kinds, including existing, intergenerationally maintained practices that are healthy, and leads to healthy identities and forms of consciousness. The traditions and practices that are not examined and named remain hidden and so do the associated forms of identity, leading those within this paradigm to believe that what is needed is the transformation of consciousness. As Freire put it, "Each generation must rename the world." To eagerly undermine traditions in favor of creating a new "transformative" subject is functionally identical to the drive within industrial capitalism for growth and new markets and the modernist worship of "progress" as linear and evolutionary. We assert that it may be more important to ask what needs to be conserved in and learned from communities where mutual aid and an understanding of earth democracy are already at work, than it is to focus solely on a transformative model of education, where the individual is seen as needing "conscientization," or a more developed form of consciousness.

By drawing on the historical notion of the "commons" where a community shares its relationship to a specific place both bioregional and cultural, a pedagogy of responsibility can ask what traditions of mutual support and of responsibility to the nonhuman environment also exist. Work like that of Wendell Berry (1995), and Wes Jackson (1987) of the Land Institute in Kansas, Frederique Apffel-Marglin and PRATEC with the Quechua peoples of Bolivia and Peru (1996), or Helena Norberg-Hodge and the International Society for Ecology and Culture with the Ladakh (1991) in northern India provides excellent examples of ways that traditions of responsibility and care have grown out of the relationships people have with the life systems of specific bioregions.

Freirean pedagogy tends to ignore the wisdom of the commons found in traditional cultures. It is dependent on a rationalistic framework found within Enlightenment thinking, and thus tends to exclude other forms of knowing sometimes used by women and people of color—for example, the emotional, the caring, and the sacred (Belenky, Tarule, & Goldberger, 1986). In fact, it often presents a deficit perspective on other cultures in its clear denial that there is ancient wisdom on how to live just and sustainable lives in those communities.

What is clear when one looks at the emotional and spiritual dimensions of knowing within Indigenous or traditional cultures is that it is partial, contextual, and nonuniversal (see, e.g., Basso, 1996; Cajete, 1994). These dimensions of knowing present a particular moral code that is context specific and grows out of unique mytho-poetic and linguistic systems born of a particular, often centuries-old relationship to the land. For example, Keith Basso (1996) told of the complex moral system created by the Apache people via oral stories about events occurring in specific geographical locations and passed down intergenerationally. Knowledge of survival, or wisdom, is taught through the telling of stories attached to the land via place names.

Hence, the Apache use the land mediated by narrative to create and teach an ethical system. For the Apache, the land holds wisdom, teaching the people how to live well together, how to survive.

For the Apache, what we would call pedagogy is what happens in this relationship among the people and the naming of places; education is in the specific moral lessons created in the stories passed on about those places. Thus the people create their community. As Basso (1996) reminded us, "What people make of their places is closely connected to what they make of themselves as members of society and inhabitants of the earth" (p. 7). Thus we see clear links between Western modernist notions of knowledge as abstract, fragmented, and objective, and our hyperseparated relationships to natural systems.

A pedagogy of responsibility seeks to realign consciousness and identity with the emotional and spiritual dimensions of knowing, recognizing that the pedagogical relationship must be built on mutuality and trust. As emotional knowing operates often at the tacit level, responsible pedagogues must learn to attend to the individual cues of emotional response. Nel Noddings's (1992) understanding of care offers a larger sense of responsibility than does a rational/universal focus on rights:

> We have to share the limited resources of earth, and, standing ready to help each other, we must also try not to put too great a strain on the contribution of others. This is where the language of care proves itself so much more practical than the language of rights and justice. If we run out of resources ... rights mean nothing. To say that all people have a right to a particular good is ridiculous in the absence of that good. But to recognize need, to respond reasonably and caringly to it, and to commit ourselves to continuing response require us to live moderately, sensitively, and responsibly. (p. 138)

The language of justice thus can meet the language of sustainability at the juncture of the local: taking responsibility to care for specific people and places and balancing rights with obligations. This is a sharply different attitude than Freirean pedagogy's single-minded focus on rights.

A pedagogy of responsibility looks to the spiritual, not only because, as Noddings noted, people have fundamental questions about the meaning of life and a longing for a sense of god, but also because a sense of the sacred provides a fundamental antithesis to the commodified world we usually experience. The truly sacred cannot be reduced to utilitarian or market values. Also, spiritual traditions can offer repositories of accumulated wisdom on how to live responsibly with each other (see, e.g., Lawlor's 1991 discussions of Australian aborigines, whose stories teach how to live in a place: "All moral codes, spiritual beliefs, and social obligations are embedded in the Dreamtime stories" [p. 236]). Of course, teachers must be cautious in bringing in spiritual matters, given the tradition of church–state separation. However, there is a long-standing freedom to teach *about* various spiritual traditions, which provides room to offer alternatives to students. Also, it is not a violation of church–state separation to encourage students to consider questions of meaning, of what their purpose is, of what's deeply important (sacred) that is not commodified.

PRINCIPLES OF A PEDAGOGY OF RESPONSIBILITY

To summarize our argument thus far, a pedagogy of responsibility asks first "to what and whom are we justly responsible?" It focuses on "the commons" (including all aspects of the environment that are shared in common—air, water, soil, animals—and all the symbolic aspects of the culture—practices, language and traditions) as important forms of resistance to forms of privatization and enclosure negatively impacting communities and natural systems. A pedagogy of responsibility looks for sources of moral authority in community traditions rather than individual judgment, while understanding that some traditions should not be maintained if they are oppressive, such as sexism, racism, and nationalism. Thus, this approach focuses on the important tension between stability and transformation, asking both what needs to be conserved and what needs to change as primary ethical questions.

The primary focus of this perspective is on the local, rather than the universal or global. The cultural, linguistic, and biological diversity growing out of local systems and contexts requires the autonomy of those living in such contexts. Thus, a pedagogy of responsibility emphasizes connection to place as necessary to the development of eco-ethical consciousness and healthy communities, and responds to diverse emotional, spiritual, and other nonrational and non-Western ways of knowing.

CLASSROOM FRAMING AND STRATEGIES

These principles outlining a pedagogy of responsibility led us to some specific paths and practices in our classroom work, where we offer alternative ways of seeing our relationship to the world, as well as teaching students how to teach. As we are committed to teaching students to think about the connections between culture and ecological concerns, the paths that we invite students to explore are framed by three very broad and interrelated concepts: diversity, democracy, and sustainability. Within this framework, teachers are encouraged to learn to see how language and tradition operate culturally, to use a dialogue of connection, and to use classroom strategies that engage students in active thinking and learning.

Framing Our Teaching: Diversity, Democracy and Sustainability:

Our first intent in teaching is to get students used to operating within two big questions: what is, and what ought to be. Rebecca generally begins from the "what ought to be," because it offers a way of pushing prospective teachers and their students to loosen their grip on cultural assumptions as inevitabilities and prepares them for a kind of comparative cultural analysis where they begin to question the *what is* of modernist, industrial cultures.

The concepts of diversity, democracy, and sustainability are addressed up front as a way of signaling that we approach social justice issues generally associated with "multiculturalism" from a cultural ecological perspective. Diversity is discussed in terms of the interrelation among biodiversity, linguistic diversity, and cultural diversity across the planet. We relate this to democracy by asking prospective teachers to imagine what principles are needed in any community where just decision making is practiced. In small groups they discuss this question, generally coming up with a short list of principles that include:

1. Everyone in the community has the right to be heard on any question, whether or not their ideas turn out to be the most viable solutions.
2. Everyone in the community has a responsibility to participate in the decision-making process to the best of their ability.
3. All decisions take into account the good of the whole community, while recognizing that this is never an easy or finished process.

This last principle generally prompts a discussion of how we define community, in particular if we are serious about the third concept, sustainability. Teachers begin to play with the notion that we could go beyond the anthropocentric notions of community that dominate our culture by considering the needs and contributions of the more-than-human world. This discussion gets the group thinking about our connections to larger natural systems and prepares us for discussing what is necessary for a community to be sustainable. We generally brainstorm this question with the help of several authors, among them Daniel Quinn (1992), Wendell Berry (1995), David Orr (1994), and C. A. Bowers (1997, 1999, 2001).

As a final step in this approach, in small group explorations and then open class discussion, we look at the ways that the three concepts are interrelated and could help us imagine ways of living that are healthy and allow the natural systems around us to regenerate. We look to Daniel Quinn's novel *Ishmael* (1992), for example. In Quinn's tale, a gorilla teaches a man about the very different ways of seeing the world among "Taker cultures" that live according to the belief that "the world belongs to us" and "Leaver cultures" that live according to the belief that "we belong to the world." We focus on the teacher-gorilla's assertion that "diversity is the strength of any community," linking what that means for natural systems as well as for democratic ones. The diversity of ideas about how to live well leads us to a discussion about fair decision making in light of differences, and the wealth of approaches across the planet that have resulted in diverse cultural systems, some of which are sustainable and some of which are not.

Language, Culture, and Thought:

This opening framing discussion leads very nicely into a closer look at the ways that culture works, in particular to a critique of modernist culture. First, it is essential that students and teachers learn to see and challenge the hidden modernist assumptions in our daily language. Therefore, we teach teachers to see the metaphors of modernity in everyday classroom and textbook language, such as the social-studies book that refers to the earth as "a treasure chest of resources," or the science book that refers to bacteria as "invaders" to be "battled."

To help teachers see the difference between sustainable and nonsustainable traditions, we watch the film *Ancient Futures*, which shows a sustainable culture in northern India that has rapidly become unsustainable under the onslaught of modernity. This film offers powerful graphic footage and ties in nicely with the aforementioned novel, *Ishmael*, by Daniel Quinn. Both sources offer students a way to challenge heavily ingrained assumptions about the "deficits" of so-called "backward" cultures, questioning what those cultures mean by "wealth," "wisdom," and "success" as a means of questioning the root metaphors in their own mindset. The class gets into rich discussion using these metaphors to analyze the way culture works, and the eco-ethical implications of the kinds of traditions resulting from different cultural mindsets.

We want to emphasize that a central aspect of good teaching is dialogue, the back-and-forth discussion, consideration, and challenge of ideas where all are invited to participate and are offered specific concepts to help open up diverse ways of seeing. Although students are encouraged to use these metaphors and concepts, it is also recognized openly that we are all still products of a particular set of historical constructs that are difficult if not impossible to let go of, and, moreover, need to be culled through because some will certainly be desirable. This makes the process clumsy sometimes, but nonetheless important as we try to take on different cultural ways of knowing.

Cultural–ecological dialogue of connection differs from the more common Freirean dialogue in focusing less on the individual as source of moral authority and more on cultural sources and ethical implications, in emphasizing tradition as a source of wisdom rather than just of oppression, and in validating sources of knowledge other than rationalism.

So although it is important to see the wisdom that may be learned from cultures that have lived in a more balanced way on the earth, we must bring it home to make it real to teachers. As an example of a dialogue of connection, we ask teachers to write about a noncommodified tradition in which they still take part, and then share their writing in a "read-around." Teachers read out stories of making bread with their mothers, learning to fish with their fathers, of religious traditions, of grandmothers who taught them to knit. After an hour, there is often not a dry eye in the house, as the emotional connections that have been made emphasize the difference between commodified and noncommodified relationships.

Next, we have our teacher education students learn a minimally commodified skill from someone else. They learn such things as gardening, canning, baking, skating, horseback riding, guitar playing, and knot tying. They write about both the learning process and the connections they made with the teacher, and to a person they voice thanks that the skill they had learned had not been lost.

Another central approach that we model for the K–12 classroom is the use of engaging pedagogy, such as simulation and role play. Although some university instructors teach about various forms of engaging activities for the K–12 classroom, relatively few actually use them in the university classroom. But to walk the talk, as well as to connect teachers at an emotional level, cultural–ecological university instructors must learn to engage with their classes.

For example, it's very difficult for most teachers to understand that technology is not a neutral tool: "Garbage in, garbage out" is a deeply entrenched mantra. To challenge its power, teachers need to see that any technology is deeply rooted in a particular culture, and that different cultural goals create different technologies. We can give students examples, but a particular simulation with paper airplanes makes the point far better. The airplanes idea comes from a simulation in a labor history curriculum (Bigelow & Diamond, 1988). Teachers become craftworkers making paper airplanes. Playing the part of the factory owner, the instructor proceeds to steal their craft knowledge and reorganize the work, first standardizing it and then bringing in assembly lines. The imposed process not only builds planes faster, it enables the boss/instructor to fire the original workers and hire unskilled workers for much lower wages.

After the simulation, the class and instructor debrief and discuss the results. After discussing the impacts of the imposed technology (the assembly line), the instructor asks, "Could this particular technology be anything other than harmful to both skilled and unskilled workers?" Teachers understand that the technology instituted by the boss/instructor was specifically designed to enhance the boss's interests. The instructor points out that the consequences were not a natural result of technology and asks them to imagine different technologies, designed with the maintenance and well-being of the community in mind. They imagine such things as tools that would enhance a collective creation of planes or that eliminate tedious steps in the process while maintaining the collective control by workers.

The results of the exercise are memorable; because teachers could feel the injustice of the lost knowledge, the experience sticks with them. In so doing, it creates a group memory to which the class and the instructor can refer later on. Thus from the simulation exercise described here, the class can return to the larger framing concepts of diversity, democracy, and sustainability, looking again at how traditions and diverse ways of knowing may contribute to the overall well-being of communities, and returning to the issue of obligation and responsibility.

Framing It in the Context of Responsibility:

The "debriefing" process just described is a way to reassert the frame of our teaching, and more generally of a cultural ecological approach. Without both debriefing/framing and the creation of context, these exercises can lose much of their power. Debriefing, as described in the preceding example, both encourages teachers to think about the ethical implications of the case and allows the instructor to try to frame students' thinking with specific questions or concepts. Careful framing from the viewpoint of a pedagogy of responsibility is essential.

In the paper airplane example, "liberation" framing would limit discussion to the need for the workers to be free from oppression by the boss. Cultural–ecological framing, on the other hand, focuses on the ways the nonneutrality of technology undermines valuable traditions and changes relationships; emphasizes the impact of these changes on community as well as individuals; and draws attention to the cultural assumptions carried in the language of progress and change.

CONCLUSION

We believe that teachers must learn to think about cultural and ecological assumptions as they learn to teach—that teachers must learn to care as much as they learn to think. Teacher educators, in turn, have a responsibility to help develop consciousness as much as they have a duty to prepare technically proficient teachers.

Developing a social justice awareness is insufficient to respond to the on-rushing ecological crisis, because it fails to challenge the ways of thinking that reproduce that crisis. Instead, an ecojustice approach incorporates social justice while recognizing the need for ecological sanity. A pedagogy of responsibility can help new generations of teachers challenge the even deeper structures of modern assumptions that degrade tradition, community, and environment. We hope that both social justice educators and environmental educators will join us in exploring that path.

REFERENCES

Appfel-Marglin, F., & PRATEC (Eds.). (1998). *The spirit of regeneration: Andean culture confronting Western notions of development.* London: Zed Books.

Basso, K. (1996). *Wisdom sits in places: Landscape and language among the Western Apache.* Albuquerque: University of New Mexico Press.

Bateson, G. (1972). *Steps to an ecology of mind.* New York: Ballantine Books.

Belenky, M., Tarule, J., & Goldberger, N. (1986). *Women's ways of knowing.* New York: Basic Books.

Berger, P. L. & Luckman, T. (1966). *The social construction of reality.* New York: Anchor Books.

Berry, W. (1995). *Another turn of the crank.* Washington, DC: Counterpoint.

Bigelow, W., & Diamond, N. (1988). *The power in their hands.* New York: Monthly Review Press.

Bowers, C. A. (1997). *The culture of denial: Why the environmental movement needs a strategy for reforming universities and public schools.* Albany: SUNY Press.

Bowers, C. A. (1999). Changing the dominant cultural perspective in education. In G. Smith & D. Willams (Eds.), *Ecological education in action: On weaving education, culture, and the environment* (pp. 161–178). Albany: State University of New York Press.

Bowers, C. A. (2001). *Educating for ecojustice and community.* Athens, GA: University of Georgia Press.

Cajete, G. (1994). *Look to the mountain: An ecology of indigenous education* (introduction by V. Deloria, Jr.). Durango, CO: Kivakí Press.

Capra, F. (1996). *The web of life: A new scientific understanding of living systems.* New York: Anchor Books.

Ellsworth, E. (1989). Why doesn't this feel empowering? Working through the repressive myths of critical pedagogy. *Harvard Educational Review, 59*(3), 297–324.

Giroux, H. (1996). Slacking off: Border youth and postmodern education. In H. Giroux et al., *Counternarratives: Cultural studies and critical pedagogies in postmodern spaces* (pp. 59–80). New York: Routledge.

Griffin, S. (1996). *The eros of everyday life: Essays on ecology, gender and society.* New York: Doubleday.

Jackson, W. (1987). *Altars of unhewn stone: Science and the earth.* San Francisco, CA: North Point Press.

Ladson-Billings, G. (1994). *The dreamkeepers.* San Francisco: Jossey-Bass.

Ladson-Billings, G. (1995). But that's just good teaching: The case for culturally relevant pedagogy. *Theory into Practice, 34*(3), 159–165.

Lakoff, G., & Johnson, M. (1980). *Metaphors we live by.* Chicago: The University of Chicago Press.

Lankshear, C. (1996). Critical pedagogy and cyberspace. In H. Giroux et al. (Eds.), *Counternarratives: Cultural studies and critical pedagogies in postmodern spaces* (pp. 148–188). New York: Routledge.

Lawlor, R. (1991). *Voices of the first day: Awakening in the Aboriginal dreamtime.* Roches-
ter, VT: Inner Traditions.
Martusewicz, R. A. (2001). *Seeking passage: Post-structuralism, pedagogy, ethics.* New
York: Teachers College Press.
McLaren, P. (1995). White terror and oppositional agency. In L. Sleeter & P. Mc-
Laren (Eds.), *Multicultural education, critical pedagogy, and the politics of difference*
(pp. ??). Albany, New York: SUNY Press.
Noddings, N. (1992). *The challenge to care in the schools.* New York: Teachers College
Press.
Norberg-Hodge, H. (1991). *Ancient futures: Learning from Ladahk.* San Francisco: Si-
erra Club Books.
Orr, D. (1994). *Earth in mind: On education, environment, and the human prospet.* Wash-
ington, DC: Island Press.
Plumwood, V. (1993). *Feminism and the mastery of nature.* London: Routledge.
Quinn, D. (1992). *Ishmael: A novel.* New York: Bantam/Turner.
Shiva, V. (1993). *Monocultures of the mind.* Penang, Malaysia: Third World Network.
Shiva, V. (2002). *Water wars: Privatization, pollution and profit.* Cambridge, MA: South
End Press.

APPENDIX: SOME ROOT METAPHORS OF WESTERN AND NON-WESTERN CULTURES, DERIVED FROM VARIOUS WORKS BY C. A. BOWERS

Root Metaphors of Western, Modern Cultures

1. *Mechanism*: Sees world and life processes as being like a machine. Exhibited in such terms as "information processing" and "feedback systems."
2. *Individualism*: Individual is seen as the basic social unit, autonomous
   from culture and tradition or struggling to escape them. Expressed in
   such terms as "be creative" and "think for yourself."
3. *Anthropocentrism*: Sees humans as at the center, and dominant over the
   rest of nature. Ignores consequences of human activity. Expressed in
   Genesis granting of dominion over nature to humans, and in such
   terms as "natural resources."
4. *Change*: Seen as linear and usually progressive, but irresistible regardless. Expressed in "you can't stop progress" and in assumptions that
   "newer is better," experimenting on nature is good.
5. *Science*: Seen as most legitimate way of knowing; objective and culture
   free; separate from morality. Reductionist—analyzes complex phenomena by breaking into parts. Knowledge is only "high status," that
   derived from rational thought and formal schooling.

6. *Commodification* or turning everything into a product for sale on the market.

Root Metaphors of Sustainable Cultures

1. *Holistic/Organic*: Sees world as interconnected like a living thing. Views humans and the rest of nature in reciprocal relationships of interdependence.
2. *Community centered*: Sees community as basic social unit. Elders conserve and pass on traditions that sustain community and ecology. Community includes rest of nature.
3. *Ecocentric*: Sees humans and other life and nonliving nature as equal participants in a moral universe. Humans have moral obligation to nature.
4. *Controlled change*: Stability is valued. All cultures change, but here change is evaluated in terms of long-term consequences. Past and future are important considerations in decisions.
5. *Science* is just one way of knowing. Science is holistic, focusing on whole systems rather than parts, on understanding relationships and patterns. Knowledge comes in many forms—tacit, folk, poetic, spiritual, technical, encoded in language, genes, plants.
6. *Noncommodified* traditions are maintained based on intrinsic value and meaning.

Chapter 5

"To Live for Art": Teaching and Learning Aesthetic Education Within Foundations of Education

Mary Bushnell Greiner

As a teacher I have been striving to develop my thoughts and beliefs on the American educational system. Personally, I am very thankful to this country for providing me with great opportunities as an immigrant student. I often feel guilty criticizing the system because it has obviously supported me and many others at Queens College. I remember sitting outside during my [undergraduate] graduation commencement looking around and thinking "… and they say there is no social mobility in this country!" I promised to be a loyal American by being thankful, but I found myself in great confusion and uncertainty after watching the documentary "Children in America's Schools" based on Kozol's book "Savage Inequalities." I couldn't believe my eyes. (Yasmine Javdanfar)

Yasmine, a master's degree student, tells me she feels that she is being anti-American when she says that schools aren't working. She struggles with her learning about schools and society, learning that occurs in the social foundations of education courses I teach, among other locations. We know each other well, as Yasmine was a student in one of my undergraduate teacher education courses, and then enrolled in my graduate foundations course during her first year as an elementary school teacher. Yasmine's struggle is not one based on a lack of ability or interest, but rather one of the stability of her philosophical foundations. How, she wonders aloud, can she criticize the very educational system that has served her so well? I designed my social foundations courses to be based on questioning and critique; she is highly adept at both. However, her

93

abilities come into conflict with her conscience when the subject is the equality of U.S. education. That is, her intellectual experiences with social foundations comingles with her emotional experiences.

Yasmine is one of the success stories of New York City and U.S. schools. Her parents left Iran for Israel following the 1979 Iranian revolution; they came to the United States intentionally seeking a place where their daughters would have opportunities for higher education. Her parents instilled in them a strong faith in the power of education to enable them to succeed, and that faith has paid off. Both of her sisters graduated from college and are successful in business; Yasmine was easily accepted into graduate school. Many of Yasmine's classmates are the first in their families to attend college, and the first to attend graduate school. For all of them, the system of education has worked. The unwritten contract between their families and the school system was met: If they worked hard, studied, and learned their academic lessons, higher education and its companion socioeconomic benefits would be available to them. Yasmine and many of her peers signed this contract and continue to believe in it because they are the living proof of its veracity.

The value of the contract gets called into question in my social foundations of education courses when we consider to what extent schooling has and has not served various populations in our society. Like her working-class and low-income classmates, Yasmine is hesitant to criticize the very system that has provided for her success. What if the system were truly faulty? Would her success be somehow less valuable? Less the result of her own hard work and effort? What would it mean to recognize some way in which she, among others, is somehow privileged over other students?

Part of why Yasmine is hesitant to criticize the social context of schooling is because she had never before been asked to question in a way in which she felt comfortable enough to respond. She, like other students, succeeded in school by giving back to her teachers precisely what they had expected of her. That is, she memorized facts and figures, which are presumed to be absolute, unchanging, and truthful. She and other New York City students "have been cultivated to believe that knowing in school means to have committed to memory information that someone else told them or that they read authored by someone else" (Bushnell & Henry, 2003, p. 40). Although many educators sing the praises of critical thinking skills, most students are not taught such skills in the push for meeting standards of information retrieval. My students know, for example, of the three branches of government, but have not learned to ask about the persistence of the two-party system, nor the ways in which the three branches of government serve the interests of groups other than working-class voters. I do not criticize my students here—they are simply working within the carefully structured system that we, their elders, created for them.

Questioning and thoughtful criticism are at the heart of social foundations, and I take the struggle of Yasmine and other students like her very seriously. The content of social foundations is clear, but must be linked to pedagogy. How do I create a classroom in which students feel safe and supported to critically analyze the very system that has served them—particularly when many of them are not working from positions of privilege in which they might take higher education and its benefits for granted? Those who are first-generation college attendees are too close to not succeeding in school to be comfortable with attacking the hand that feeds them. In short, how do I help create a pedagogy of engagement in the classrooms of an urban, underfunded, traditionally working-class and immigrant institution of higher learning?

A SNAPSHOT OF AN ENGAGED CLASSROOM

Another semester, another social foundations course: My undergraduate students are telling each other their own experiences of encountering prejudice. As one student describes her account, another transcribes her story onto paper. A third student makes notes about the speaker's gestures, vocal tone, cadence, and volume. The second student then retells the story following the direction to recreate the original qualities of presentation—in essence, to faithfully mimic the first speaker. In a round robin, students attempt to step into each other's shoes. Some students visibly display emotion, reflecting that in the act of saying someone else's words, they had a visceral sense of being that person and feeling her struggles. We then, as a class, walk into a black box theater to view *Twilight: LA (1992)*, a play by Anna Deavere Smith (1994) about the violence in Los Angeles following the Rodney King verdict. The students write reflections after the performance:

"[In the workshop] I came to understand and see more clearly how our bodies play an important role with what we see, hear, and feel .... When watching the performance, I felt that I became a part of the characters .... My body was connecting to what I was seeing and hearing all around me."

"In school, I read and talk about many different issues but don't experience the readings firsthand .... Whereas going to the workshop and viewing the play gives you an emotional connection."

"I experienced the pain inside others that was so real. I didn't think I would be so affected by one person portraying another."

"[Through the performance I learned] the real emotion behind racism, not just an overview of it."

"I have learned that the activity in a classroom greatly affects what happens in society and that there are ways to change it .... We can make a difference in our classroom by learning from experiences of that past."

Twilight: LA (1992) opens a classroom discussion about race, gender, class, and privilege that spills over to the ensuing weeks. The initial responses, just excerpted, grow as we read the "Letter from Birmingham Jail" of Martin Luther King, Jr., and the students engage in that reading with vigor. It is a discussion in which students display their anger, frustration, disappointment, and sadness; it is a discussion that in other semesters students have been reluctant to engage. This work of art, this play, has brought down students' resistance to openly exploring the darker issues that lie at the heart of a social foundations of education course.

Over the last few years I have become increasingly involved in this kind of teaching and learning known as aesthetic education (Bushnell Greiner, 2003). In moving with my class into emotional spaces such as that just described, we are collectively locating one possible way in which a pedagogy of engagement may be fostered. In this chapter I describe my interpretation of the elements of my work with the Lincoln Center Institute for the Arts in Education (LCI) that have become most important to me to date. Using a method of inquiry developed by the Lincoln Center Institute, my students and I experience works of art through a multistep process that includes description, analysis, and interpretation, as well as direct experience with art making. Through the process, my role as teacher shifts to more fluid roles of participant, guide, explorer, *and* teacher. It is not insignificant that I am not only a teacher of aesthetic education, I am a learner. In the earlier manifestations of teaching aesthetic education in my classrooms I emphasized the three-step inquiry process. I latched on to the pedagogy as a means of creating a more engaging classroom space. What I slowly learned is that the pedagogy of inquiry is not the point: The point is to apply that inquiry to works of art. As I delve further into aesthetic education I have become increasingly aware of the importance of placing works of art at the center of our inquiry. It is by living for art that my classroom has become a place of both emotion and intellect, in which all of us can bring our full selves to our work.

AESTHETIC EDUCATION AS PHILOSOPHY

Moving into aesthetic spaces is not how I learned social foundations of education in graduate school, if by that I mean the literal pedagogies and curricula revealed to me then. Aesthetic education has become a central part of my social foundations classroom as an extension of my graduate training that taught me to describe, analyze, and interpret from multiple disciplinary perspectives. My courses were filled with faculty and students from the full range of foundational disciplines, including sociology, anthropology, philosophy, history, political science, international relations, and economics. As an anthropologist, I was continually, and respectfully, reminded that there were other intellectual lenses through which to view the educational world and its context. I now consider it my responsibility, as an instructor of social foundations, to bring those perspectives to the classroom; I believe to some extent I succeed. Yet there is so little time in one semester—how can I create a space for my students to recognize their "ontological stability" (Gilmour, 1986, p. 181) and to be willing to shake its foundations? In aesthetic education I have found an answer that works for my teaching.

Aesthetic education utilizes art as both a means and a subject. More than the working in multiple modalities, aesthetics involves the exploration of art as a means of exploring one's place in the world. When we immerse ourselves in works of art, we enter a world created out of the intersection of imagination and experience. As Gadamer wrote, "Of all the things that confront us in nature and history, it is the work of art that speaks to us most directly. It possesses a mysterious intimacy that grips our entire being, as if there were no distance at all and every encounter with it were an encounter with ourselves" (Gadamer, quoted in Gilmour, 1986, p. 179). I find Gadamer's assertions about art entirely appropriate, as I have experienced and witnessed the openings achieved through meaningful experiences with works of art. Art, simply because it is art, implicitly holds the potential for circumventing any mediation between ourselves and our world. The aesthetics that is art taps directly into our senses in an opening of experience.

Yet what I have written is not quite accurate, for such openings become possible only if we are able to create them. Simply viewing a work of art does not constitute an aesthetic experience if in the viewing we keep ourselves detached from it, as most of us have learned to do. A colleague of mine regularly revisits one of Mark Rothko's color-block paintings in a museum. She may sit before it for up to an hour at a time, opening herself and her changing moods, experiences, and growth with the experience of viewing the painting. While she sits with "her" painting (as she likes to call it), other museum visitors stop for a few seconds and then move on. Her immersion in an artwork is uncommon in a U.S. culture that puts a premium on quantity of art visited, rather than the depth of experience. The vast majority of us need to "learn to know, to see, to hear more by exploring the languages and gestures out of which plays (as an example) are made" (Greene, 1988, p. 54). We need to learn this in our social foundations of education classrooms because earlier learning, in school, at home, and on the streets, did not teach us that we can embrace our own ontological event that is constructed in the encounter with a work of art. As Rosenblatt (1978) argued, a poem is merely text on a page until a reader interacts with it and enables it to be a transitory "event in time" (p. 12). "A specific reader and a specific text at a specific time and place: change any of these, and there occurs a different circuit, a different event—a different poem" (Rosenblatt, 1978, p. 14).

Notice that to date I have named painting, theater, and poetry: three media of art. The particular medium is not so relevant here; nor is the genre, whether Baroque, Impressionist, surreal, or abstract. We might experience a Chinese opera or listen to a quartet playing Poulenc. What is relevant is that the artwork have enough depth to invite an experience. It is beyond my capacity and desire to define art, although I adamantly assert it is not found only in museums and performance halls.

As art is a direct encounter with human perception and experience, it cannot hold a singular and final meaning; the possibilities of interpretation are as varied as life on earth. Rosenblatt's (1978) reader response theory is built on Dewey and Bentley's (1949) theory of transactionalism, which recognizes that knowings are always incomplete, tentative, and of the moment. In encountering works of art with others, therefore, we must become open to understanding the explanations and ontologies created as they experience the work of art. Such openness can be particularly challenging for those of us taught to seek a single correct answer (known, of course, by the teacher). Girod and Wong (2002) described one such student who remained focused on identifying a single right answer throughout an aesthetic learning experience that encouraged him to explore "beauty and artistry" instead. "He knew what to do to get good grades, had a career goal in mind, and behaved in ways that garnered him the support and admiration of his teachers" (Girod & Wong, 2002, p. 222). A single aesthetic learning experience was not enough to overcome 4 years of learning about knowledge as complete and static. By the time students are in college, they are thoroughly inculcated into a fixed epistemology. Aesthetic education intends to undo such work.

Greene carefully pointed out that aesthetic education goes far beyond merely ushering in young people into an "elite community" that is Art. The point is not to "appreciate Art that others have defined as masterpieces. On the contrary, it is to challenge awed passivity or a merely receptive attitude or a submergence in pleasurable reverie" (Greene, 1988, p. 53). We do not maintain a passive, observing relationship with art that relies on accepting the verdicts others place on it. Through aesthetic education, students delve into active relationships with specific works of art including (and perhaps especially) art that they do not initially "like." Greene encouraged us to "move deliberately into what can be called an aesthetic space, where the familiar becomes unfamiliar" (2001, p. 69), and to develop "a peculiar kind of attentiveness" (1988, p. 54), which opens all of our senses to feelings and thoughts previously held under wraps.

AESTHETIC EDUCATION AS PRACTICE

In our aesthetic education work in the social foundations classroom, we experience a work of art in depth and in a manner that is grounded within the curriculum of the course. Because our collaborative is with the Lincoln Center for the Performing Arts, we usually observe performing art such as dance, theater, or music, but we may instead interact with visual artwork such as paintings, sculpture, and photography, or written art such as poetry and fiction. Our activities in the classroom are grounded in the chosen work of art. For example, in fall 2002 my students traveled to the Lincoln Center to watch a performance of "Shadow's Child," a Lincoln Center-commissioned performance by the Urban Bush Women and the National Song and Dance Company of Mozambique. In advance of the performance, a Teaching Artist (herself a dancer) visited my class on the college campus and led the students through a dance workshop designed to deepen their experience of the performance. Immediately following the performance we convened in a studio at the Lincoln Center and held a second workshop to process the experience. The pattern of preperformance workshop, performance, then postperformance workshop may vary each semester, but the essence of the preperformance workshop always remains. LCI has found that such preliminary experience opens students' observational and analytical abilities concerning a work of art.

During the preliminary workshop, students create a work of art related to the featured performance. In the case of a dance performance, students may explore a series of movement activities that often result in us dancing in our classroom. In the case of a visual arts piece, students might construct a collage or painting. The idea is for the students to directly engage with the process of art creation. In so doing they shift from being passive observers or consumers of the artwork, to fellow creators. They must solve some of the problems "real artists" face, and make some of the decisions inherent to the medium and its limitations and possibilities.

Throughout the workshops, the Teaching Artist and I lead the students through a three-step inquiry process to describe, analyze, and interpret. This process is applied not only to the performance, but to the workshop itself. "Describe," I might say to the students, "what kinds of activities we did in class today. What happened? What did you notice?" We continually ask students to ground their descriptions in the concrete, so that descriptions are literal and uninterpreted (the interpretation comes later). By focusing on description first, we remove the evaluatory component of interpretation that often shuts down some students' responses. We never ask "Did you like the performance?," as one student's dissenting voice may become lost in a chorus of "It was wonderful!" The Teaching Artist and I document the students' comments on large chart papers taped to the walls. Through the documentation, students' words are removed from their individual speakers and become part of the collective knowledge of the classroom.

After the work of art is sufficiently described, we move to analysis by asking students to examine the relationships between elements in the work of art. Students might explore the relationship of the rhythm in the music to the dancers' movements, or how the lighting contributes to the overall story and emotional content. They may begin to consider the choreographer's choices about when dancers came on stage and then off, touched, or moved independently. They may discuss how the storyteller's stance on stage mimicked the content of his story, and how his eyes looked at each person in the audience.

Interpretation seeks to explore the meanings embedded in the work of art and the students' interactions with it. Students may speculate on the artist's intentions, how the work of art connects to their own lives, or the personal meanings they take away from it. The Teaching Artist and I encourage students to consider the meanings of the work of art for the larger society, or for groups of persons unlike themselves. We endeavor to validate all interpretations, although we require students to provide evidence in the artwork for their arguments. For example, while exploring a Chinese silk scroll painting, most observers found the artwork to be very peaceful. One man, however, said that he interpreted the work as angry because of a large red splotch in one area that reminded him of blood. Although no one else in the group shared his interpretation, everyone understood his experience because he grounded it in the work of art through specific notations of those objective elements from which he drew his subjective conclusions. Students must, in other words, provide a basis for their opinions in the work of art.

Interpreting the experience of a work of art in this manner makes use of Rosenblatt's (1978) assertion that the meaning of a work of art is found not in the piece itself, but in a person's interaction with the work of art. With the interaction as the focal event, the personal contexts of each individual influence interpretations as each person brings unique knowledge and experience to the art experiencing. We then identify where we will go next with the work of art by asking students questions such as, "What more do you want to know (about the work of art, the artist, connections that were raised in class, etc.)?" "What resources might you make use of to learn more?" Using their responses as a springboard, we construct follow-up research activities to extend our learning and interactions with the work of art.

The activities just described might be engaging in themselves; they are worthwhile in the classroom as means of creating new physical and linguistic spaces for students and instructors that do not resemble a lecture-based classroom of teacher-based epistemology. The real strength in the activities is because they are built on works of art. We fully realize the possibilities of such aesthetic work when we take the time to reflect on what we have done together. I was taught in yoga that the most important part of the practice is not found in the twisted postures and exercises; rather, it is found in the moment of relaxation after a posture, when the body is allowed to fully breathe and absorb the impact of the physical activity. Likewise, reflection in the classroom enables the learning to become fully absorbed in the selves of the students and teachers as we articulate to ourselves and others what has occurred. Catherine Lewis (1995) similarly chronicled the centrality of reflection or "hansei" in Japanese classrooms where even preschool students develop the abilities to consider the events of the day and the actions, feelings, and thoughts of the persons involved.

As the heart of professional practice, reflection involves an attentiveness to particularities and the asking of questions about practices, ideas, and assumptions (e.g., Schön, 1983). Reflection is not necessary when utilizing scripted curricular materials; indeed, as the antithesis of a scripted interaction in the classroom, reflection requires continual inquiry into what happened, what might have happened, what was said and not said. One day in a workshop for teacher educators our activities were so compelling that we ran out of time to conduct a reflection on our work together. In describing the workshop to a colleague afterward, I found my usual enthusiasm absent. Struggling to figure out what was "wrong" with the activities, I recognized that without the reflection, the activities remained outside of my personal experience and therefore did not result in any shift of identity or ontological awareness of the world. The workshop was fun, but not a learning experience. Since that time, I have redoubled my efforts to always make the time for reflection in my classroom.

Over several years of aesthetic education in my foundations classrooms, I am noticing subtle shifts in my students and significant shifts in my teaching, including how I teach other courses that are not connected with the Lincoln Center Institute. There are several forms of shifts in my students: physical, experiential, emotional, and, I hope, intellectual. The physical shifts are easiest to recognize as we literally move around the classroom: We are up out of our seats, dancing, stretching, playing musical instruments, leaving far behind the static desks and chairs. Students stand around large tables working on collaborative collages. They recreate scenes from a play. And the physical shifts go even further when we take a "field trip" each semester, traveling by subway to Manhattan to watch a performance and visit a museum. We travel together on the subway, or share cabs across Central Park, which affords new opportunities for social interactions among students, and between the students and myself. They learn that I don't own a car. I learn that their parents have warned them away from subways and Manhattan.

The experiential shifts occur because our work is located outside of the everyday, commonplace college classroom. One semester we viewed a Chinese opera—a highly unusual art form for most college students and their professors in this country. The presence of the artists was palpable as we sat in the small theater, only a few feet from their movements and singing on stage. Students also have learned U.S. history (e.g., Black migration to the North; the Depression; the Harlem Renaissance) while viewing the Jacob Lawrence retrospective at the Whitney Museum of American Art. Instead of textbooks or lectures, they learned through paint and collage. They experienced multiple ways to tell a story and to convey struggles and ideas. (Consider, for example, the learning possibilities inherent in Barbara Kruger's social issues graphics, or Carrie Mae Weems's photographs revealing our challenges with race.)

Emotional shifts occur as we allow emotions to become part of the classroom social environment. Students need not maintain objective masks to hide themselves; rather, they are encouraged to connect aesthetic experiences with their own lives and aspirations. Emotions are present in every classroom, yet often hidden behind façades of lecterns, note taking, hand raising, and silence. Years ago, before I knew of aesthetic education, I was unable to hide from my students the depth of my sadness after the massacre at Columbine High School. Abandoning the day's planned lesson, we spent the hour sharing what we knew and how we felt about it. I had no answers for them, only more questions. After the class was over, one of my students commented to me, in a tone that expressed surprise, "Gee, professor, you sure are upset about this." I was angered by his response. Of course I was emotional! But my emotion was not comprehensible to him in the context of a "regular" classroom, where he expected me to be a giver of facts and truths. I had never allowed emotion to enter our classroom before that day, so it took us all by surprise. I now realize that the content of the social foundations course is inevitably emotional. The exploration of hegemonies of race, class, and gender involve students' and teachers' lived emotions that are often stifled. By honoring the import and value of emotions through aesthetic experiences, I am trying to welcome students' (and teachers') whole selves into the room.

My learning and teaching has been supported considerably by the program managers and Teaching Artists at the Lincoln Center Institute. Their summer and winter workshops for teacher education faculty, as well as ongoing seminars with Maxine Greene (LCI's philosopher in residence), brought me to this work and continue to enable its growth. Social foundations faculty without the resources and expertise of LCI can still venture into aesthetic education, first by returning to our roots in philosophy. Dewey's (1934) *Art as Experience* and Greene's lectures (2001) and essays (1978) describe aesthetic education and its import directly. In addition, LCI is part of the Association of Institutes for Aesthetic Education, which has affiliates throughout the world. Most important, however, is to trust the art and the artist. Find a work of art that compels you—even if you cannot articulate at the outset how or why it does so. Bring that artwork to your classroom and explore *along with your students* using all of your senses. If that painting were a piece of music, what would it sound like? Transform a movement of dance into a line of poetry. Take a page from a play and draw it in crayon. Above all, refrain from saying "I (don't) like it" or "Now that's (not) art!"

For Yasmine and her classmates, aesthetic education becomes part of the construction of a classroom in which questioning and critical inquiry are fundamental. Aesthetic education furthers students' experiences with art, and with the inquiry process, by engaging them as artists. Using their bodies, musical instruments, drawings, and other media, students are empowered to be artists and thereby represent and see their world in new ways. In the end, students begin questioning why a classroom so often looks like a classroom. They wonder why it can't look otherwise and they begin to live a classroom that *does* look otherwise. Aesthetic education contributes to classroom community building that provides a safe space for students to conduct such questioning as it emphasizes multiple right answers, process learning, and the decentering of authority. A safe space does not completely ameliorate Yasmine's struggle between her conscience and her intellect, but it does provide a location in which that necessary struggle can occur.

When Yasmine brought her concerns to our class, I knew only to respond to them with words. This privileges those students who are particularly adept with scholarly communication, but it leaves out the very quiet student who, after not saying a word all semester, created a collage of images and drawing that communicated the depth of her intellect and feeling. All of the class, including, I must admit, the professor, had paid little attention to this silent undergraduate. But her artwork revealed previously unknown depths to which we could then connect; for the first time I saw her potential as a teacher.

The most important element of all of our classroom efforts is the experience of original works of art. As an expression of imagination, art connects the psyche and the intellect in surprising and conceptually jolting ways: "To live for art ... is to live a life of questioning. And if you believe, as I do, that to live for art demands that every other part of life be moved towards one end, then the question 'How shall I live?' is fierce" (Winterson, 1996, p. 161). A work of art, with its authenticity and depth, provides expansive opportunities for personal and social transformation if we allow ourselves to be open to that transformation. I would mislead you to say that my classroom enacts creativity and imagination at every moment. My students (and I) remain challenged to understand that aesthetic education is much more than simply incorporating the arts into one's lessons—we are all slowly learning that aesthetic education is a full sensorial embracing of our multi-leveled experiences with works of art that are enactments of imagination.

I do not know yet, except for anecdotes, the long-term effects aesthetic education will have on my students when they are classroom teachers. Do their students learn more? Score higher on standardized tests? Stay in school longer? Are they happier in their lives? These and other questions need to be answered in time, but for now I rely on epistemological assumptions to justify this ongoing work.

I am learning how to teach aesthetic education, and, like all learning and knowing, it is perpetually incomplete. It is not insignificant that I am a student of aesthetic education just as I am a teacher of it. This is activist teaching, as I believe what we are doing is more ethically viable than teaching students that there is one right answer, or one correct authority. I find aesthetic education to be more intellectually, emotionally, and socially enriching for me than a sole emphasis on "traditional" academic pursuits. I believe aesthetic education helps students assert their view of the world and how they name the world and describe it, rather than accepting the world as it has been described to them. This stance assumes that students' power to name the world is at the heart of their own capacity and authority to engage in that world. Even more, their direct engagements with the arts are radical actions in these dark times of society. With this in mind, although Adrienne Rich was writing of poetry, I find her words applicable for all of the arts: "A [work of art] can't free us from the struggle for existence, but it can uncover desires and appetites buried under the accumulating emergencies of our lives, the fabricated wants and needs we have had urged on us, have accepted as our own. It's not a philosophical or psychological blueprint; it's an instrument for embodied experience" (Rich, 1993, p. 13).

REFERENCES

Bushnell Greiner, M. (2003). Learning representations and interpretations: Aesthetic education in dark times. *Educational Studies, 34*(4), 424–445.
Bushnell, M., & Henry, S. E. (2003). The role of reflection in epistemological change: Autobiography in teacher education. *Educational Studies, 34*(1), 38–61.
Dewey, J. (1934). *Art as experience.* New York: Perigee Books.
Dewey, J., & Bentley, A. F. (1949). *Knowing and the known.* Boston: Beacon Press.
Gilmour, J. (1986). *Picturing the world.* Albany: State University of New York Press.
Girod, M., & Wong, D. (2002). An aesthetic (Deweyan) perspective on science learning: Case studies of three fourth graders. *Elementary School Journal, 102*(3), 199–224.
Greene, M. (1978). *Landscapes of learning.* New York: Teachers College Press.
Greene, M. (1988). What happened to imagination? In K. Egan & D. Nadaner (Eds.), *Imagination and education* (pp. 45–56). New York: Teachers College Press.
Greene, M. (2001). *Variations on a blue guitar: The Lincoln Center lectures.* New York: Teachers College Press.
Lewis, C. (1995). *Educating hearts and minds: Reflections of Japanese preschool and elementary education.* Cambridge: Cambridge University Press.

Rich, A. (1993). *What is found there: Notebooks on poetry and politics*. New York: W. W. Norton.

Rosenblatt, L. M. (1978). *The reader, the text, the poem: The transactional theory of the literary work*. Carbondale, IL: Southern Illinois University Press.

Schön, D. A. (1983). *The reflective practitioner: How professionals think in action*. New York: Basic Books.

Smith, A. D. (1994). *Twilight: Los Angeles (1992)*. New York: Anchor Books.

Winterson, J. (1996). *Art objects: Essays on ecstasy and effrontery*. New York: Vintage International.

Part III

DEVELOPING TEACHER EDUCATORS WITH/IN SOCIAL FOUNDATIONS

Chapter 6

Identity (Re)Construction and Student Resistance

Dan W. Butin

In America, the seeds of racism are so deeply rooted in the white people collectively, their belief that they are "superior" in some way is so deeply rooted,
that these things are in the national white subconscious … it isn't the American white man who is a racist, but it's the American political, economic, and
social atmosphere that automatically nourishes a racist psychology in the
white man. (Malcolm X & Alex Haley, 1975, pp. 363, 371)

I begin with this quote from Malcolm X to introduce the sociology of education and multicultural education unit of my social foundations of education
course. Students come into class already having read the *NAACP Call for Action in Education* (2002) and Sleeter and Grant's (1999) opening chapter "Illusions of Progress," both of which focus on the continued inequities in
schools and society for lower-class, non-White, and nondominant youth.

We have just completed a unit on the philosophy of education; idealism,
theoretical debates of what it means to be educated, and hope are in the air.
My students are well-meaning, White, predominantly female, middle-class
and upper middle-class undergraduates just beginning our teacher education program. And so they are hit, and hit hard, with these harsh words,
harsh numbers, and harsh realities.

The first class of this unit is thus spent grappling with what these words
and statistics might mean and how they could still be accurate today, 40
years after the birth of the civil rights movement, half a century after *Brown
v. Board of Education*. One-on-one, small-group, and whole-class discussions

are raw, emotional, and often defensive. They range from claims of wholesale racism in our society to unequivocal rejections of such perspectives.

Irrespective of students' ideological positioning, though, a consistent theme runs through the discussions: issues of, for example, inequity, racism, and privilege always seem to be about someone else. "Society" is inequitable. "People" are small-minded. "We" are all moving slowly but surely toward a better future.

I am prepared for this. An extensive literature base within antioppressive education and Whiteness studies has explicated how students consistently resist, reject, and obscure notions of their own privileged positions (Hytten & Adkins, 2001; Kumashiro, 2000, 2002). So for the next class I assign an additional task: to take a short "implicit association test" on racial preference (www.implicit.harvard.edu).[1]

"Explosive" is an understatement to describe the next class. Every single student comes back with results of having a slight, moderate, or strong preference for Whites rather than Blacks. I immediately tell my class that I had a "moderate" preference when I took the quiz; I also tell them that many non-White students often have either slight or moderate preferences for Whites as well. It is here that my unit on the sociology of education and multicultural education really begins; it is here that we must begin to address not only the inequities and disparities of our schools and society, but the very real possibility that these inequities and disparities are structured into how we think and act and that we are somehow complicit.

This chapter investigates students' resistance to theoretically complex, politically volatile, and culturally debated educational issues similar to the one just outlined. I explore four prevalent conceptualizations for such resistance: resistance as failure, resistance as unknowing, resistance as alienation, and resistance as uncaring. Although each offers a useful framework by which to understand student actions, none provide an evident means to truly overcome such resistance. All, I show, maintain static notions of identity and knowledge and thus perpetuate a zero-sum struggle between students and teacher. Instead I suggest an alternative perspective—resistance as identity construction—in order to better comprehend, subvert, and refocus my students' resistance. By understanding resistance as the constant (re)constructing of identity, alternative pedagogical and curricular strategies become possible, allowing fuller engagement with issues of inequity and social justice within a social foundations classroom.

---

[1]It is beyond the scope of this chapter to explore the methodological, epistemological, and political assumptions and implications of this research. See the extensive bibliography linked to this website. My goal here is to provoke my students into engaging the possibility of structural inequity and racism, rather than convince them that they (or I) are racist.

WHAT IS RESISTANCE?

Student resistance is a central and problematic aspect of daily classroom life (Bidwell, 1965; Giroux, 1983; Lortie, 1975; Waller, 1932). Whether active or passive, student resistance disrupts learning and teaching in the classroom by questioning teacher authority, defying specified tasks, questioning the value of compliance, and fomenting peer emulation of said resistance. The consequences of student resistance can be as far-ranging as student failure, teacher withdrawal, and the near-total stoppage of meaningful classroom work.

It is therefore crucial to theorize student resistance. The prevalent discourse on student resistance is within critical theory (Giroux, 1983; MacLeod, 1995; McLaren, 1999; Willis, 1981); nevertheless, the contemporary literature on resistance spans a wide range of theoretical and disciplinary perspectives (Fine, 1991; McFarland, 2001; McIntyre, 1997; Ogbu, 1992; Schutz, 2004; Tatum, 1992). I thus outline four distinct conceptualizations for understanding student resistance: resistance as failure, resistance as unknowing, resistance as alienation, and resistance as uncaring.

Resistance as Failure: Conservative and Liberal Perspectives

My students' "resistance" to grappling with the potential for structural inequity and racism could be viewed in a seemingly "commonsensical" way: My students simply didn't "get it." Their apparent failure to comprehend, articulate, or engage with the course content can be viewed as just that—students' inability to master content knowledge. This perspective is in fact the dominant framework by which our society understands students' actions in the classroom. This perspective has "conservative" and "liberal" strands (Collins, 1992); the former focuses on explanations internal to the individual whereas the latter focuses on the individual's local environment. Both, though, operate under a deficit perspective that succumbs to a "blame the victim" approach to students' failure (Valencia, 1997).

Conservative perspectives focus on two distinct explanations for student failure: genetic and psychological. Genetic perspectives view students' failure as the inevitable outcome of the variable distribution of intelligence across populations (Hernstein & Murray, 1994). Schools are presumed to be meritocratic institutions sorting and selecting students through objective measurements of ability, which is understood to be a unitary attribute distributed along a normal curve. Accurate school sorting of students "above" and "below" the norm inevitably separates students according to a seemingly inevitable pseudo-Darwinian "cognitive partitioning." As Hernstein and Murray (1994) argued, "In a universal education system, many students will not reach the level of education that most people view as basic," given the range of cognitive variation across a population (p. 436).

While continuing to view failure as inherent within the individual, psychological perspectives focus on students' lack of motivation, willpower, and/or internal fortitude. Individual failure becomes a moral lack, a lack of willingness to self-improve and to self-sacrifice toward betterment. Those who fail are admonished for living in the moment, unwilling to delay immediate gratification, unable to think ahead.

Contrarily, liberal perspectives relocate blame from the individual onto her surroundings. The *culture-of-poverty* and *devaluation of education* arguments, in specific, suggest that variables such as peer groups, family, drugs, urban blight, pregnancy, cultural incongruities, and lack of English language competency are to blame for student failure.

The culture-of-poverty argument suggests that the conditions of urban and rural neglect foster and sustain unproductive habits of living, thinking, and acting that in turn maintain a vicious and unbreakable cycle of degradation (Lewis, 1966). Even the most well-meaning and motivated individuals are faced with insurmountable pressures to conform to negative norms that endanger and destroy genuine opportunities for betterment. Although exceptional "success stories" of overcoming poverty continue to be laudable, a liberal perspective argues that these exceptions actually prove the rule of the inadequate social, economic, and political support networks for the vast majority of residents in such conditions (Wilson, 1997).

The analogous devaluation-of-education argument further suggests that some families, groups, and cultures do not value education and thus do not promote academic success for their children (Thernstrom & Thernstrom, 2003). Such devaluation could be the result of cultural incongruities between immigrant and American norms, the lack of belief in the efficacy of the schooling process, or a distrust in the neutrality and beneficence of the educational system (Ogbu, 1992).

Although there are clear distinctions between the conservative and liberal perspectives of school failure, both maintain a "blame the victim" mentality by positioning individuals, groups, and cultures within a deficit perspective. A singular, neutral, objective, and normative yardstick is presumed to exist to measure the "best way" of teaching, learning, and doing school. This paternalistic and assimilationist argument denies the viability and variability of other ways of being and negates the possibility that students' inability to master content knowledge may actually be a legitimate consequence of rational actions by students to specific classroom practices and structures (McFarland, 2001). Academic failure may thus be viewed as one consequence of student resistance, but the two cannot be conflated.

Resistance as Unknowing: Racial Identity Development

To take student resistance as a legitimate set of actions (rather than as a mode of failure) is to explore how and why such resistance is enacted in the first place. One answer is that student resistance to issues of inequity and social justice is due to (White) preservice teachers' lack of (self) knowledge: "Teachers are genuinely unaware of culturally contrasting worldviews, and they are likely to deny that race or ethnicity play any part in the development of the child" (Noel, 2001, p. 4). This perspective is grounded in the notion that all individuals develop a racial identity (Helms, 1990), and that understanding one's position along specific developmental stages allows for greater comprehension and openness to diversity and difference.

Although there are several "stage" theories of racial development (see, e.g., Cross, 1991; Phinney, 1989), all focus on a progressive upward movement from an unexamined identity to some form of identity crisis to a concluding reintegration stage of nonracist or antiracist identity positioning. Helms (1990), for example, provided a six-stage racial identity development model: (a) contact–denial/obliviousness; (b) disintegration–disorientation; c) reintegration–distortion; (d) pseudo-independence; (e) immersion/reeducation; (f) autonomy/nonracist. The key for educators is the confrontation with and resolution of the fact that different racial and ethnic groups not only have distinctive identities and cultures, but that such identities and cultures have historical, social, cultural, and political contexts of oppression, suppression, and/or privilege (Lawrence & Tatum, 1997; Tatum, 1992).

Thus White teachers' failure to acknowledge their own racial identity "becomes a barrier for understanding and connecting with the developmental needs of children of color"; alternatively, "progression along Helms's continuum is necessary for teachers to be successful first learning about and then teaching in ways that constitute antiracist pedagogy" (Lawrence & Tatum, 1997, pp. 163, 164). From this perspective, preservice teachers' resistance to antiracist pedagogy and content can be viewed as a simple by-product of residing at a lower stage in the racial identity developmental process. The goal for teacher educators becomes the systematic elevation of students' consciousness of their particular stage along the developmental progression. Students are able to realize that they are not "racist"; rather, they have not been exposed to such issues before, they have not realized the alternative stages of where they could/should be, and they have not been given an opportunity to work their way through the necessary stages.

Positioning resistance as a stage along a continuum of racial identity development demystifies and seemingly neuters preservice teachers' hostility, disregard, and rejection of culturally contentious dilemmas and debates.

"Racism" (or sexism or classism) becomes a lower stage that someone can just move through with adequate support and guidance. Although an identity development framework is helpful for theorizing resistance (it provides educators with concrete steps that can be taken to overcome students' antipathy to difficult issues), it also reinscribes a mythical and highly modernist notion of education and resistance.

Students' resistance becomes positioned as something that teachers are able to work through, given enough dialogue, data, and reflection. Such a perspective suggests that if we talk enough, if we are presented with enough convincing evidence, and if we deeply reflect on our own situation, we can overcome our deep-seated prejudices. This is the prototypical "the truth will set you free" argument. Unfortunately, it is also beholden to several problematic assumptions: namely, that learning and teaching are rational, linear, and progressive endeavors, and that all participants come to the process with the same aspirations, assumptions, and desires to "overcome" their negative behaviors and beliefs.

Although these assumptions may hold under traditional teaching conditions, highly contentious and volatile issues may be viewed as limit cases under which traditional norms break apart. As Jones (2001) argued, there is a strong "passion for ignorance" among White students when confronted with issues of privilege and inequity. To further presume that students "want" to change is to reject that students may be comfortable with their present positioning or that students even understand why such change is necessary (Butin, 2002; Rattansi, 1999).

The upward movement across stages thus feeds into our myths of education as a civil and rational progression and resistance as amenable to logic and reflection. Yet civility and reflection may in fact perpetuate the very conditions meant to be overcome (Mayo, 2002; Webb, 2001); the final "stage" of identity development may promote a paternalistic "friend of Black people" positioning that focuses on individual self-help while masking fundamental structural inequity and racism. A racial identity development model for resistance is a useful yet flawed heuristic.

Resistance as Alienation: Critical and Resistance Theory

Probably the most cited articulation of resistance is through the work of critical theorists. Grounded primarily in neo-Marxist discourses, critical theorists have long focused on how students' resistance is due to an alienation from the normative schooling process (Giroux, 1983; McLaren, 1999; Willis, 1981). Students' resistance and subsequent failure are understood as the rejection of the singular and hegemonic attributes of school as a White, middle-class, and body-less institution. Students' alienation from school is thus something done *to* students by external structures and norms as well as something done *by* students as an explicit rejection of such external structures and norms.

Resistance in the classroom is viewed as a multifaceted attempt to maintain one's cultural identity against the hidden curriculum of schooling; it is a rejection of the implicit assimilationist emphasis of schools as socializing agents (Freire, 1992; Giroux, 1983). Fundamentally, this resistance is due to the mismatch between the cultural capital of lower-class and non-White youth and the cultural capital of the school (Bourdieu & Passeron, 1977). Through resistance, students display and reinforce their allegiance to particular identity markers (e.g., masculinity, working class) while at the same time dismissing any claims of authority by the dominant school discourses of what constitutes a "successful" individual.

Critical theorists thus articulate resistance as a disruption of the "total institution" of schooling, which emphasizes order, control, and passivity; resistance becomes a strategic move of empowerment devoted to displaying other modes of agency, intelligence, and self, even if at the same time such actions disempower and alienate these youth from the dominant "culture of power" (Davidson, 1996; Willis, 1981).

Viewing student resistance as alienation provides critical theorists with a coherent framework by which to modify educational policies and practices: Alienation can only be transformed if oppressive conditions are fundamentally altered by reversing traditional power relations at all levels of the system. Kumashiro (2001), for example, challenges us to "imagine an assignment where students are helped to resist repeating their and their teachers' knowledges, identities, and practices, and to engage in the discomforting process of resignifying knowledges, identities, and practices" (p. 9). Students must be given voice and power in what is taught in the classroom and how it is taught (Shor, 1996), teachers must be able to control their own curriculum (Gatto, 2002), and schools must foster spaces for border crossings rather than races for consumerism.

A resistance-as-alienation perspective offers a forceful and clear vision for overcoming seemingly oppressive conditions in order to achieve a more just educational system. Yet the strength and clarity of this vision are also its main problem: Critical theorists have been persistently critiqued for engaging in the exact same form of oppression upon others that they have themselves decried (Butin, 2002; Ellsworth, 1997; Gore, 1993; Lather, 1998).

Critical theorists argue forcefully and directly for overpowering oppressive pedagogy. Yet the epistemological certainty of critical theorists' arguments denies a self-reflective hesitancy about whether other antioppressive strategies may be useful or that their own strategies may be flawed. As Ellsworth (1989) succinctly stated in her oft-cited essay, "Why Doesn't This Feel Empowering?," concerning the seeming empowerment of silenced voices: "I cannot unproblematically bring subjugated knowledges to light when I am not free of my own learned racism, fat oppression, classism, ableism, or sexism. No teacher is free of these learned and internalized oppressions" (quoted in Gore, 1993, p. 99).

Moreover, the forcefulness of critical theorists' arguments all too easily slides into a righteousness of the support of the "oppressed." I am not arguing against the reality that oppression is all too often a daily and humiliating reality for many. Rather, I want to suggest that this championing glosses over the hierarchies and problematics within the "oppressed" groups themselves—the homophobia within African-American culture, the racism within the first-wave women's movement, the "color-coding" of skin darkness across many non-White groups.

Finally, such denunciations of alternative pedagogical and theoretical perspectives diminish opportunities for alternative conceptualizations and reformulations of potentially effective and empowering strategies. The continued attacks on postmodern pedagogy and theory may be theoretically eloquent (Hill, McLaren, Cole, & Rikowski, 2003); yet they do little to promote actual pedagogical or theoretical change (Butin, 2004).

Resistance as Uncaring: Whiteness Studies

A final form of resistance can be conceptualized: student resistance as the uncaring rejection of ones' own complicity in the culturally contentious issues under discussion, specifically in relation to one's privilege of Whiteness. Although a critical perspective viewed student resistance as a noble undertaking, Whiteness studies sees student resistance as the refusal and avoidance of the realization of White privilege and how it is embedded within our society's very practices, structures, and thoughts (Fine, Weiss, Powell, & Wong, 1997; Frankenberg, 1997; Levine-Rasky, 2002; McIntyre, 1997).

Whiteness studies have mapped out the means by which such resistance occurs—namely, students disclaim the charge of White privilege as both invisible and inevitable. Student resistance manifests itself as the misappropriation of a presentist and acontextual argument that sees all forms of racism, discrimination, and prejudice as something that happened "long ago," to "someone else," and thus has "nothing to do with me." Moreover, because it has to do with outward appearances—with identity markers not as easily changeable as hair length or clothing—one's whiteness is presumed to simply exist and thus not be open for discussion or contestation.

Whiteness studies scholars use strategies analogous to those found in racial identity development and critical theory. An antioppressive rhetoric is linked to identity stage developments to argue for the efficacy and legitimacy of coming to understand and ultimately to reject the inherent privileging of one's whiteness.

Yet interestingly, Whiteness studies provide a diametrically opposed conception of resistance from critical theory. For critical theorists, student resistance is conceptualized as occurring due to nondominant students' rejection of the *maintenance* of the hidden and/or explicit social, cultural, and academic structures and practices of the school that privilege and sustain White, middle-class norms. For Whiteness studies, student resistance is conceptualized as occurring due to dominant students' rejection of the *exposure and analysis* of these same hidden and/or explicit social, cultural, and academic structures and practices of the school that privilege and sustain White, middle-class norms.

In both cases, student resistance can be understood as mode of identity politics, an attempt at sustaining a particular cultural identity. Yet the divergence of perspective is sharp: From a critical theory perspective, student resistance is a legitimate practice against an oppressive pedagogy; from a Whiteness studies perspective, student resistance is an illegitimate practice against an antioppressive pedagogy. In both cases student resistance is conceptualized as a static, either-or dichotomy with no middle ground: Either resistance occurs due to oppressive pedagogy (even if such pedagogy is conceived by the teacher as antioppressive) or resistance is overcome by an antioppressive pedagogy (even if it is taught in an oppressive manner due to its desire to overcome resistance).

The irony here is that both sides of the binary—students and teacher—have been essentialized as either teacher imposition or student opposition. This combative zero-sum positioning allows only one side, either the student or the teacher, to emerge as victor in the encounter. As such, it is to presume that only one side in the relationship—either the student or the teacher—has legitimacy on its side. Either the students have legitimacy to resist seemingly oppressive pedagogy, or the teachers have legitimacy to impose antiracist theories upon recalcitrant students. There is no middle ground.

What all four conceptualizations of resistance (as failure, as unknowing, as alienation, and as uncaring) demonstrate (either wittingly or not) is a disregard for the contextual and changing nature of when and why student resistance emerges (McFarland, 2001). Viewing student resistance as a fixed response—be it due to cognitive inadequacy, lack of racial identity self-comprehension, or desire to maintain a privileged status—commits oneself to a fixed notion of the individual and to the notion of what transformations may or may not be possible.

This is a troubling scenario for teacher educators committed to an agenda of social justice. If the social foundations of education classroom provides one of the few opportunities for prospective teachers to grapple with the weighty and contested issues of our educational system, and if that one opportunity is precluded due to student resistance and teachers' subsequent engagement with the resistance rather than with the content, then a social justice emphasis all too quickly disappears from the curricular horizon. The next section offers an alternative conceptualization of student resistance and thus a different means by which to allow social justice issues to pervade the social foundations classroom.

RESISTANCE AS IDENTITY (RE)CONSTRUCTION

Rather than begin with students' resistance, I suggest that it is more fruitful to view such resistance as the ongoing positioning of identity. This is what Foucault (1982) termed the "subjectification" of the self, where the individual is both constructed and constructs herself or himself as a subject and subjected to predefined categories of what constitutes an appropriate (and inappropriate) self.

This poststructuralist perspective is grounded in the decentering and fragmentation of the seemingly stable and unitary self. Identity is no longer seen as an innate consciousness; rather, our notions of identity and subjectivity are relocated within an external network of shared symbols, discursive practices, and structural conditions.

The self as fixed and stable, for example, as specific binary sex and gender positions, can thus be understood as the performative moves of specific gestures and acts employed to produce seemingly coherent narratives of identity. The repetitive enactment of specific (and specified) identities purportedly develops a sense of identity. My biological sex can thus be understood as the male "body signs" by which I read my body type and in turn by which I discursively define and am defined as masculine. In Judith Butler's (1999) phrasing, "My argument is that there need not be a 'doer behind the deed,' but that the 'doer' is variably constructed in and through the deed" (p. 142). The will-to-coherence for a stable and secure identity fosters the internalization (and reconstitution) of external cultural, historical, and political schemas for self-definition of what it means to be male.

If identity can be understood as the tactical deployment of a presumptive self, then student resistance can be reconceptualized as a student's attempted maintenance of a particular identity through the refusal and/or inability to see themselves in an alternate identity. Moreover, such resistance can be understood as the performance of an ongoing process of decisions meant to obscure the constant destabilization and reconstruction of a purportedly coherent identity. In other words, my students refuse to see themselves in "someone else's shoes" because it would reveal the frayed construction of their own sandals.

The pedagogical implications of such a perspective are profound. Critical theory and antioppressive/antiracist pedagogy attempt to directly confront and address the social justice and inequity issues within our schools and society. Yet in so doing, they position such teaching as engaging students' performative identities as stable, conscious, and amenable to persuasion and change. This disregards that the performative identity is a by-product of a process of always-ongoing identity reconstruction.

Pedagogy committed to encouraging social justice, I thus suggest, is better focused at engaging the student's process of identity construction and reconstruction than at simply propounding content knowledge at the student. The direct teaching of contested content knowledge presumes that what we perform is who we are. The accurate teaching of content knowledge is presumed to help individuals better understand themselves (as in racial identity development) or their misunderstandings (as in critical theory and Whiteness studies). This is accurate to the extent that the identity we deploy is a reinscription of our identity-in-process (see Abowitz, this volume). Yet this conflates our performative identities with our "true" selves, thereby essentializing and reifying a nonstatic process of an always-ongoing identity reconstruction.

An unbridgeable clash thus occurs if students resist certain contested content knowledge and the self is presumed to be stable: a clash between students' identities and specific content knowledge. From a "resistance as failure" perspective, the clash is between students' cognitive inabilities and the neutral content knowledge; from a "resistance as unknowing" perspective, the clash is between students' racial development and the contested content knowledge; from a "resistance as alienation" perspective, the clash is between students' cultural identities and hegemonic content knowledge; from a "resistance as uncaring" perspective, the clash is between students' privileged identities and a liberatory content knowledge.

These are all zero-sum setups. Either the student or the teacher (who is delivering the content knowledge) has to lose. If the resistance is successful, students maintain their "true" identities (be they "cognitively impaired," alienated, or privileged) and the content knowledge is not learned. If the teacher is successful in teaching the content knowledge, students are forced to change their "true" identities. In either case, the presumption is of a fixed and direct inverse correlation between student identities and contested content knowledge.

Teaching for identity destabilization and reconstruction—for exposing the process of how we learn content—offers an alternative methodology for overcoming resistance and fostering the potential of students' engagement with more diverse and contested perspectives. Resistance to contested content knowledge can be viewed as a proxy for students' desire for stability and certainty. Students resist that knowledge and truth (and by extension who they are) are contested, ambiguous, and changing "language games." Put otherwise, as students' understanding of the epistemology of knowledge changes, so does their epistemology of selfhood.

The proposition is as follows: Identity destabilization enhances tolerance of ambiguity of selfhood; such enhanced tolerance of ambiguity in turn widens the scope of openness to alternative and/or opposing perspectives of selfhood; such openness to alternative perspectives offers the potential for the reconstitution and redeployment of one's identity. This is what Lather (1998) termed a "pedagogy of not being sure," of working from a condition of doubt. Social justice from such a perspective is not at the heart of the message of the pedagogy; it instead becomes one by-product of the pedagogy.

An obvious implication is that the intended results of the impartment of contested content knowledge are not certain. We cannot expect that students will "get it." But this seeming problem—that we cannot promise that what we teach is what is learned—is in fact just the explicit acknowledgment that education is never a certain linear process of content knowledge transfer. This articulation simply makes this situation visible, discussable, and thus (hopefully) modifiable. The question thus becomes how to destabilize identity. How do we work from a condition of doubt? The next section offers some means to teach for identity destabilization and reconstruction toward the goal of social justice as a by-product.

SOCIAL JUSTICE AS A BY-PRODUCT

Let me offer one activity I have my students engage in approximately halfway through the semester: staring at a toilet. I ask my students to look at a toilet for 10 minutes sometime before the next class. They are to look at the toilet from the following perspectives and think about some of the questions listed:

- Functional/technical—How does the toilet work? Why is it built the way it is? Open the lid—what do all those parts do?
- Aesthetic—There is a toilet in the Museum of Modern Art in New York City. Why? How can the toilet be an object of art?
- Spiritual—What makes an object holy? Is it the materials, the location, the atmosphere? Is there something different/special about a cross, a star of David, a candle?
- Sensual—Can you view the toilet in a sensual/sexual way? Does it give and/or promote pleasure?
- Anthropomorphic—Does the toilet have an identity? If the toilet was a person, would it be male or female? Old or young? Outgoing or shy? What would it say if interviewed?

This activity is highly destabilizing. We have used a toilet every single day of our lives from the age of 3 or so, yet this is probably the first occasion where we have carefully examined this object. Why is something so ubiquitous so un-thought-of?

My students' discomfort during class discussion is palpable. I attempt to settle them (slightly) by focusing initially on the more obvious implications of this activity: our daily habituation of an activity precludes critical and thoughtful analysis; the "taken for granted" quality of an object inheres the status of normalcy. Outhouses, latrines, open holes in the ground, buckets, are all viewed as "strange." Yet going to the bathroom in a private enclosure that minimizes sights, sounds, and smells through the non-hands-on disposal of waste to an unknown location is "natural."

Just as "natural," I remind them, as a teacher-centered, classroom-based, age-graded, textbook-driven, discipline-fractured educational system. Just as we presume to know our toilet, so too do we presume to know our educational system. Yet the very ubiquity of both of these objects—the toilet and the educational system—diminishes our critical and sustained analysis of what it is, why we use it in the way we do, and what other functions it may have. My students "get it." In reflective notes written at the end of class they write that they have learned to look at things from multiple perspectives, never to take things for granted, and to be critical of the seemingly "natural." For them this is what the liberal arts are supposed to be all about—expanding our understanding of the world.

But there is more to this activity. The more disturbing aspect of this activity rests on the realization that I had my students stare at a toilet, rather than a more "neutral" object such as a tree, a light bulb, or a Diet Pepsi can. A toilet is an, if not *the*, archetype of the unclean in our society (Douglas, 1974). It connotes disease and dis-ease, something embarrassing not to be spoken of in public, much less in an undergraduate classroom. I then explain to my class how a toilet is actually cleaner than our kitchen sink: how there are 200 times more fecal bacteria on our cutting boards than on our toilet seats due to the type of materials used and the way and amount we clean each of these objects (Gerba, 2001). You are risking your health, I summarize, by eating in the kitchen; the toilet seat would be a much better place for lunch.

The shock value here is obvious—but so are the scientific data. So I push the issue. I quickly extend my right hand out to the nearest student, who obligingly shakes it. I then rub my left hand vigorously on the bottom of my shoe and extend it out to the same student. This time she refuses to shake hands. I explain that the chances of coming into contact with pathogenic bacteria are much greater from my hand than from the dirt under my shoe. I attempt to shake hands again. She refuses to take either hand now.

The disturbing aspect of this activity is that the truth does not set us free (at least not immediately and certainly not easily). The debriefing of this activity makes clear that we are all constrained and work within certain social norms and standards. We may become more self-conscious about some of them, but this in no way suggests that we can or will disregard them.

My students initially resist this. They want to see themselves as autonomous, radically free agents in a world of their own making and choosing. So I keep asking them where they will have lunch; I keep offering my left hand to shake. This is in fact metaphoric for much of my course. I engage in a wide variety of such activities throughout the semester: through reading, in-class discussion, and experiential learning activities. Most function at two levels—by providing clearer comprehension of the texts under discussion and at the same time by revisiting the question of our sense of identity as stable and internal, as somehow "our own."

My students slowly begin to understand. They begin to see that they are a part of a larger social system where they are not radical free agents but embedded within powerful, complex, and implicit normative frameworks and social habits. The hidden curriculum we talk about at the beginning of semester (Henry, 1963; Jackson, 1990) has now with the toilet become personal; there is a hidden curriculum to life. Students may not be willing to fully accept that the system plays them rather than that they are playing the system (Gadamer, 1989), but they no longer find such ideas preposterous. They are willing to contemplate that their identities are not as much their own as they originally believed.

So does it work? Do such activities foster students' sense of doubt about themselves, and thus of their definitional and categorical sense of others, and thus, ideally, enhance their willingness for renewed engagement with the contested positions engaged in throughout the social foundations of education course? I'm not sure.

But I have noted the following: If they can no longer be certain of the dichotomy of gender (Butler, 1999; Sondergaard, 2001), they are no longer willing to categorize girls as being only a certain way; if they can no longer define success by a unitary grade-based measure (Neill, 1960; Spindler, 2000), they are more tolerant of different definitions of what it means to be educated; if they come to realize their own compliance with unstated norms about toilets, they can no longer simply discount that there are other ways by which unstated norms may also work in the classroom (Heath, 1983).

To put the argument succinctly, I disrupt students' sense of identity as a means of fostering engagement with contested educational issues. Students can resist the academic content in and of itself if such content is threatening or disruptive to how they see the world and themselves. Yet if the world and they are already disrupted, if my students come to understand that their notions of the fixity of such things are a social construction, then the academic content I teach need no longer be so threatening or disrupting. My point is not to suggest that because everything is a social construction, everything is changeable. I am aware that social constructions become just as fixed and permanent as so-called "reality." My point instead is to begin a discussion about ourselves, our educational system, and our world as constructed, processional, and intersubjective creations.

In so doing, I embrace the notion of the student as always in a process of becoming. This allows me to bypass the direct confrontations of student resistance to academic content knowledge. It opens up the opportunity to engage with some of the most pressing issues within the social foundations of education curriculum. I have a different response at the conclusion of the semester when I again read the passage from Malcolm X:

> In America, the seeds of racism are so deeply rooted in the white people collectively, their belief that they are "superior" in some way is so deeply rooted, that these things are in the national white subconscious ... it isn't the American white man who is a racist, but it's the American political, economic, and social atmosphere that automatically nourishes a racist psychology in the white man. (pp. 364, 371)

My students may still not embrace such an articulation of the structural conditioning of our racial psychology (although some will). But what almost all of them can do is understand Malcolm X's position, why he says what he does, and how they too might think and act in an unacknowledged racist ways based on cultural and societal conditionings. A conversation has finally begun. Without resistance.

REFERENCES

Bidwell, C. (1965). The school as a formal organization. In J. G. March (Ed.), *Handbook of Organization* (pp. 972–1022). Chicago: Rand McNally.

Bourdieu, P., & Passeron, J.-C. (1977). *Reproduction in education, society, and culture.* London: Sage.

Butin, D. (2001). If this is resistance I would hate to see domination: Retrieving Foucault's notion of resistance within educational research. *Educational Studies, 32*(2), 157–176.

Butin, D. (2002). This ain't talk therapy: Problematizing and extending anti-oppressive education. *Educational Researcher, 31*(3), 14–16.

Butin, D. (2004). A review of Dave Hill, Peter McLaren, Mike Cole, and Glenn Rikowski's (editors) *Marxism Against Postmodernism in Educational Theory. Teachers College Record, 106*(2), 389–392.

Butler, J. (1999). *Gender trouble.* New York: Routledge.

Collins, R. (1992). *Sociological insight: An introduction to non-obvious sociology.* New York: Oxford University Press.

Cross, W. (1991). *Shades of black: Diversity in African-American identity.* Philadelphia: Temple University Press.

Davidson, L. A. (1996). *Making and molding identities in schools.* Albany, NY: SUNY Press.

Douglas, M. (1974). *Purity and danger: An analysis of concepts of pollution and taboo.* New York: Taylor & Francis.

Ellsworth, E. (1989). Why doesn't this feel empowering? Working through the repressive myths of critical pedagogy. *Harvard Educational Review, 59*(3), 297–324.

Ellsworth, E. (1997). *Teaching positions: Difference, pedagogy, and the power of address.* New York: Teachers College Press.

Fine, M. (1991). *Framing dropouts: Notes on the politics of an urban public high school.* Albany, NY: State University of New York Press.

Fine, M., Weis, L., Powell, L., Wong, L. M. (Eds.). (1997). *Off-white: Readings on race, power, and society.* New York: Routledge.

Foucault, M. (1982). Why study power: The question of the subject. In H. Dreyfus & P. Rabinow (Eds.), *Michel Foucault: Beyond structuralism and hermeneutics* (pp. 208–216). Chicago: University of Chicago Press.

Frankenburg, R. (1997). Introduction: Local whiteness, localizing whiteness. In R. Frankenburg (Ed.), *Displacing whiteness: Essays in social and cultural criticism* (pp. ??). Durham, NC: Duke University Press.

Freire, P. (1992). *Pedagogy of the oppressed.* New York, Continuum.

Gadamer, H. (1989). *Truth and method.* New York: Crossroad.

Gatto, J. T. (2002). *Dumbing us down: The hidden curriculum of compulsory schooling.* Gabriola Island, BC: New Society.

Gerba, C. P. (2001). Application of quantitative risk assessment for formulating hygiene policy in the domestic setting. *Journal of Infection, 43,* 92–98.

Giroux, H. A. (1983). *Theory and resistance in education: A pedagogy for the opposition.* South Hadley, MA: Bergin & Garvey.

Gore, J. (1993). *The struggle for pedagogies: Critical and feminist discourses as regimes of truth.* New York: Routledge.

Heath, S. B. (1983). *Ways with words.* Cambridge: Cambridge University Press.

Helms, J. (Ed.). (1990). *Black and White racial identity: Theory, research, and practice.* Westport, CT: Greenwood Press.

Henry, J. (1963). *Culture against man.* New York: Random House.

Hernstein, R. J., & Murray, C. A. (1994). *The bell curve: Intelligence and class structure in American life.* New York: Free Press.

Hill, D., McLaren, P., Cole, M., & Rikowski, G. (Eds.). (2002). *Marxism against postmodernism in educational theory.* Lanham, MD: Lexington Books.

Hytten, K., & Adkins, A. (2001). Thinking through a pedagogy of Whiteness. *Educational Theory, 51*(4), 433–450.

Kumashiro, K. (2000). Toward a theory of anti-oppressive education. *Review of Educational Research, 70*(1), 25–53.

Kumashiro, K. K. (2001). "Posts" perspectives on anti-oppressive education in social studies, English, mathematics, and science classrooms. *Educational Researcher, 30*(3), 3–12.

Kumashiro, K. K. (2002). Against repetition: Addressing resistance to anti-oppressive change in the practices of learning, teaching, supervising, and researching. *Harvard Educational Review, 72*(1), 67–92.

Jackson, P. (1990). *Life in classrooms.* New York: Teachers College Press.

Jones, A. (2001). Cross-cultural pedagogy and the passion for ignorance. *Feminism & Psychology, 11*(3), 279–292.

Lather, P. A. (1998). Critical pedagogy and its complicities: A praxis of stuck places. *Educational Theory, 48*(4), 487–498.

Lawrence, S., & Tatum, B. (1997). Teachers in transition: The impact of antiracist professional development on classroom practice. *Teachers College Record, 99*(1), 162–178.

Levine-Rasky, C. (2002). *Working through Whiteness: International perspectives.* Albany: State University of New York Press.

Lewis, O. (1966). *La vida: A Puerto Rican family in the culture of poverty—San Juan and New York.* New York: Vintage Books.

Lortie, D. C. (1975). *Schoolteacher: A sociological study.* Chicago: University of Chicago Press.

MacLeod, J. (1995). *Ain't no maki' it.* Boulder, CO: Westview Press.

Mayo, C. (2002). The binds that tie: Civility and social difference. *Education Theory, 52*(2), 169–186.

McIntyre, A. (1997). *Making meaning of Whiteness.* Albany: State University of New York Press.

McFarland, D. (2001). Student resistance: How the formal and informal organization of classrooms facilitate everyday forms of student defiance. *American Journal of Sociology, 107*(3), 612–678.

McLaren, P. (1999). *Schooling as a ritual performance.* Lanham, MD: Rowman & Littlefield.

NAACP (Call For Action in Education.) (2002). Available at www.naacp.org/work/education/educalltoactn2.pdf

Neill, A. S. (1960).*Summerhill: A radical approach to child rearing.* New York: Hart.

Noel, J. (2001). Examining the connection between identity construction and the understanding of multicultural education. *Multicultural Perspectives, 3*(2), 3–8.

Ogbu, J. (1992). Adaptation to minority status and impact on school success. *Theory into Practice, 31*(4), 287–295

Phinney, J. (1989). Stages of ethnic identity in minority group adolescents. *Journal of Early Adolescence, 9,* 34–39.

Rattansi, A. (1999). Racism, "Postmodernism" and reflexive multiculturalism. In S. May (Ed.), Critical multiculturalism: Rethinking multiculturalism and antiracist education (pp. 77–112). Philadelphia: Falmer Press.

Shor, Ira. (1996). *When students have power: Negotiating authority in a critical pedagogy.* Chicago: University of Chicago Press.

Shutz, A. (2004). Rethinking domination and resistance: Challenging postmodernism. *Educational Researcher, 33*(1), 15–23.

Sleeter, C., & Grant, C. (1999). *Making choices for multicultural education: Five approaches to race, class, and gender* (3rd ed.). New York: John Wiley & Sons.

Sondergaard, D. M. (2001). Poststructuralist approaches to empirical analysis. In *Qualitative Studies in Education, 15*(2), 187–204.

Spindler, G. D. (2000). Beth Anne—A case study of culturally defined adjustment and teacher perceptions. In G. D. Spindler & L. S. Spindler (Eds.), *Fifty years of anthropology and education, 1950–2000: A Spindler anthology* (pp. 111–126). Mahwah, NJ: Lawrence Erlbaum Associates.

Tatum, B. (1992). Talking about race, learning about racism: The application of racial identity development in the classroom. *Harvard Educational Review, 62*(1), 1–24.

Thernstrom, A., & Thernstrom, S. (2003). *No excuses: Closing the racial gap in learning.* New York: Simon and Schuster.

Valencia, R. (1997). *The evolution of deficit thinking: Educational thought and practice.* Philadelphia: Taylor & Francis.

Waller, W. (1932). *Sociology of teaching*. New York: Wiley & Sons.

Webb, P. T. (2001). Reflection and reflective teaching: Ways to improve pedagogy or ways to remain racist? *Race Ethnicity and Education, 4*(3), 149–156.

Wilson, W. J. (1997). *When work disappears: The world of the new urban poor.* New York: Vintage.

Willis, P. (1981). *Learning to labor.* New York: Columbia University Press.

X, Malcolm, & Haley, A. (1975). *Autobiography of Malcolm X..* New York: Random House.

Chapter 7

Confronting the Paradox of Autonomy in a Social Foundations Classroom

Kathleen Knight Abowitz

What does it mean to teach critical thought—requiring self-knowledge, degrees of detachment, and self-critique—in a class that explicitly rejects the myth of autonomy and teaches the pervasiveness of structural and cultural processes which construct reality itself? In teaching future teachers, how can we teach toward a sense of autonomy that positions students as free thinkers, capable of understanding and acting on the cultures and structures that shape them?

THE PARADOX OF AUTONOMY
IN THE FOUNDATIONS CLASSROOM

The social foundations undergraduate course that we teach at my institution is not unlike many courses across the country. It is the sole required social foundations offering for Miami University students wishing to become licensed to teach in our state. More than 300 students each semester take the class (EDL 204: Sociocultural Foundations of Education) in small sections of 22, and experience a syllabus that has been influenced by progressive, critical, feminist, antiracist, and multiculturalist discourses (see Appendix I). As the syllabus states, "EDL 204 is an introduction to the social foundations of education that applies a cultural studies approach to the investigation of selected educational topics." The typical student is from the midwestern U.S., a sophomore, 19 years old, white, female, and from a middle- or upper-middle-class culture. Miami University is a selective public university with a relatively elite population—57% of the class of 2006 came from homes where the estimated total annual income of parents was $100,000 or more; 20.8% of this same class came from homes with annual income of $200,000 or more; and 32.6% of this group came to Miami with a high school GPA of an "A" or "A+" (Higher Education Research Institute, 2002).

A course setting out to teach a critical perspective on educational history, philosophy, and sociology, drawing on and often unsettling the lived experiences of students who have largely known schools to be places of achievement and success, clearly has an ambitious agenda. At Miami we rely on the traditions of social foundations itself—the interpretive, normative, and critical perspectives on education (Council of Learned Societies, 1997, p. 7)—to set the stage for this work. In EDL 204, schools are studied through an issue-based approach that examines the role of schooling versus education more generally; purposes and philosophies of education; the various social constructions that shape schooling and its differentiated outcomes, such as class, gender, race, ethnicity, and sexuality; and some contemporary issues that are read through lenses of history, politics, and ethics, such as the resegregation of public schooling, bilingual education, and tracking. Primary and secondary sources are used to make these issues become more meaningful, and first-person narratives also bring useful and often moving perspectives to the other kinds of texts in the course reader (Rousmaniere & Knight Abowitz, 2002).

The primary assignments for the class also explicitly attempt to challenge commonsense views of schooling through a critical framework we call text analysis. Students are asked to look at all texts to identify their arguments, rhetoric, historical, and philosophical contexts, their political and moral claims, and their potential implications for readers. Students are also asked to identify their own biases, experiences, and beliefs that help them to interpret the text—they work to name the lenses of experience and meaning that help them interpret the text that they are reading. Students use this same framework in their pedagogical group projects, where they analyze a contemporary issue related to education and subsequently engage in some form of action (building a web page, writing a letter to a legislator or other official, etc.) in order to participate in the public dialogue around their issue.

A traditional aim of the social foundations curriculum has been to help teachers understand the cultural and structural contexts in which they labor. Yet there are also continual assumptions made that teachers will use their understanding of these contexts to shape, challenge, and shift the status quo in schools. This is a paradoxical agenda. Kincheloe (1999) described the process of critical education this way:

We begin to understand and *disengage ourselves* from the social, political, and educational structures *that shape us*. We begin to expose the cultural stories (the metanarratives) that have grounded dominant ways of making sense of the world in general and education in particular. Our ability to see from a variety of perspectives forms the basis of a conversation about the unstated assumptions of the culture (a metadialogue) with ourselves. (p. 79, italics mine)

Through disengagement, social foundations instructors wish to both promote free thinking and critical reflection, yet we also fight against the myth of autonomy that circulates as radical individualism in our culture. We rely on some notion of autonomy, however, in believing that students can detach from their perspectives and views through critical analysis. We want "free thinking," but many of us also want students to be transformed by the curriculum into critical educators. For some instructors, critical, "free" thinking is not a cognitive exercise for neutral purposes—it is a tool in the critical, reconstructionist vision of schooling. Yet our politically conservative undergraduate students are typically fighting such transformations, what we call "resistance" in critical-speak. I would argue that there may be good reasons for resistance, if our conceptions of our students do not grant them some degree of autonomy, or the capacity to govern themselves to varying degrees, to be truly "free thinking" in ways that we do not share.

Joel Feinberg (1989) stated that autonomy is "an ideal complex of character traits" and described 12 virtues of autonomy: self-possession, individuality, authenticity or self-selection, self-creation or self-determination, self-legislation, moral authenticity, moral independence, integrity, self-control, self-reliance, initiative, and responsibility for self. Autonomy is touted as an essential virtue of liberal citizens (Callan, 1997) and as an important universal pinnacle of human development (Kohlberg, 1984; Perry, 1970). Yet other contemporary theorists decry autonomy as a set of Western delusions. Communitarians deny that the self can be detached from its historical roles, communities, and traditions (MacIntyre, 1981). Cultural or difference feminists call autonomy a myth promoted by a radically individualist patriarchal culture that suppresses human interdependence and relation, those more feminine of human ideals (Miller, 1976). Critical multiculturalists view autonomy as a White, Eurocentric cultural ideal, which, in its posing as an American virtue, endangers the bonds of community and culture of minority cultures (Kymlicka, 1989). Poststructural critics argue that autonomy symbolizes a Western investment in the belief of rationality over the murky, messy workings of the largely unconscious and nonrational world of human mind and language (Kristeva, 1982). Social foundations instruction reflects these conflicts over autonomy. As U.S. citizens, many of us also have a deep and mostly unconscious belief in the myth of autonomy, yet as social foundations scholars, we are well versed in the ways that individuals are *not* autonomous beings.

What notion of autonomy, if any, could social foundations instructors envision for a course that utilizes critical pedagogies to undermine western narratives of individualism and the autonomous self? This question focuses the inquiry here. I begin by laying out some of the pedagogical challenges faced by typical social foundations teachers in negotiating the terrain of autonomy, critical thinking, and teaching. To explore these problems, I have created two composite characters, Tim and Andrea, who in their respective classrooms are faced with questions of autonomy, indoctrination, teacher authority, and resistance. To contextualize the narratives of Tim and Andrea, I then turn to a brief review of the philosophical debates about the role of autonomy as an educational aim. Drawing from the feminist reconceptualizations of liberal notions of autonomy, I argue that the student is a subject-in-process whose views are to be respected, but not necessarily because those views represent the product of fully realized self-reflection or human agency. Rather, we need to appreciate and respect the immense task that we expect students to take on in our classes and in other experiences in their college life: the task of self-authorship (Baxter Magolda, 2001; Cooke, 1999). I frame a conception of autonomy that benefits from the reconstructions of the concept of autonomy by feminist and poststructural philosophers, and later, using constructivist theories of development, explore how an understanding of student autonomy as understood through the process of self-authorship might guide practice in the social foundations classroom.

TEACHER AUTHORITY AND STUDENT AUTONOMY IN A SOCIAL FOUNDATIONS CLASSROOM

Tim, a doctoral student who has for the past year been strongly influenced by the ideas of critical theorists in education, is teaching a section of EDL 204 for the first time this semester. He assigns Henry Giroux's essay, "Are Disney Movies Good for Your Kids?," from the course reader. The essay introduces a critical view of media culture, especially children's media. Tim is shocked at his students' reaction to the reading in class discussion. Almost all the students disavow Giroux's argument, and tell their own stories about magical moments and positive lessons they've experienced through Disney movies, stories, and characters. Tim, in response, spontaneously delivers a 20-minute lecture on the history and role of critical theory in education today. Tim also describes some of his own experiences of marginalization and discrimination as an African American male in a society whose dominant media narratives did not include his face or culture in realistic portrayals. His empassioned viewpoints seem to engage the students, but many shift in their seats uncomfortably at times when he takes different points they have made earlier in the conversation and explicitly denounces them using the work of critical theorists and his own experiential knowledge. Afterward, Tim asks for responses or questions from the class, and no one raises a hand.

Tim could be accused of silencing the questions and critiques of students in favor of his own point of view. Yet Tim's decision to deliver a speech to counter the dominant understandings of Disney and media culture might be embraced by critical pedagogues as justifiable in a conservative society where "free thinking" about Disney or anything else has been suppressed. Tim's move to bring his own convictions and knowledge to bear in this situation represents a kind of rationalized attempt to indoctrinate that is explicitly or implicitly sanctioned by many within the critical tradition in education. As Westheimer and Kahne (2003) noted, there are important political and moral reasons for the teacher to avoid taking a neutral stance toward knowledge. "Too often when educators have focused on how to avoid indoctrinating by remaining 'neutral,' they have instead paved the way for a kind of education that serves the interests of those with power" (p. 2). Tim, in attempting to challenge the disproportional influence of the Disney mythology in popular culture, engages in a kind of justified indoctrination.

To indoctrinate is to "imbue with a partisan or sectarian opinion or point of view." The verb *imbue* is particularly telling here. To imbue is "to permeate or influence as if by dying ... to tinge or dye deeply" (Merriam-Webster, 1988). As Macmillan (1998) noted, some indoctrination is inevitable in human learning because what we know as children are the stories of culture and family which are typically propositions taken as true without question. Thus, as the culture instructs my young daughter about what it means to be a woman, she is deeply colored by these lessons. "Our most basic world pictures must be achieved by non-rational teaching and learning," Macmillan wrote, but as children grow up, "they learn how to reason—a complex, long-term process, needless to say—[and through this process] students become able to question all beliefs, standards, and customs" (p. 10). When Tim teaches, he is working against many powerful forces that have already deeply colored the worldviews of these students. As the students in EDL 204 study the history, philosophy, and politics of schooling in the United States from a critical perspective, we are attempting to help them question their beliefs not just about education, but about the very cultural and structural arrangements that order the hierarchies of society, schools, and their own existence. The critical perspective that influences our EDL 204 curriculum and teaching is perhaps only leveling the playing field in a society where critiques of the dominant culture are rarely heard, as Westheimer and Kahne argued, but it is not a perspective that is readily embraced by our students. Their resistance leads to Tim's attempt to interject his worldview more powerfully into the classroom discourse. This leads to more resistance, or more learning, or more evasive moves, such as performing.

It is all too common in our grade-conscious environment of higher education for students to simply "read" the instructor's beliefs and commit-

ments and to perform those commitments back to him or her in an effort
to please and conform to the classroom authority. Tim's move may provide a way for students to question and investigate Disney as a cultural
icon, but in the context of a place like Miami, it is just as likely to promote a
shutting down, an unwillingness to authentically reflect on and struggle
with one's own views.[1] Mirroring the instructor and performing what is
seen as desired by the teacher is far easier than actually doing the work of
self-reflection and cultural investigation. Despite these dangers, teacher
testimony is seen as pedagogical ammunition for many teachers in social
foundations classrooms. When students' first inclinations are to repel the
truths of social reproduction, for example, or to reject a deep understanding of the racist assumptions that are built into the historical and contemporary fabric of public education, many social foundations instructors
may respond with variations on Tim's theme of "testify and deliver," seen
as justified indoctrination by some educators, but perhaps also viewed by
students as "the party line" that they are to toe for the duration of the
course. In such a passive form of resistance, or even in more aggressive, direct forms of resistance, students guard their autonomy, their right to
have a different belief system than the one held by the instructor. The
trouble is, in evading Giroux's critique, their beliefs are no more reflec-
tively held than they were before they read the essay. Learning thus is successfully avoided, with their own comfortable identities, knowledge, and
values left undisturbed (Kumashiro, 2002).

Teachers who question the moral, political, or pedagogical virtues of testimony or testimonial forms of education, and who are heavily invested in
the rights of the student as an autonomous person, deal differently with student resistance. Andrea is another fictive teacher of EDL 204, and her story
represents another approach to teacher authority and student autonomy.

Andrea, a new social foundations instructor with feminist convictions, has
students read Peggy McIntosh's essay, "White Privilege and Male Privilege:
A Personal Account of Coming to See Correspondences Through Work in
Women's Studies," in the class reader. Andrea also requires students to write
a journal response to the reading. The journals are described in the syllabus
as places to "engage the reading and your ideas about the class readings and
concepts," and are not assigned letter grades but are evaluated through the
"Class engagement" portion of the total grade. Jane, a White conservative
Christian, is a sophomore in Andrea's class, and fills three single-spaced
pages regarding her views on McIntosh's article. Jane denounces racism using her Biblical point of view, but she also rejects McIntosh's claims about the

---

[1]Walker (1999) wrote that when there is no genuine agreement to participate in learning,
there is no self-control in respect to learning. "A student in disagreement with a teacher may
well exercise self-control, in the sense of self-discipline, by restraining negative emotional reac-
tions which are not in their own interest .... This self-control ... masks, through suppression,
relevant aspects of the student's true self and so hinders authentic self-expression" (p. 118).

role of women in society. Her critique of feminism is especially detailed, articulate, and is grounded in quotes from the Bible and conservative theologians. There is little evidence that Jane has seriously considered feminism from the viewpoint of authors such as McIntosh who are within the feminist paradigm, however. Andrea reads Jane's journal entry and because she has "engaged the reading," she gives Jane full credit, raises a few questions in the margins in response to her claims or accusations, and hands the paper back to Jane. Andrea feels discouraged that she gave students the opportunity to "engage" the readings in such a free-form manner, but does not feel it would be fair to assign Jane a low grade on this journal assignment simply because her views are wrong according to Andrea's perspectives. Jane did, after all, fulfill the guidelines of the assignment.

Andrea's response to Jane's conservative Christianity could be read as one that completely respects her autonomy as a student and a person. Andrea does not wish to use her authority as teacher simply to override or silence Jane's conservative views, so she goes in the opposite direction by allowing Jane to use her "voice" to argue against McIntosh's thesis. Andrea remembers what it was like when she was a sophomore in college and encountered for the first time an openly socialist professor of economics who opened a world of critique against capitalism that was shocking and mind-boggling to her. Like Garrison (1998), she is sensitive to the existential earthquakes she is hoping to bring about in her students' lives.

> Recall an occasion when you first realized an object, end, or institution dear to you was doomed: how did it feel? I have had many graduates of Falwell's Liberty Baptist University in my classes. They are responsible and hard working students. I try to remember my feelings when I left the Church of God I grew up with in Georgia. In my classes I am effectively telling some good people to abandon the beliefs and values of just about everyone and everything they love. You cannot do such a thing and confidently predict it will always come out well. Remember, our beliefs and values are who we are, they are embodied and held passionately; they constitute our very identities. Have you ever heard the sound of your dearest value breaking? (p. 23)

Garrison empathized with students who are, as MacIntyre (1981) reminded us, "born with a past" (p. 221). Although Kumashiro (2002) argued for the value of "learning through crisis" as students work through uncomfortable knowledge and spaces, the intimidating, belief-shifting potential of this (identity) work puts both instructor and student in very difficult positions (p. 74).

Andrea knows Jane is fighting hard to prevent her dearest values from breaking, to prevent her current worldview and relational webs from breaking and changing. Andrea is both sympathetic to the reasons for Jane's resistance and respectful of the articulate manner in which Jane has responded to the reading. Yet in fashioning an assignment that compels her to treat student "engagements" as complete and final statements of their beliefs, Andrea has undermined her authority to help students *fashion* rather than *find* their identities and voices within the context of social foundations of education (Maher & Thompson Tetreault, 2001, p. 19). Andrea seems to view autonomy as a human right rather than as a capacity to be learned and developed through critical reflection. Because Jane provides evidence for her views, and articulates them with depth and conviction, Andrea believes her role as teacher is limited in terms of challenging the content of her beliefs.

Andrea and Tim confront student resistance to the critical perspectives of EDL 204, and make pedagogical decisions that are based, in part, in their assumptions about student autonomy. Tim responds by passionately defending and explaining a critical position so that students might see more clearly how their worldviews are not neutral but influenced by dominant perspectives. He will move some students to reason through their perspectives on the media more carefully, but he will drive others underground with their true views in hopes of earning a good grade. Andrea, on the other hand, respects student autonomy to disagree with texts that are explicit in their ideological bent, but is left wholly unsatisfied, believing that Jane has not learned about some important aspects of gender and education that are part of the class objectives.

The responses of these two teachers are perhaps too neatly and diametrically opposed, but their actions represent those of countless EDL 204 instructors over time, including myself. I suspect social foundations faculty from across the country will find familiar themes in their stories. The difficulty in negotiating resistance in our classrooms hinges on a confusion over teacher authority, and our students' rights and abilities to define and determine themselves. A definition of autonomy is needed that can help instructors view students as subjects requiring respect and that can help them shape pedagogy that positions students as subjects-in-process.

THINKING ABOUT AUTONOMY

> For the proper and inestimable worth of an absolutely good will consists precisely in the fact that the principle of action is free of all influences from contingent grounds, which only experience can furnish. This lax or even mean way of thinking which seeks its principle among empirical motives and laws cannot too much or too often be warned against, for human reason in its weariness is glad to rest upon this pillow. (Kant, 1981, p. 34)

Kant said that only a priori principles can undergird truly moral action, and that experience, emotion, and desire are not to be trusted. Although many liberal philosophers today wish to distance themselves from much of Kantian thinking, autonomy remains a mainstay in liberal thinking and in conceptions of liberal education. The goal of schooling, for many liberal philosophers, is to teach the capacities and habits of autonomous thinking, to push students off their "pillows" of socialization, common sense, and sectarian views into more objective and reasoned perspectives on their world and lives. Various critical, poststructural, and feminist critiques have taken steady and repeated aim at the autonomous subject of the liberal tradition, finding it to be a dangerous fiction that promotes a universal atomistic male subject as the model of personhood. Schools organized to promote autonomy as an educational aim may be reproducing a way of thinking and acting that leads to further domination of women, people of color, and other groups. Yet while recognizing the limits and illusions of a liberal, universal, abstract, separated, self-directing, autonomous liberal individual, many feminist, poststructural, and critical theorists still recognize the need for some reconstructed vision of an ideal of self-governance and individual agency. Through exploring some of these reconstructions of autonomy here, I hope to pave the way for an understanding of student autonomy capable of guiding social foundations instructors in their pedagogical dilemmas with student-as-subject.

Liberals, concerned with human freedom, often "think of autonomy as a characteristic of persons essential to the maintenance of a free society" (Callan, 1988, p. 25). Kenneth Strike, for example, believed that autonomy is a right of students. "Human beings are ends in themselves and are moral agents who are responsible to choose wisely on their own behalf and act justly with respect to others" (Strike, 1982, in Kerr, 2002, p. 19). The right to autonomy has three components, according to Strike: "the right to self-determination, or the freedom to choose one's own beliefs, lifestyle, and so on; the right to participate in collective choices; and psychological freedom which is the ability to exercise rational judgment and self-control" (p. 19). Strike conceived of autonomy as a moral ideal in which a person is responsible to choose wisely for themselves and in their actions toward others—justice sets the context of the autonomy ideal. In addition, justice requires not only psychological freedom and self-determination, but also the right to participate in collective choices and be governed by these choices. "He or she is willing to be fair and cooperate so long as others are also willing to abide by the terms of cooperation" (Kerr, 2002, p. 24). Autonomy is only as powerful as the just society—the fair processes and procedures that are worked out through democratic deliberations by citizens and their leaders.

Citizens in a liberal democracy are pluralistic, and this is another reason why autonomy is an important aim for liberal conceptions of education. Like other philosophers in the liberal-egalitarian tradition (Rawls, 1971, 1993), Strike viewed our liberal democracy as undeniably and unalterably pluralistic, and believed schools need to reflect and teach about the diversity of worldviews that exist in our culture in order to foster the tolerance and multicultural knowledge necessary for deliberation and shared governance.[2] "The justice we need under pluralism requires us to think for ourselves in much more radical way than we must when all can take for granted the same conception of the good and the right" (Callan, 1997, p. 43). In our country, families bring up children according to many different traditions, cultural norms, and moral codes. One of the roles of a liberal education is to help students put their background, traditions, and worldviews into a larger context so that, when required, they can reason with diverse others who do not share their worldview and norms, knowing that their worldview is only one among many legitimate ways of life.

Although many critics of liberalism question the liberal individual as an unrealistic construction void of interpersonal relations, cultural contexts, and traditions, liberals respond by saying that detachment from one's original goals is not the purpose of education, but that critical reflection on one's goals and societies is an aim of democratic schooling. Communitarians criticize that such an education would position students as unencumbered by any ends prior to choice (Sandel, 1982); that is, such a liberal education assumes students can cognitively step away from their cultural and moral perspectives by choosing to do so—all ends are chosen. Callan (1997) stated that this important critique of liberal thinking on autonomy does not require that people detach themselves from their ends, but to engage in self-reflection about what those ends are and what values they hold in a public, pluralistic society. "Whatever reflection autonomy requires does not demand that we can detach ourselves from all our ends. The requirement is only that we be capable of asking about the value of any particular end with which we currently identify and able to give a thoughtful answer to what we ask" (p. 54). Such a requirement does not require a rejection of one's beliefs, for example, about schooling in a democratic society, but requires that the acceptance of one's beliefs be an informed choice among alternative beliefs, not a result of ignorance, chosen or unchosen. Callan (1997) called this responsible choice, and it does not require that our students have detachable commitments to their beliefs, but that they have the capacity to "choose on the condition that what we embrace merits choice, and that means we must be ready to reconsider should we come to see that we were mistaken" (p. 59). Winch (2002) named critical reflection "the ability to assess the worthwhileness of ends from a point of view that is detached, in the sense that it is free from quotidian concerns and involves a long-term perspective on one's life" (p. 33).

---

[2]There is not space here to discuss the differences among liberal philosophers regarding autonomy. I am discussing the liberal tradition here as it is articulated through the liberal-egalitarian philosophies of John Rawls, but even within this tradition there is diversity of thinking about the importance and scope of autonomy. See Kerr (2002) and Winch (2002) for examples.

Liberals emphasize detachment from commitments and worldviews as not the ultimate goal but as a part of a good liberal education. They are not alone in this emphasis. Many theorists who criticize the liberal paradigm, such as feminist and poststructural thinkers, rely on some notion of detachment. Communitarians, on the other hand, point out the limits and even dangers of detachment. Identities are constructed as layers of history and belief and cultural practices from which detachment is extremely difficult and not always desirable. Detachment endangers these cultural beliefs and practices, because rational reflection may result in many abandoning their practice. Still, liberals and others who are interested in critical reflection are not necessarily committed to detachment as an end goal, but as an important cognitive ability.

For many social foundations instructors, detachment is an important process toward unlearning the beliefs that result in educational and social injustices. Return to the case of Tim, who upon encountering resistance to Giroux's perspective on Disney gave his students a lecture on critical views of media and culture. In a certain sense Tim is trying to push students away from their views about Disney in hopes of making them critical educators. Part of providing students with alternatives to their commonsense understandings of culture and schooling is a project of passionate argument and persuasive talk. Liberal education, in this sense, is not treating students as autonomous beings, but as autonomous beings-in-process; it is helping students to see the reasonable alternatives to their own ideologies and beliefs about schooling. Feinberg (1998) said "freedom of association" is an important principle of public education in a liberal democracy, holding that students have the rights to choose their alliances, but that "children are not to be treated as if they were *destined* to relive the lives of their parents" (p. 11, italics in original). Tim's actions could be interpreted, through a liberal definition of autonomy, as helping students to see and respect an alternative view about culture and schooling than the one that most of his students were raised to believe, whether by parents, media, or popular culture. He is advocating and urging the importance of critical reflection, as Winch defined it, by helping them take a larger perspective on an issue about which they have deeply held, although probably not carefully examined.

But remember the earlier definitions of critical thinking—thinking toward social transformation in the critical theorist's tradition. Tim's likely desire to teach detachment is not simply a cognitive commitment, but a step toward his goal of making these conservative students into something like himself: a critical educator committed to leftist ideologies about education. Such an educational aim would violate most liberal thinking about autonomy, because students in Tim's class would not be respected as beings with rights to or capacities for independent thought and self-determination. Critical education, for philosophical liberals, is not the same as critical reflection for critical theorists of the Frankfurt tradition. Liberals typically embrace critical reflection as a process that better enables students to choose among a variety of legitimate life forms and ideologies. Critical theorists in the Frankfurt tradition believe that the result of critical reflection ought to be a form of political transformation, moving in the general direction of right to left. So "critical thinking," as it transpires in social foundations classrooms, will sometimes look like liberal critical thinking (with more emphasis on autonomous reasoning) and at other times looks like neo-Marxist critical thinking (with more focus toward progressive critique).

But an analysis of autonomy and its place in teaching would not be complete without an examination of feminist views. Feminist thinkers have criticized the Western philosophical tradition of autonomy on a number of fronts. Autonomy is seen as a normative force that requires women to give up affiliation and relation in order to become separate and self-defined (Gilligan, 1982; Miller, 1976). The force of autonomy in our culture as a moral pinnacle of human development is a result of an androcentric view, normalizing what may be a preferred masculine way of being over other ways of being. The liberal understandings of an autonomous self became further normalized and sanctified through prominent human development theorists (Kohlberg, 1984; Perry, 1970) who echoed the liberal view of self as a unified, unfolding self assumed to be originating within a subject that is "unpolluted by conditioning or manipulation" (Di Stefano, 1996, p. 97). "Feminists have argued that the Kantian approach must be rejected if ethical theory is to recognize the moral importance of emotions, close personal relationship, social relationships generally, and the non-impartial nature of any actual ethical standpoint" (Friedman, 2000, p. 212).

Agency for men and women might best be constructed by dropping the standard concept of autonomy itself, as Noddings (2002) argued. Difference feminists in education have offered productive critique that undermines the importance of autonomous reasoning and promotes attention to "contextual detail and interpersonal emotional responsiveness" (Friedman, 2000, p. 206). Noddings defined the self as "a sort of co-constructed script that directs and interprets the activities of the organism. Together, the organism and this scriptlike self constitute a person" (p. 117). This organic, relational, shifting self is a far cry from the liberal person who is entitled to rights of self-determination. If self is a relation, as Noddings (2002) claimed, then the distinctions between an autonomous and a heteronomous life fade away. Noddings wanted a relational notion of self to reconstruct the educational system and society. To correct for schooling that promotes radical individualism and competition, "we *must allow* ourselves to be affected by the needs and predicaments of others," instead of trying to foster an independent self through critical detachment (p. 112). Only in encounters with others do we see ourselves and do we find the "building blocks of the self under construction" (p. 12). Liberal notions of autonomy imply the self is found through an internal search—Noddings suggested that perhaps the concept should be abandoned for a more useful concept of reflection, a process of self-examination and evaluation experienced in encounters with others. Reflection, at least, has none of the Western legacies of the individualistic self (p. 116). Yet reflection alone may not recover forms of agency that are necessary for feminist and other goals of social justice. Feminist critiques of autonomy, argued Huntington (1995), should not be simple corrections for the "Cartesian subject" ruled by rationality and free will; rather, "feminist theory needs to pave a way between subjecting women to the very normative conception of autonomy that led to their oppression and recovering the agency denied them by masculinist views of subjectivity" (p. 39).

Poststructuralist feminists share some of Noddings's misgivings of the atomistic liberal self, but disagree with the essentialistic notions of women as relational beings that undergird the arguments of difference feminists like Noddings. Poststructuralists believe that an atomistic self represents Western humanity's desperate wish for self-direction and control that is largely impossible in a world constituted through the prisons of language and social constructions of identity. "The poststructuralist feminist claims that, while subjects do have 'agency' in a weak situated sense, their possibilities for agency are posited only through and thus restricted by the competing discourses that comprise their world." (Huntington, 1995, p. 41). There is little that humans can directly control, and encouraging students to critically reflect in order to know themselves, to understand and order their own views in a more coherent fashion, erroneously imagines the self as an "inner space" that is pure and powerful.

In contrast, the poststructural self is split between the unconscious and the conscious, and constructed not through an autonomous, rational journey of self-development but through the language and performances that we create using the tools of the social world around us. We live in and through discursive constructions not of our making. But agency is not lost. The social world gives us language and multiple discourses, our humanity gives us the power to imagine, and we are therefore not impossibly imprisoned by our social contexts. Kristeva's notion of subjects-in-process (also translated as subjects-on-trial) reminds us that identity is a process of differentiation, between our own diverse selves and between ourselves and others (Kristeva, 1984). Because there is no "inner self" that is continuous, stable, and consistent, human subjectivity is a creative process of opening and renewal (McAfee, 2000, p. 69).

Feminist and poststructuralist thinking helps retool autonomy as a creative, relational, ongoing process of encounters with persons or texts that demand we see the world differently than we did prior to such encounters.

This notion of self seems well designed for teaching any subject matter, because part of the pedagogical encounter assumes some sort of openness to encounters with other people and ideas. Remaining open and to creative innovations of self requires vulnerableness, derived through love or psychoanalysis, according to Kristeva (1987). Noddings's relational self also requires openness, called reciprocity in the caring relation between teacher and student. Such vulnerability goes against the norm in many college classrooms. Jane, the conservative Christian in Andrea's class, is fighting against the openness and renewal that could be possible in her encounter with McIntosh's ideas. What Andrea is inviting her to do through an engagement with feminism feels dangerous to Jane. The subject-in-process is "always on trial and precariously poised between subjecthood and disintegration. Alterity always promises and beckons but threatens the borders of the self" (McAfee, 2000, p. 77). Jane's resistance, like that of many of the students in EDL 204, is in some ways an understandable reaction to the haziness that a good liberal education brings about, in educational contexts. The foreigner, the strange idea or radical ideology, is on all sides.

> Confronting the foreigner whom I reject and within whom at the same time I identify, I lose my boundaries, I no longer have a container, the memory of experiences when I had been abandoned overwhelm me, I lose my composure. I feel lost, indistinct, hazy. (Kristeva, 1991, in DiStefano, 1996, p. 109)

Feeling lost is what we experience when we venture too far from home. But leaving home, said Martusewicz (2001), is at the heart of becoming educated. Martusewicz, in her work on a poststructuralist approach to education and ethics, wrote that to become different from who we have been, we must leave the familiar and encounter the disruptive, creative world of difference. But this leaving is not an abandonment of attachment itself. "Detachment is at the heart of education and thus of our ability to think of a better world. We leave home as we search for different relations and ways of being on the earth" (Martusewicz, 2001, p. 34). Detachment is provoked by "flashes from unpredictable sources" and is "necessarily painful" (p. 37), but is not designed to push the student back onto an individualist sense of anomie or atomism. It is to help the student reframe (although not necessarily radically transform) her or his understanding of self, schools, and society within an enlarged view of her or his context, interdependencies, and possible obligations. Detachment and reframing are useful metaphors for liberal education in a college setting, where many students have physically left home in order to begin an educational journey full of encounters with difference in the classroom and cocurricular contexts of college and university life. It is difficult to imagine the liberal arts college experience without some notion of "leaving home," if not literally then certainly figuratively. But this leaving is not something done alone, as a lone traveler on a dangerous journey—it is a journey traveled with others, including teachers, who best serve students when they are in tune with the demands of this trip.[3]

LIMITS OF TEACHER AUTHORITY: CONTENT-NEUTRAL OVER SUBSTANTIVE AUTONOMY

Detachment and reframing in a relational context may be a helpful rearticulation of liberal autonomy, but these concepts alone do not help us understand the limits of teacher authority in the Kantian quest to push students off their pillows of common sense and familiar belief. In order to successfully engage Jane in the content of Peggy McIntosh's essay, must Andrea's goal be to move Jane from conservative Christianity to some form of feminism? Friedman (2003) raised this question in her discussion of content-neutral versus substantive conceptions of autonomy:

> Does autonomy require someone to have commitments of a particular sort or that fall within certain guidelines? Some philosophers have argued that someone is not autonomous unless she chooses in accord with certain values. In particular, she must choose in accord with the value of autonomy itself, or, at least, choose so as not to undermine that value. This is the "substantive" conception of autonomy. (p. 19)

By this account of autonomy, one cannot be autonomous while choosing subservience. By many feminist accounts, this is what Jane would be doing by embracing a conservative Christianity against a feminist view on equality. However, Jane might be considered autonomous by a content-neutral understanding of autonomy, wherein the manner in which she chooses her brand of Christianity is what matters. Friedman (2003) used the example of a woman giving up her own future autonomy by joining a religious order. "She will become nonautonomous in her behavior after making and adhering to that sort of choice, but this does not mean that she was nonautonomous when first making the choice" (p. 19).

In working with young adults in a public context, content-neutral autonomy is a preferable threshold for self-determination for several reasons. First, substantial autonomy is an ideal that potentially violates the relational self. Following the feminist account of the related self, Jane's commitments are likely formed in her past encounters with others, and represent more than simply a habitual socialization to heteronomy. They

---

[3]The language here directly reflects the influence of my colleague Marcia Baxter Magolda. Baxter Magolda's (1999) understanding of intellectual development has shaped my thinking in the area of autonomy and learning.

represent relationships and commitments, and are not to be taken lightly, even if they are not to be taken at face value, either (a point I address later). Second, the goal of substantive autonomy assumes too much—it assumes that it is desirable to value autonomy more highly than many other moral ideals, like friendship, trust, or care. To teach with the aim of developing substantive autonomy in students is to choose *for* students the desired outcome of their liberal education—an oxymoron, to be sure. Third, an ideal of substantive autonomy further propels a unified, undivided, coherent self, rationally choosing choice above all else. In a class that teaches theories of social reproduction, histories of segregated schooling, and educational legacies of meritocracy, the vision of substantive autonomy as an ideal simply defies the powerful evidence that human choice and agency are always limited, often repressed and constrained by one's position, status, skin color, and other identifications.

Friedman (2003) acknowledged that content-neutral autonomy represents a lower standard than substantive autonomy. But this lower standard reflects the fact that students arrive in classrooms with a range of commitments—familial, religious, ethnic, political—that may be inconsistent with a primary valuing of personal autonomy. Content-neutral autonomy does not require students to give up these commitments, necessarily, in favor of substantive autonomy, but it does require that students become minimally self-determining. What self-determination would require, for content-neutral autonomy, still represents serious work, however:

> It is indeed a significant threshold for someone with a stable array of deep and persistent concerns to become capable of reflectively reaffirming her deeper concerns and to behave in ways that accord with those concerns partly because of those reflections. A major qualitative difference emerges with behavior that begins to be self-reflective in this way. That something matters deeply to a person when she attends to it, and that this concern partly directs her choices and actions, imparts a special significance to her behavior that it is appropriate to call determination by herself as the self she is. (Friedman, 2003, p. 21)

Friedman reminded us that even content-neutral autonomy requires considerable personal, interpersonal, cognitive, and affective abilities. If our beliefs define us, then to establish the cognitive distance necessary for reflection and possible adjustment of those beliefs is hard work. The work has been recently named self-authorship (Baxter Magolda, 1999; Cooke, 1999).

Cooke (1999) did not wish the metaphor of self-authorship to imply that the self is formed absent the "determining influences of heredity, environment, contingency, and the prelinguistic and non-linguistic dimensions of human agency" (p. 266). Self-authorship is the metaphor for becoming responsible and accountable for one's own actions, for one's own judgments and goals, and with an independence that "forbids over-reliance on the opinions and judgments of others in one's views of the world, relationships to others, self-definitions and narrative constructions of identity; it also calls for the attempt to free oneself from the pernicious influence of one's own earlier lives" (p. 267). As Baxter Magolda (1999) showed, this work is not simply cognitive, or how students' make meaning of knowledge. It is also involves interpersonal (how students view themselves in relationship to others) dimensions as well as intrapersonal (how students perceive of their sense of identity) components (p. 10). The metaphor of self-authorship conceives of the development of autonomy in a social, relational context.

Freedom for liberals, for feminists, and for poststructuralists involves a detachment from the familiar, an internal distancing from what they currently understand to be true, into the haze of uncertainty. The goal is not creating autonomous persons in a substantive way by evaluating students based on the distance they've come from their original beliefs about schooling and society. Neither is the goal to create uncertain, ambiguous relativists who are unsure about everything. Content neutrality demands that we create environments where genuine reflection on one's beliefs about schooling is possible. Because students are often only beginning their work of self-determination, we must acknowledge and respect their current views and belief systems as their current *selves* while understanding that they have often not formed these views in a deeply reflective way. Students are, like all of us, subjects in process, working toward self-authorship—but as cognitive developmental experts tell us, we as teachers are in a different place in the process of crafting a self. Traditional-aged college students are often experiencing fundamental shifts in how they view themselves, what they believe, and why they believe it.

ENGAGING SUBJECTS-IN-PROCESS: PEDAGOGY IN THE HAZE

> Respecting someone's autonomy means not interfering unduly with her choices or behavior (assuming her behavior is not harming others). It means giving her the freedom to choose and act unimpeded by such hindrances as deception, manipulation, and coercion. *In case someone's autonomy has not yet matured, respecting her autonomy calls for treating her in ways that promote the development of autonomy competency, for example, encouraging her to explore what she wants and supporting her initiatives.* (Friedman, 2003, p. 75; italics mine)

Friedman noted that one cannot be autonomous while being impeded by deception and manipulation, and this certainly is relevant to social foundations classrooms, where preservice teachers are often confronting for the first time the popular half-truths and untruths of schooling in America. Part of our role as social foundations instructors is to reveal knowledge about schooling that contests and troubles these popular myths, thereby providing students with knowledge that enables them to be less likely to be deceived or coerced by "common sense" about schooling. Part of the way in which this deception and coercion is battled is through reading the history and sociology of education as is presented in our course reader (see Appendix I for class readings). Another way is through a process of thinking that teaches habits of analytical scrutiny. The text analysis assignment that provides the structure for two major assignments in the class requires that students examine a text carefully, in terms of its argument(s) and rhetorical style, its historical and social contexts, and its political and moral meanings and consequences. The text analysis process invites students to see any text as a social product subject to interpretation and competing claims. We seek to convey that *all* texts, including themselves, their peers, and their teacher, are to be read in this way.

If we look at the studies of intellectual development, the importance of the text analysis becomes clear. Students typically arrive at college as what Baxter Magolda (1999) called "absolute knowers" who believe knowledge to be absolutely certain and held by authorities. In their quest toward self-authorship, students must come to see that knowledge is uncertain and subject to various interpretations (Baxter Magolda, 1999, pp. 44–46). The text analysis process helps students break away from the authority of textual truth and to see American schooling as a series of contested truths about humanity, democracy, and educational aims.

Cognitive developmental theorists have much to offer us in our efforts to understand college students. Baxter Magolda's longitudinal study, since 1986, followed the intellectual development of an original sample of 101 Miami University students through qualitative interviews. Baxter Magolda (1999, 2001) argued that students move toward self-authorship through a complex process that typically includes several phases of thinking about knowledge and knowing. The first phase is absolute knowing; the second is transitional. The third is called independent knowing, in which "authorities are no longer the only sources of knowledge in an uncertain world but instead become equal with students, who for the first time view their opinions as valid" (1999, p. 48). Most students in Baxter Magolda's study did not move into this phase of knowing until late in college and developed this understanding of knowledge further in their years after college. It was only as students reached ages in their late 20s and 30s that Baxter Magolda saw evidence of the final pattern of intellectual development that she called "contextual knowing," in which both expert advice, personal reflection and evaluation of one's own and others' perspectives, and personal choice are collectively used to determine truth.

> Contextual knowers felt that rationality in terms of consulting experts and processing evidence was necessary but simultaneously valued working

through their perspectives by accessing their own experiences and others' perspectives. Contextual knowing involved constructing one's perspective in the context of one's experience, available information, and the experiences of others. (Baxter Magolda, 1999, p. 51)

Baxter Magolda's work suggests that a class like EDL 204, in which mostly college sophomores are enrolled, will not result in students' achievement of a mature self-authorship, in which the views of experts, self, and others determine valid beliefs. Rather, students in EDL 204 are most likely only beginning to see knowledge as political, contextual, and open to question and interpretation. They are also only beginning to question the cherished beliefs of their childhood. As Friedman's (2003) quote at the opening of this section suggests, students who are developing their capacity for independent thought require encouragement and opportunities to define and articulate what they believe, and why. Jane, in Andrea's class, was asked to articulate her beliefs on feminism, and did so with vigor.

However, as Friedman (2003) also pointed out, this process of encouragement is not all that is involved in teaching for self-authorship. Andrea should, based on her knowledge of social foundations of education, help Jane and her classmates explore the educational consequences of their beliefs. Friedman put it this way:

> To respect someone's autonomy does not require supporting or conforming to the contents of the choices she makes. She may choose foolishly or badly. To respect her autonomy is to take her perspective seriously, to regard it as the stance she chooses to take up in the world, to hold her responsible for it, and to treat her appropriately in virtue of what she wants and values. (Friedman, 2003, pp. 75–76)

How might Andrea take Jane's response to the McIntosh reading seriously? By only commenting minimally on Jane's response, Andrea is not holding her completely responsible for it. Jane should be pushed to explore the consequences of these beliefs. Andrea could help Jane explore a series of questions that relate to gender and education, such as: Should girls and women be given equal funding for sports programs in high schools and colleges? Do women and men receive equal educations in public schools today? Have women always had access to the kind of education that Jane herself is privileged enough to experience? Through seeking answers both empirical and philosophical, Jane's antifeminism might be taken seriously enough to allow her to explore the consequences of her views. This requires some trust between Andrea and Jane, but it also requires the Kantian kind of *push* that is a combination of encouragement and of well-designed assignments that call for students not simply to "talk back" to texts, but to talk *with* the authors of texts and their fellow students.

Fashioning one's self and selves will require more than simply reacting to texts and ideas, as Andrea's journaling assignment proves. There is nothing in the assignment that helps Jane fully engage the ideas of McIntosh's article. Instead she poses a counterargument to McIntosh, using her reasoning to reject the feminist viewpoint in the essay. Peter Elbow (1986) wrote about problems of our frequent tendencies to use methodological doubt, or critical argument, rather than methodological belief as a way of learning:

> Everyone agrees in theory that the only way to assess an interpretation is to try it out. But actually the practice is rare: either people don't really try out interpretations they don't like—they don't really try believing or experiencing them; or they think that "trying it out" means arguing against it and seeing how it holds up. But if you take seriously the banal principle that you cannot assess a reading without experiencing it, then an unusual "method" emerges—and one that is difficult because it has rules and takes discipline. (p. 260)

Imagine students in Andrea's class sitting around discussing their interpretations of McIntosh, and each person presenting his or her views about the text. When instructors can facilitate well and students are prepared, a lively discussion emerges in which arguments for and against various interpretations of McIntosh are compared and contrasted. Yet Elbow pointed out that in this form of academic inquiry we have skipped the step of methodological belief. The question that should begin the inquiry is not "defend an argument" but "how can my vision be enlarged by this perspective?" Elbow said that we must not ask "What are your arguments for such a silly view as that?" but rather "What do you see when you see the text so? Give me the vision in your head. You are having an experience I don't have: help me to have it" (p. 261).

What do classrooms look like where belief precedes doubt as the method of inquiry? Course authors, students, and teachers are, at first, approached with an empathetic, open engagement in the spirit of belief. As students move through belief and into more critical investigations of doubt, they utilize both cognitive and affective dimensions of thinking to explore various views and their educational consequences. In EDL 204 we employ various readings—some analytical, some more personal narratives—that help students see different visions of education. We should also honor their visions and commitments through an exercise of methodological belief that we ourselves as instructors undertake. We must do for them what we ask they do for us—engaging and *learning*, from the inside out, a perspective on society or schooling that is Other. Elbow argued that "you may not reject a reading till you have succeeded in believing it." Jane may know her views on feminism, but she has not tried on McIntosh's argument in order to see it from an insider's perspective. Andrea may know "conservative Christianity," but she does not know Jane's perspective on her beliefs. Tim may feel he knows well the feelings of childhood innocence and endearment that Disney inspires, but he may not be aware of the way his students make meaning of various Disney representations. Classroom activities and exercises that tap into these kinds of questions would inspire more methodological belief and lead to more productive forms of methodological doubt and critique. But the object of methodological belief is not simply to share and trade beliefs. It is to *first* believe with the end of an enlarged understanding, and then to subsequently *doubt* one's own and others' views through *self-reflection* and *argument* that attempt to analyze and reflect on what sorts of educational consequences result from one's current beliefs.

Methodological belief can be used with a variety of approaches that foster self-exploration as an important primary stage in self- and cultural critique. Bushnell and Henry (2003) wrote about the exercise of autobiography as a way to connect learning to a student's own experience to promote both self-awareness and the ability to detach from one's own life to the degree necessary to narrate it to a reader. A readiness to listen to and understand the views of others (through methodological belief), and a willingness to explore oneself and experiences to promote an understanding of identity in a social and historical context (through autobiography and other forms of self-reflection), pave the way for the more typical kind of argument and critique that may form the primary pedagogical vehicle in many of our social foundations classes. Beginning with arguments and counterarguments will not necessarily give students the help they need to detach from current understandings and begin to reconstruct those beliefs based on others' views. Teaching a critical curriculum, inclusive of feminist and multicultural views, requires instructors who both challenge and support their students' autonomy as a formation in process, not a fully formed entity. Self-authorship demands cognitive, interpersonal, and intrapersonal work. Social foundations instructors can focus on the metaphor of self-authorship to help students begin to fashion an identity as an educator that takes seriously—but does not necessarily adopt in the ways that critical theorists would hope—a fully (in)formed critical stance.

REFERENCES

Baxter Magolda, M. B. (1999). *Creating contexts for learning and self-authorship.* Nashville: Vanderbilt University Press.

Baxter Magolda, M. B. (2001). *Making their own way: Narratives for transforming higher education to promote self-development.* Sterling, VA: Stylus.

Bushnell, M., & Henry, S. E. (2003). The Role of reflection in epistemological change: Autobiography in teacher education. *Educational Studies, 34*(1), 38–61.

Callan, E. (1988). *Autonomy and schooling.* Kingston: McGill–Queen's University Press.

Callan, E. (1997). *Creating citizens: Political education and liberal democracy.* New York: Clarendon Press.

Cooke, M. (1999). Questioning autonomy: The feminist challenge and the challenge for feminism. In R. Kearney & M. Dooley (Eds.), *Questioning ethics: Contemporary debates in philosophy* (pp. 258–282). New York: Routledge.

Council of Learned Societies in Education. (1997). *Standards for academic and professional instruction in foundations of education, educational studies, and educational policy studies.* San Francisco: Caddo Gap Press.

Di Stefano, C. (1996). Autonomy in the light of difference. In N. J. Hirschmann & C. Di Stefano (Eds.), *Revisioning the political: Feminist reconstructions of traditional concepts in Western political theory* (pp. 95–116). Boulder, CO: Westview Press.

Elbow, P. (1986). *Embracing contraries: Explorations in learning and teaching.* New York: Oxford University Press.

Feinberg, J. (1989). Autonomy. In J. Christman (Ed.), *The inner citadel: Essays on individual autonomy* (pp. 27–53). New York: Oxford University Press.

Feinberg, W. (1998). *Common schools/uncommon identities: National unity and cultural difference.* New Haven, CT: Yale University Press.

Friedman, M. (2000). Feminism in ethics: Conceptions of autonomy. In M. Fricker & J. Hornsby (Eds.), *The Cambridge companion to feminism and philosophy* (pp. 205–224). New York: Cambridge University Press.

Friedman, M. (2003). *Autonomy, gender, and politics.* New York: Oxford University Press.

Garrison, J. (1998). The paradox of indoctrination, pluralistic selves, and liberal communitarianism. *Educational Foundations, 12*(1), 17–28.

Gilligan, C. (1982). *In a different voice.* Cambridge, MA: Harvard University Press.

Higher Education Research Institute. (2002). *Freshmen survey: Results for the first-year students at Miami University.* Berkeley: University of California.

Huntington, P. (1995). Toward a dialectical concept of autonomy: Revisiting the feminist alliance with poststructuralism. *Philosophy and Social Criticism, 21*(1), 37–55.

Kant, I. (1981). *Grounding for the metaphysics of morals* (J. W. Ellington, Trans.). Indianapolis: Hackett.

Kerr, D. (2002). Devoid of community: Examining conceptions of autonomy in education. *Educational Theory, 52*(1), 13–25.

Kincheloe, J. L. (1999). Critical democracy and education. In J. G. Henderson & K. R. Kesson (Eds.), *Understanding democratic curriculum leadership* (pp. 70–83). New York: Teachers' College Press.

Kohlberg, L. (1984). *Essays on moral development. Volume 1: The philosophy of moral development.* New York: Harper and Row.

Kristeva, J. (1982). *Powers of horror: An essay on abjection* (L. S. Roudiez, Trans.). New York: Columbia University Press.

Kristeva, J. (1984). *Revolution in poetic language* (L. S. Roudiez, Trans.). New York: Columbia University Press.

Kristeva, J. (1987). *Tales of love* (L. S. Roudiez, Trans.). New York: Columbia University Press.

Kumashiro, K. (2002). Against repetition: Addressing resistance to anti-oppressive change in the practices of learning, teaching, supervising, and researching. *Harvard Educational Review, 72*(1), 67–92.

Kymlicka, W. (1989). *Liberalism, community and culture.* New York: Oxford University Press.

MacIntyre, A. (1981). *After virtue* (2nd ed.). Notre Dame, IN: University of Notre Dame Press.

Macmillan, C. B. J. (1998). The inevitability of indoctrination. *Educational Foundations, 12*(1), 7–16.

Maher, F., & Thompson Tetreault, M. K. (2001). *The feminist classroom: Dynamics of gender, race, and privilege*. Lanham, MD: Rowman & Littlefield.

Martusewicz, R. A. (2001). *Seeking passage: Post-structuralism, pedagogy, ethics*. New York: Teachers College Press.

McAfee, N. (2000). *Habermas, Kristeva, and citizenship*. Ithaca, NY: Cornell University Press.

Merriam-Webster's dictionary, 9th ed. (1988). Springfield, MA: Merriam-Webster.

Miller, J. B. (1976). *Toward a new psychology of women*. Boston: Beacon Press.

Noddings, N. (2002). *Starting at home: Caring and social policy*. Berkeley: University of California Press.

Perry, W. G. (1970). *Forms of intellectual and ethical development in the college years: A scheme*. Troy, MO: Holt, Rinehart, & Winston.

Rawls, J. (1971). *A theory of justice*. Cambridge, MA: Harvard University Press.

Rawls, J. (1993). *Political liberalism*. New York: Columbia University Press.

Rousmaniere, K., & Knight Abowitz, K. (Eds.). (2002). *Readings in sociocultural studies in education* (4th ed.). New York: McGraw-Hill.

Sandel, M. J. (1982). *Liberalism and the limits of justice*. Cambridge, MA: Harvard University Press.

Strike, K. A. (1982). *Liberty and learning*. Oxford: Robertson.

Walker, J. (1999). Self-determination as an educational aim. In R. Marples (Ed.), *The aims of education* (pp. 112–123). New York: Routledge.

Westheimer, J., & Kahne, J. (2003, April 21). *Teaching justice: Indoctrination, neutrality, and the need for alternatives*. Paper presented at the American Educational Research Association, Chicago.

Winch, C. (2002). Strong autonomy and education. *Educational Theory, 52*(1), 27–41.

Chapter 8

Social Foundations Within Teacher Education

Jeff Edmundson

Mary Bushnell Greiner

As the climate of educational reform and politics turns again to teacher-proof pedagogies, high-stakes testing, and uniform curricula, our students may be all the more likely to dismiss courses in their teacher education programs that don't seem directly applicable to the K–12 classroom. These students (and some of their future employers) may ignore theoretical ideas that do not appear to lead directly to a technique of teaching. In this environment, it's all too easy for teacher education programs to avoid theory in the name of being relevant and practical. But as foundationists as well as teacher educators, we know that to claim to ignore theory is only to reproduce the status quo, because our lives are lived in a context of theory. Most of that theory, of course, is taken for granted, assumed subconsciously as "just the way things are" (see, e.g, Berger & Luckmann, 1966). When teachers carry what are in fact theoretical assumptions into the classroom, they reproduce social inequality and also reproduce the cultural assumptions underlying the ecological crisis.

As teacher educators dedicated to social and ecological justice (ecojustice), we are convinced that theories—the attitudes and ways of thinking that students carry into the classroom—are as important as any particular techniques they might acquire. In this chapter we argue for the importance of theory and, in so doing, for the centrality of social foundations within teacher education (see also deMarrais, this volume). We want this understanding of theory to take hold for our students, so that they recognize their daily lives are filled with theory. Naming the theories we utilize in our daily lives can be an awakening experience for students who may come to college having been taught that their own lives have little to do with school knowledge.

But it is not sufficient simply to be aware of theory. We want students to be able to change their assumptions and change their actions in the world—and especially in the classroom. What good will it do them, or their future students, if they can name theory but are unable to rewrite the scripts through which they live and act in the world? Active use of theory involves a potential alteration of one's attitude and being in the world. Thus, they need to be able to think about and analyze their actions within a framework that offers ethical guidelines as well as analytical ones. Students need to question the scripts in which they have lived, so as to recognize the subjectivity of such scripts and the potential to change them.

However, neither is it sufficient for students to only be able to change. We also want them to be aware of what is worth conserving—that is, what cultural and educational traditions should be maintained in the face of a dominant culture that worships the new and that relentlessly undermines those traditions not easily turned into commodities. For example, we should look to conserve traditions as varied as gardening and face-to-face mentoring for their enhancement of community. Conservation can emerge by understanding the consistencies of our educational history; it can even more powerfully take part in an ethic of care for those fragile aspects of our world that in their absence would leave us diminished at best, and irretrievably damaged at worst.

This call for theoretical awareness may appear to be similar to what is often called Reflective Practice (Schön, 1983; Zeichner, 1992). We believe it is a deeper conception, because it asks students to become aware of their intimate social, political, and cultural assumptions and to determine their actions in ethical responses to these assumptions, and because it focuses on conservation as well as change. Reflective practice as we present it here explicitly opens up cultural assumptions of the practitioner and those assumptions operating in the larger situational context of schooling and society. The theoretical awareness we favor is not a generic one. First, our stance is framed by a commitment to social justice (Mary) and ecological justice (Jeff; see Martusewicz & Edmundson, this volume). Our perspectives differ, but we believe our differences offer nuance rather than contradiction, recognizing that ecojustice pushes the concepts of social justice to a broader embracing of justice.

As part of the route to social/ecological justice, we hold *questioning* central as an epistemology and a way of being in the world, within which the status quo of sociological structures and of expertise remains open to challenge.

Questioning the status quo is necessarily an unending process that does not hold any constructs of knowledge as absolute and final. We endeavor to steer clear of absolutes, such as presumptions about what a democracy is and what its benefits may or may not be to certain populations at certain times. Questioning, therefore, remains entirely situated in its constancy of change. However, a nuanced understanding sees that challenge and change must be part of a dialectic with conservation of those structures and traditions that support justice. We do not advocate change merely for the displacement of the old and the delight of the new.

An epistemology of questioning implies that teaching and learning involve knowing what one does not know and how to look for it. In this construct teachers do not constitute absolute knowers or final authorities. Further, it involves interrogating one's own cultural assumptions that may influence how one defines what is worth knowing. It also involves honoring the knowledge students bring into the classroom, and shaping an environment in which students can actively construct understandings with the cultural tools that are available to them. Such teaching is the hallmark of a professional educator who remains critically aware of her place in the particular situation of a classroom, rather than an automaton who presumes to objectively deliver content.

Finally, we privilege democracy in its ideal representation of a deep democracy in which rights and responsibilities are truly shared. This should not suggest that we consider democracy to be a political panacea for all persons and societies; rather, a nuanced understanding acknowledges its roots in Western culture and recognizes it can be colonizing for indigenous peoples. We are aware, for example, that when the U.S. Bureau of Indian Affairs imposed supposedly democratic elections on Native Americans, it undermined the place of tribal elders, and thus contributed to the decline of Indian communities. As a complex and continually renegotiated construct, democracy requires an ongoing understanding of the ways schools reproduce the status quo of class, race, and gender oppression and of ecological crisis; it thus invites us to challenge that status quo and overcome it.

SOCIAL FOUNDATIONS OF EDUCATION IN TEACHER EDUCATION

Our primary argument in this chapter assumes that as foundationists we are working to widen the reach of justice, that our schools are ideal locations to conduct such an enterprise, and that the social foundations classroom sets the path for prospective teachers to embark on that journey.

Working for justice presumes an active being in the world to promote social and economic equity, to resolve differentials of power, and to use power for the benefit of those without. It is an active rejection of the hierarchical status quo in which some persons live without basic necessities, rights, and possibilities. These ideas are rooted in the work of Rawls (1971) and Nussbaum (1999), who articulated a conception of justice for human beings that accords dignity, rights, and equity to all persons. Nussbaum takes a broader approach than Rawls, as Nussbaum does not consider the civil society to be a necessary precursor to the distribution of justice to all persons. Despite this difference, both political philosophers have advanced the public recognition of justice as attainable and necessary.

Nancy Fraser moves our thinking beyond Rawls and Nussbaum as she provides a critical view of justice. She argues that the last several decades of political projects for justice have moved from a "politics of redistribution" to a "politics of representation." That is, earlier concerns were with mapping democratic justice to all persons whereas later concerns focused wholly on racial, ethnic, gender, and/or sexual identity. In her more recent work, Fraser (2003) argued that identity politics must remain inextricably bound to a politics of justice and redistribution to create a democratic politics of recognition that conjoins a politics of social equality with a politics of representation.

Tangentially, but relevant to our work in teacher education, Maxine Greene (e.g., 1978) writes continuously of the need to "imagine things as if they would be otherwise" as she constructs an existentialist philosophy that struggles with the challenges and possibilities of our current sociohistorical context. She asserts that such other-imagining must be rooted in the moral stance of imagining a world of justice. Influenced by such social intellectuals as Hannah Arendt and Maurice Merleau-Ponty, Greene insists on the responsibility of each individual to question and act with moral purpose.

Such assumptions of justice parlay directly into the classroom, where children (and adults) live daily lessons of inequity and social reproduction. Social reproduction research and theory pervade much of the last few decades of sociological, political, and economic research on education. Theorists (and practitioners) such as Henry Giroux and Paulo Freire have clearly identified the school as a location in which all of the inequities and injustices of society play out and are replicated over successive generations. Schools do not only mirror societal events; they actively create them through smaller classroom practices such as silencing students' voices (Fine, 1991), as well as larger structural practices such as tracking (Oakes, 1985).

We would like to complicate the concept of justice, however, by offering the concept of ecojustice. As developed by Bowers (2001) and discussed elsewhere in this volume (Martusewicz & Edmundson), ecojustice extends the consideration of justice beyond humans to the natural world and to the protection of cultural diversity, particularly those cultural traditions that offer ecological wisdom. An ecojustice lens sees schools as not only reproducing social and economic inequity, but also reproducing the ways of thinking that hasten ecological destruction.

Despite these dark possibilities, schools have the potential to be sources of just social and structural change if they involve an education that critiques existing practices and values and actively constructs ethical alternatives. In the crucible of the classroom, students develop their social and ethical selves through the interaction of their home and neighborhood lives. A teacher's "awesome power" (Raywid, 1995) can dramatically alter young persons' conceptions of their selves in the world, so that they can change their location within the demeaning reproduction of social life.

In addition to advocating and working for needed structural changes to our school system, as teacher educators we are predominantly concerned with developing teachers' abilities to be subversive within their own classrooms. Such grass-roots action may be more immediately effective than attempting to change school organization, funding, and accountability. Many teachers enter the profession with the intention to be change agents, but do not have the skills or institutional support to do so. Other prospective teachers carry a romanticized view of teaching based on their own positive school experiences. Without the interpretive abilities to ask thoughtful questions about their students and their cultural context, these teachers will likely continue to reproduce the inequities and cultural assumptions of the schooling they experienced. Developing the skills and sensibilities to be socially active teachers can ideally occur within the social foundations classroom, with its critical content and emphasis on exploring causes, implications, and imaginative possibilities.

Teaching social foundations of education as a justice/ecojustice agenda occurs within the current context of teaching and teacher education that is overwhelmingly concerned with technical rationality. Uniform standards and high-stakes testing arrive masked in a cloak of equity which presumes that sameness can substitute for fairness. Proponents of such schooling argue that if all children are given the "same" opportunities, then all have an equal chance of success. Despite decades (and even centuries) of evidence decrying sameness as a substitute for equity, such consistency of curriculum and resources endures as the dominant distribution of presumed educational opportunity. This context of conservative persistence presents a challenge for social foundations to thrive, as the ambiguities and uncertainties inherent to social foundations do not find a home in uniformity. At the same time, the field of social foundations of education becomes all the more urgent in this current context.

In a master's or doctoral degree program in social foundations of education, such issues can be explored from a range of perspectives with some intellectual leisure. Research- and theory-oriented programs provide natural homes for the critical analyses of social foundations. But most social foun-

dations courses exist within teacher education programs, where their presumed value may not be readily apparent. The present authors' experiences have been positive as our departments embrace the value of social
foundations in teacher education and accordingly weave it in to our programs and/or our national accreditation processes. However, other social
foundations faculty in teacher education programs may find themselves
having to justify their intellectual existence by proving the positive impact
of foundations on school practice (see again deMarrais, this volume).

CREATING A PRACTICE-ORIENTED VISION
OF SOCIAL FOUNDATIONS

For a separate social foundations course to impact teacher education, we
believe that two components are key: Students must be provided with intellectual tools that can be carried into other courses as well as their own teaching. In addition, the theory must be translated into practice so that students
connect abstract concepts to their lived schooling experiences. We discussed earlier the intellectual tools students need: a habit of questioning, a
commitment to ethical judgment and social justice, and an ability to see the
theoretical assumptions underlying any school activity. In order to develop
these tools in themselves, however, the second component becomes central—students must *experience* theory being translated into practice. Social
foundations becomes an integral part of teacher education when theory is
more than an intellectual exercise, and when students see theory as having
some relevance to their lives as teachers.

In order to accomplish such integration it is necessary to ground theoretical viewpoints in classroom reality in at least three ways: Theory must be
translated into accessible language—language that is part of students' everyday conversation; theory must be shown in the university classroom—we
must "walk the talk"; and students must be able to see how theory is played
out in actual K–12 classrooms. There are, of course, other means, but these
are some of the experiences with which we have been occupied. We offer
here a few examples of social/ecojustice teaching that provide concrete representations of what our work looks like in practice.

Translation does not necessarily mean direct paraphrase of difficult theoretical material, although that may sometimes be appropriate. Often we
offer students a direct paraphrase of a concept in everyday language. Beyond this, it means that we help students make sense of theory through pedagogical techniques. This can be as simple as explaining key vocabulary or
framing a reading with guide questions. To open a semester by asking students to define "democracy" can lead to an invigorating discussion about
ideals and reality that provides an articulated backdrop for explorations
into schooling and society. It can mean offering analogies. In our classes, it

often means asking students to write a piece applying a certain section of text to their own experiences. This pushes students to read a section closely enough to make an application, rather than giving up and dismissing the material as pointless. For example, we might have students write educational autobiographies or genealogies to explore their own identity in relation to the sociohistorical context of the United States and schools (Bushnell & Henry, 2003). Or we might have students write about their experiences with tracking and then share those with other students, producing a rich classroom text that makes the dry reading come alive.

We can also approach translation through modalities other than writing. To advance their understanding of the history of schooling, Mary's students may read children's books about historical periods (e.g., Fireside, 1997; Littlefield, 2001; Stanley, 1992), then use the information in those books to draw or collage a collective mural of educational and historical events. We then discuss the mural jointly, pulling out major themes and issues from the last several centuries. Most importantly, we discuss who is not included in most historical accounts, and what the visibility or invisibility of certain populations reveals about power relations in our society. The activity also provides an opportunity to critique children's (and adults') books for their representations, nonrepresentations, and misrepresenations of historical events and persons. In another drawing and group discussion exercise, students use crayons to create a visual image of teaching. Inevitably these images reveal traditional and dated presumptions of lecture-style elementary school classrooms in which the teacher stands at the chalkboard, pointer in hand, in front of neat rows of identical students. Weber and Mitchell's (1995) detailed account of teacher education students analyzing and critiquing similar images, as well as images from popular culture, demonstrates the potency of such reflection into and awareness of cultural norms.

Next, the importance of walking the talk cannot be underestimated. Students are quick to smell hypocrisy if we read Dewey and talk about the importance of democratic community while lecturing and imposing top-down structure on the students. Instead, we endeavor to model the kind of classroom community we want students to try to create in their own classrooms: one based on respect, on dialogue, and on an expectation that we can all learn from each other. Through videotapes or direct observation, students may analyze teachers' classroom practices to identify those teachers' underlying philosophies and beliefs about students and learning. This exercise leads to students writing their own educational philosophies that they will revise throughout their teacher education program. The social foundations classroom serves as a valuable source of data for such an analysis—which requires the foundations instructor to remain comfortable with students pointing out those aspects of the university classroom that are *not* democratic. Students and their instructor can then reflect on that discrepancy in an exploration of the tension between the ideals of a philosophy and its execution in the classroom. To model respectful teaching, the foundations professor needs to reveal his or her own ongoing struggle with overcoming entrenched educational practices.

Finally, for students to take theory seriously, they must see what it looks like in actual K–12 classrooms. This "seeing" can include observation of exemplary teachers, who demonstrate by example that teachers "really can" step outside the ordinary. If students are not yet placed in classrooms, we may take field trips to classes or schools that offer a clear alternative to the familiar teacher-centered classroom. Field trips, of course, may need to be virtual if the local schools do not demonstrate progressive or alternative practices, or if such journeys are not feasible because of time, financial limitations, or other constraints. Although limited, videotapes can be useful windows into a range of classroom practices. The series from the Developmental Studies Center in Oakland, CA are particularly useful, as are the films *Why Do These Kids Love School?* (Fadiman, 1995), and *It's Elementary* (Chasnoff & Cohen, 1996).

Certain readings reveal classroom practices more openly than others and enable students to visualize teachers' and students' interactions, particularly when they are comparative studies or accounts of classrooms that may be unfamiliar to students. As a small sample of such readings, Catherine Lewis's (1995) ethnographic study of Japanese preschools repeatedly cracks open students' assumptions about classroom management and how a teacher holds authority. The interrelationship of schooling and culture and the impact of a dominant culture on an autonomous cultural group are apparent in McCarty's (2002) historical and contemporary examination of schooling in the Navajo nation. The group Rethinking Schools has put out several books (e.g., Bigelow, Christensen, Karp, Miner, & Peterson, 1994; Bigelow, Harvey, Karp, & Miller, 2001), as well as the journal *Rethinking Schools*, full of writing by teachers about specific ways they challenge the societal and educational status quo. This work ranges from a teacher who leads her students to critique biases in fairy tales (Christensen, 1994) to a teacher who explores ways to teach diversity in a math class (Zaslavsky, 1994). Lastly, Sue Books (2003) assembled a compelling collection of studies of "invisible" students in our schools. By exploring unfamiliar schools, students may more easily take an anthropological stance of observing the strangeness of their own schooling experiences, and thereby be able to connect to the theoretical assumptions that undergird those practices.

Seeing the theory made real can also be accomplished through modeling lessons or teaching techniques that are directly applicable in the K–12 classroom. Jeff, who is still a practicing secondary teacher as well as a university faculty member, commonly models lessons from his secondary teaching that explicitly challenge economic inequality. For example, we'll do a simulation of the process by which Third World farmers are forced into the global economy and deprived of their land by foreign corporations. Invariably, students ask how one can "get away with that," which leads to robust conversation about the relative autonomy of the classroom, about self-censorship and about the façade of "balance" that obscures the day-to-day reproduction of social injustice in schools and society.

REALITIES OF TEACHING SOCIAL FOUNDATIONS IN TEACHER EDUCATION

Some institutions may have constructed a social foundations course within teacher education to be little more than an "introduction to teaching"—which is not the equivalent of a foundations course. Other teacher education programs have become bound by state and federal measures to standardized pedagogy that seemingly belies the need for the questioning, ethical, and democratic stance taken in foundations courses. In smaller departments, a foundations professor may be the only faculty member in a department teaching a single required foundations course. In these and other departments, social foundations faculty in teacher education programs may need to cope with intellectual and administrative isolationism.

We suggest that above all, foundations faculty remain committed to the importance of social foundations of education as an integral component of teacher preparation. In a climate of uniform pedagogy, and a culture that values quick results, teacher education programs may marginalize foundations because of its seeming lack of relevance at best. At worst, colleges may shy away from foundations courses that are, inherently, about questioning institutional structures and a status quo that privileges a consistent elite. Foundations faculty may need to advocate social foundations not merely as a required course, but as the location of ideas central to all aspects of a teacher education program. What this kind of infused approach can look like is described later.

The centrality of foundations ideas in teacher education may become most evident in the creation of students' educational philosophies. Through writing and rewriting, the philosophy enables students to articulate, refine, and reexamine their assumptions about schooling and society. The written philosophy can thread through the courses and practica of a teacher education program. Initiated in a social foundations course in the context of a strong grounding in philosophical traditions, the philosophy can be drawn on in later courses as students are invited to rewrite their texts for eventual submission to a portfolio or hiring committee. The philosophy of education exemplifies the intersection of theory and practice, as well as the integral role of social foundations in teacher education.

Social foundations faculty can collaborate with departmental and campus colleagues to develop ways in which other threads of foundational topics, often introduced in a first semester course, might be woven into methods and curriculum courses. If in the social foundations course students begin to develop intellectual tools such as questioning, a commitment to justice, and an awareness of theory, those tools will become more fully functional if they are are welcomed and actively called for in other teacher education courses. Consistent with a foundations commitment to ongoing inquiry, we can open our syllabi and our classrooms to share our philosophies and methods with colleagues. To do so often involves taking a risk, perhaps particularly so for untenured faculty, but isn't such risk taking precisely what we are encouraging our students to undergo in their own classrooms?

As Tozer and Miretzky reveal (in this volume), the current standards movement has involved social foundations as an element of teacher preparation. Social foundations faculty should become familiar with the Council on Learned Societies in Education (CLSE) standards, which were created by social foundations scholars, and utilize those standards to support the ongoing role of social foundations in teacher education (Council on Learned Societies in Education, 1996). These standards speak to the necessity for discrete foundations courses taught by faculty with advanced study in one or more foundations areas. All of this work can be supported by developing relationships with colleagues who provide intellectual, emotional, and institutional support through professional associations, such as the American Educational Studies Association.

A MODEL FOR INFUSING SOCIAL FOUNDATIONS OF EDUCATION IN TEACHER EDUCATION

We would also like to offer another approach: infusing foundations concepts into an entire teacher education program. Foundations as we have discussed them are as germane to an educational psychology or learning class as is developmental psychology, as much part of methodology as writing lesson plans.

The continuity required for an infusion model can be hard to accomplish in a conventional teacher education program. Jeff teaches at Portland State University, whose Graduate Teacher Education Program is built on the cohort model (Peterson et al., 1995), in which student teachers go through the year-long program in groups of about 30. Each cohort is largely autonomous, which means that faculty members do not need to reach consensus before variant approaches are tried, as long as they meet the requirements of the university and state regulations. Further, the continuity of students allows for an individual cohort to have a consistent theme across the courses, and to be taught by a small group of faculty, thus allowing a coherent infusion of concepts of culture, diversity, and social and ecological justice. Once essential concepts are introduced, they can be reinforced and reinterpreted within individual courses.

When each class is taught through foundations lenses, it is transformed from narrow practice into examination of the implications of practice. For Jeff's cohorts, the key concept is culture, seen as the meanings that humans construct within the frames of race, gender, class, and ecology. In our classes, it becomes part of a teacher's daily job to try to understand the often constrasting meanings that students bring in and that the institution of school imposes.

In a course called Classroom Instruction, we teach teachers how to structure units and write lesson plans, but we also teach the cultural biases of conventional lesson plans: They tend to enhance a linear and teacher-centered vision of teaching, for example. In teaching about objectives, we teach about the ways that the teacher can be a gatekeeper in choosing how students are introduced to a topic—so we have teachers write two sets of objectives: one standard set and one that consciously helps students become aware of hidden social and cultural assumptions, thus opening up a challenge to the social status quo. In teaching how to translate subject matter into accessible language, we also emphasize the metaphorical nature of thought and focus on thoughtful examination of the language being used in the classroom. Finally, the very first unit that students construct, an interdisciplinary group effort, is required to be on a topic of social or ecological justice.

In a Teaching and Learning class, the conventional material is all examined through sociocultural lenses. We look at adolescent development through a cultural frame by looking, for example, at the ways modern culture has created "adolescence" as a stage that did not exist in earlier cultures. Students are asked to consider the different ways some of their students may experience adolescence, such as those who have formal coming-of-age ceremonies or who are conferred with adult responsibilities when other cultures would consider them still children.

We teach teachers about the concepts of IQ and multiple intelligences, but we problematize the concept of intelligence and its roots in the need to sort students by race and class. This leads directly to consideration of the fairness of various forms of assessment. If certain forms of assessment can be discriminatory, how should we assess students? Rather than this being a theoretical discussion, we try out and examine a wide range of classroom assessments. When student-teachers' creation of assessments is rooted in a conception of antidiscrimination rather than simple grade giving, their discussions center on how assessment can accurately show what a child has learned, and even on how assessment can improve learning rather than just measure it.

Next, the framework of culture asks that teachers see "intelligence" as existing culturally rather than simply in people's heads. For example, because most conceptions of intelligence are culturally biased in favor of White middle-class experience and logico-mathematical thinking, we help students create assessments that reflect other cultures and other "intelligences," such as musical and intrapersonal. Further, we look at various exemplars of the intelligences, such as Michael Jordan and kinesthetic intelligence, and examine what cultural constructs were necessary to enable them to achieve at extraordinary levels. For the classroom level, this is translated into considering the cultural conditions that allow different student "intelligences" to flourish.

We teach about cognitive scaffolding, but also about affective scaffolding: that is, the ways that a teacher can, through understanding students' cultural backgrounds, anticipate students' emotions, help them develop trusting relationships, and help them gain access to material that is otherwise too remote (Rosiek, 2003). For example, as Rosiek described, a math teacher might draw Latino students into an algebra lesson by framing it within the planning of a quinceñera celebration (15th birthday coming-of-age), thus both making it more accessible and connecting it to student lives.

Rather than teach about "best practices," we ask teachers to understand the cultural context for their teaching. The concept of "culturally relevant" teaching (Ladson-Billings, 1994) helps teachers see that the teaching practices that are best for some aren't necessarily best for all. Teachers can learn from students, families, and other teachers in a school the methods that may work for their particular situation. At the same time, we ask teachers to reflect on the practices in their schools—to see that perhaps, in fact, the standard practices are based in low expectations of poor and minority students.

We problematize the very name of the Classroom Management course, looking at the ways that the "management" metaphor is rooted culturally and historically in the factory model and in capitalism. We consider the social and cultural issues involved in classroom management—for example, through role-playing interactions between a teacher and a student who won't make eye contact (possibly from different cultural meanings of eye contact) or a student who doesn't bring the book to class (possibly due to peer pressure). We generate various responses and talk about which ones might be most successful with different students, and why.

Even the Multicultural Education course can be broadened to be more foundational. For example, we consider class as a category of analysis along with ethnicity. To see class in a cultural sense means to ask questions about the meanings a working-class student enters the classroom with, the same as we would ask about an African American or Native student.

Class, all too often unmentioned in teacher education, is brought into many courses. In the Teaching and Learning course, thinking about class can mean considering how to make a topic relevant to students who don't see themselves going to college. It means helping student teachers see the lack of academic confidence often exhibited by working-class students.

In methods courses, class is offered directly as a category for analysis in social studies and language arts. For example, we demonstrate simulations and role plays that put issues of class directly in front of students (e.g., Bigelow & Diamond, 1988). We then ask students to write lessons that expose class issues. In more subtle attention to class, we focus on ways to bring working-class students into discussions without stigmatizing them.

In the various courses where gender is discussed, we don't leave it at the simple level of "the problems girls face," and "the problems boys face," but look at how class affects those problems. Student teachers learn to see that poor and working-class boys often have different issues than boys from affluent homes. Working-class boys may have a peer culture that discourages serious effort in school, or may have pressure to go to work to help pay family living expenses. Student teachers learn not only to anticipate the problems, but to consider solutions, such as ways to help students work around the peer culture and how to use work experience to connect to class experience.

Once the cohort begins student teaching, its members are expected to put their learning about social and ecological justice into action. Student-teachers are required to investigate the class and ethnic background of their students. In their regular reflective writing, they are expected to locate and interrogate assumptions about students and about language that occur in their classroom. Where possible, given the limitations of the student-teaching situation, students are asked to include social and ecologial justice issues in their teaching. Finally, university supervisors look for attention to gender, race, and ethnicity by student-teachers, from the simple "who gets called on" to the more subtle uses of language that either invite students or discourage them.

Many of these approaches are probably used in various teacher education courses. What we believe is different in this infusion model is the systematic effort to consider foundations concepts in nearly every course. When student-teachers are regularly asked to consider aspects of culture, it starts to become a routine part of their lesson planning. When they are consistently pressed on questions of social and ecological justice, students begin to look for assumptions in their teaching or obstacles that can inhibit their students. When they write unit plans that focus on social and ecological justice, role play interactions where class plays an issue, and then teach with awakened attention to justice issues, there is a substantial hope that justice will become an integral part of their teaching career.

CLOSING

The work described here assumes a stance in which we actively and knowingly engage in political work, as all teaching is political. We do not have the hubris to believe that our politics are right above all others, and we do not presume they will not continue to develop, but we do believe that our openness about our activism engenders a pedagogical honesty that prospective teachers need.

We have emphasized in this chapter that the theoretical insights offered by a justice-oriented foundations perspective offer essential directions for teacher education programs. Teachers who learn to use such theory, we believe, are better equipped to offer education that opens up the world for students, that is sensitive to cultural differences, that challenges a society that is increasingly destructive of community and ecological stability, and that strives to construct alternatives to such a society.

We wish to underscore, however, that this work is driven by the assumption that teacher education provides a powerful intellectual home for social foundations. Not only does teacher education need social foundations, but in this dialectic, social foundations of education remains honest to its endeavors by relying on teacher education for its connections to the pragmatic realities of schooling and society. Teacher education challenges foundationists to remain painfully awake to the implications (and limitations) of theory as well as practice. As our lives are lived in a context of theory, so social foundations of education remains situated in the theories we bring to K–12 and higher education.

REFERENCES

Berger, P. L., & Luckmann, T. (1966). *The social construction of reality: A treatise in the sociology of knowledge.* Garden City, NY: Doubleday.

Bigelow, W., Christensen, L., Karp, S., Miner, B., & Peterson, B. (1994). *Rethinking our classrooms.* Milwaukee, WI: Rethinking Schools, Ltd.

Bigelow, W., & Diamond, N. (1988). *The power in their hands.* New York: Monthly Review Press.

Bigelow, W., Harvey, P., Karp, S., & Miller, L. (2001). *Rethinking our classrooms* (Vol. 2). Milwaukee, WI: Rethinking Schools, Ltd.

Books, S. (Ed.). (2003). *Invisible children in the society and its schools.* Mahwah, NJ: Lawrence Erlbaum Associates.

Bowers, C. A. (2001). *Educating for ecojustice and community.* Athens: University of Georgia Press.

Bushnell, M., & Henry, S. E. (2003). The role of reflection in epistemological change: Autobiography in teacher education. *Educational Studies, 34*(1), 38–61.

Chasnoff, D., & Cohen, H. J. (1996). *It's elementary: Talking about gay issues in school* [videorecording]. San Francisco: Women's Educational Media.

Christensen, L. (1994). Unlearning the myths that bind us. In B. Bigelow, L. Christensen, S. Karp, B. Miner, & B. Peterson (Eds.), *Rethinking our classrooms* (pp. 8–13). Milwaukee, WI: Rethinking Schools, Ltd.

Council on Learned Societies in Education. (1996). Standards for academic and professional instruction. In *Foundations of education, educational studies, and educational policy studies* (2nd ed.). http://members.aol.com/caddogap/standard.htm

Fadiman, D. (1990). *Why do these kids love school?* [videorecording]. Santa Monica, CA: Pyramid Film & Video.

Fine, M. (1991). *Framing dropouts: Notes on the politics of an urban public high school.* Albany: State University of New York Press.

Fireside, H. (1997). *Plessy v. Ferguson: Separate but equal?* Springfield, NJ: Enslow.

Fraser, N. (2003). Social justice in the age of identity politics: Redistribution, recognition, and participation. In N. Fraser & A. Honneth (Eds.), *Redistribution or recognition? A political–philosophical exchange* (pp. 7–109). New York: Verso.

Greene, M. (1978). *Landscapes of learning.* New York: Teachers' College Press.

Ladson-Billings, G. (1994). *The dreamkeepers: Successful teachers of African American children.* San Francisco: Jossey-Bass.

Lewis, C. (1995). *Educating hearts and minds: Reflections of Japanese preschool and elementary education.* Cambridge: Cambridge University Press.

Littlefield, H. (2001). *Children of the Indian boarding schools.* Minneapolis, MN: Carolrhoda Books.

McCarty, T. L. (2002). *A place to be Navajo: Rough rock and the struggle for self-determination in indigenous schooling.* Mahwah, NJ: Lawrence Erlbaum Associates.

Nussbaum, M. C. (1999). *Sex and social justice.* Oxford: Oxford University Press.

Oakes, J. (1985). *Keeping track: How schools structure inequality.* New Haven, CT: Yale University Press.

Peterson, K., Benson, N., Driscoll, P., Narode, R., Sherman, D., & Tama, C. (1995). Preservice teacher education using flexible, thematic cohorts. *Teachers Education Quarterly, 22*(2), 34–52.

Rawls, J. (1971). *A theory of justice.* Cambridge, MA: Harvard University Press.

Raywid, M. A. (1995). A teacher's awesome power. In W. Ayers (Ed.), *To become a teacher: Making a difference in children's lives* (pp. 78–85). New York: Teachers College Press.

Rosiek, J. (2003). Emotional scaffolding: An exploration of the teacher knowledge at the intersection of student emotion and the subject matter. *Journal of Teacher Education, 54*(5), 399–412.

Schön, D. A. (1983). *The reflective practitioner.* New York: Basic Books

Stanley, J. (1992). *Children of the Dust Bowl: The true story of the school at Weedpatch Camp.* New York: Crown.

Weber, S., & Mitchell, C. (1995). *"That's funny, you don't look like a teacher!" Interrogating images and identity in popular culture.* Washington, DC: Falmer Press.

Zaslavsky, C. (1994). Bringing the world into the math class. In B. Bigelow et al. (Eds.), *Rethinking our classrooms* (pp. 76–78). Milwaukee, WI: Rethinking Schools, Ltd.

Zeichner, K. (1992). Conceptions of reflective teaching in contemporary U.S. teacher education program reforms. In L. Valli (Ed.), *Reflective teacher education: Cases and critiques* (pp. 161–173). Albany, NY: SUNY Press.

Chapter 9

Reflections on a Social Foundations
Approach to Teacher Education[*]

Kathleen deMarrais

Kathleen deMarrais is a professor and coordinator of the Qualitative Inquiry Program in the Department of Educational psychology, University of Georgia, Athens, Georgia. She gratefully acknowledges the contributions of Jamie Lewis, University of Georgia, and Sally Oran, Northern Arizona University, for their contributions to the Urban/Multiculrural Teacher Education Program discussed in this article and to previous publications and presentations based on the program.

What is the role of social foundations faculty in the preparation of professional educators? Since the origin of the field in the 1930s, scholars have held differing interpretations, viewpoints, philosophies and approaches toward social foundations in the preparation of teachers. Some scholars in the field promote "the idea that Foundations of Education should be assembled around educational issues, using the issues as curriculum-selecting and curriculum-organizing principles."[1] This perspective takes an interdisciplinary approach rather than the more disciplinary stances of those social foundations scholars who hold close disciplinary ties to fields such as philosophy, history, sociology, anthropology, political science, and comparative education. Despite the differing positions taken by individuals in social foundations, there has been a general consensus about the purpose of social foundations for the preparation of professional educators as evidenced in the Council of Learned Societies in Education's (CLSE) *Standards for Aca-*

---

[*]Reprinted by permission of Caddo Gap Press.

demic and Professional Instruction in Foundations of Education, Educational Studies, and Educational Policy Studies. These Standards state that the purpose of study in the social foundations is to "bring these disciplinary resources to bear in developing interpretive, normative, and critical perspectives on education, both inside and outside of schools."[2] The Standards are worth quoting at length to provide a common understanding of the role of social foundations in teacher education:

> The aim of such study is not simply to describe accurately the connection between the internal organization of schools and their socializing mission. Foundations also refers to a tradition of academic inquiry that seeks to expose and make explicit the relationship between educational methods and values .... A foundational approach to the study of education assesses the logical connections between the educational goals we select and the means we employ to achieve them. Foundational study, therefore, contains a prescriptive as well as a descriptive dimension: to consider in tandem what schools are doing and what they ought to be doing. Such study focuses on the ways schools carry out their mission of preparing individuals to occupy productive roles in our society. A common theme is discernment of educational aims that are implied in current school practices as well as in recommendations for modifying such practices. Foundational study serves to gradually deepen the ability of prospective and veteran teachers to answer the overarching question: Why do American schools operate the way they do?[3]

Although social foundations faculty are clear about the purpose and value of foundational study in professional education, there is a sense within the field that our work is slipping away from us, pushing social foundations faculty further to the margins of teacher education.[4]

In recent years, many teacher education programs replaced the social foundations course(s) with a general Introduction to Education course offered to students their freshman or sophomore years. This course is more often than not taught by curriculum and instruction faculty who may or may not be prepared to engage students in developing interpretive, normative, and critical perspectives on schooling. Using the Introduction to Education course as a substitute for a social foundations course flies in the face of the CLSE Standards that stipulate that social foundations courses "shall NOT be equated with 'Introduction to Education' coursework unless such study clearly addresses the perspectives indicated in this Standard and is taught by individuals specifically trained in Foundations of Education."[5] In addition to the dwindling number of social foundations courses offered, state regulations which previously mandated a specific course or set of courses in foundations of education have moved to performance-based standards for the preparation of teachers that do not link the content with specific courses within the curriculum. While social foundations has played a peripheral role in teacher education, the field is struggling to find a place for itself in light of these policy changes.

The purpose of this article is to explore alternatives for social foundations faculty in working within teacher education. Through the use of one teacher education program, the Urban/Multicultural Teacher Education Program, I describe how social foundations can be central to the preparation of professional educators. Following a description of various aspects of the program—core goals, selection of partnership schools and school faculty, the construction of the instructional team at the college, the selection of students for the program, and the key knowledge and understandings built into the program components—I move to a discussion of state and national standards that have impacted our work in social foundations.[6] I conclude with a challenge to social foundations scholars to reposition themselves more centrally in the task of preparing teachers for today's schools, particularly in light of the performance-based standards movement in teacher education.

The Urban/Multicultural Teacher Education Program

The Urban/Multicultural Teacher Education Program[7] was developed as a collaborative effort among school district teachers and faculty in the College of Education at the University of Tennessee, Knoxville (UTK) within a context of major college restructuring. Faculty in the college were reorganizing departments toward a more interdisciplinary team structure around small, cohort-based teacher education. A colleague referred to this approach in which students chose from an array of programs as the "boutique" approach to teacher education. Concurrently, the college became involved with the Urban Network for the Improvement of Teacher Education (UNITE),[8] whose primary goal was to prepare high quality teachers for urban schools.

I had been on the faculty at UTK since 1987 in social foundations of education and taught the social foundations course for the professional core sequence: Teachers, Schools, and Society. Prior to moving to Tennessee, I served as a field coordinator in Bethel for the University of Alaska-Fairbanks X-CED program. This program infused anthropological perspectives and Native Alaskan knowledge and experience throughout the teacher education program as it prepared students to work in their home communities. The work in my doctoral program at the University of Cincinnati in sociology and anthropology of education prepared me well for this sociocultural approach to teacher education. A masters degree in special education and fourteen years of public school teaching in both rural and inner-city contexts provided the experiential and knowledge base I needed to inform my practice in this unique teacher education program. I served as the director of the Urban/Multicultural Teacher Education from 1992–96.

When the College of Education at Tennessee was invited to participate in the UNITE project, I was keen to build a program similar to the X-CED program, but one aimed at educating teachers for inner city schools, using social foundations as the "real" foundation. Tozer reminds us that

> ... if social foundations instruction is to have a genuine impact on teachers' meaning-construction in professional practice, then students will have to be engaged in forming and articulating meaning for themselves in their foundations coursework. They enter their professional programs well practiced in understanding educational phenomena in non-scholarly ways, well-practiced in seeing teaching and learning with eyes that have learned to see in ways the dominant culture has trained us all to see. If students are to learn to evaluate those traditional and sometimes inadequate ways of constructing meaning, if they are to learn to construct meaning anew, then they should be given as much opportunity as possible to practice such new interpretations. Ideally, they should do it in every course, and this remains an unmet challenge for most teacher education programs.[9]

In October 1993 the faculty at UTK began to work with local teachers and administrators to develop plans for a small, cohort-based teacher education program to meet the UNITE goal of preparing high quality urban teachers at the local level in Knoxville's inner-city schools. To be consistent will all other teacher education programs within the college, this one would be a fifth-year program. Students were required to complete the majority of a liberal arts degree prior to entry into the program and began their professional education course sequence during the final semester of their senior year. Coursework and a year-long internship during the fifth year were graduate courses and served as the beginning of a masters degree. The internship represented the students' first year of teaching; although they were not paid, the experience was recognized by the state as one year's teaching experience on the career ladder. Interns were viewed as co-teachers by both school faculty and students rather than student teachers. Students completed the requirements for a teaching certificate during the internship year; many completed requirements for a masters degree the following summer with four additional courses.

One of my goals for the Urban/Multicultural Teacher Education Program was to demonstrate that social foundations could serve as the basis for this teacher preparation. The program turned around the whole notion of traditional teacher education. Rather than segregate social foundations content to one or two discrete courses, this entire program was framed in the disciplines of Social Foundations, particularly history, philosophy, policy studies, sociology and anthropology of education and utilized this knowledge base to prepare teachers for their work in schools. The program offered a multidisciplinary theoretical and experiential base for educators.

We expected students in the Urban/Multicultural Teacher Education Program to gain the following knowledge and abilities:

1. to develop knowledge and understandings of their own cultural backgrounds;
2. to develop understandings in the history, philosophy, sociology, and anthropology of education;
3. to develop knowledge and understandings of diverse students, particularly from Appalachian and African American families;
4. to develop knowledge and understandings of children from impoverished families;
5. to better understand the problems and concerns of children and teachers in urban school settings;
6. to understand the social service programs and agencies involved with the families in the communities in which they will teach;
7. to develop an understanding of the structures and policies of urban schools; and
8. to develop a repertoire of teaching practices appropriate to the education of children in urban contexts.

We[10] examined schooling through sociological analyses of school structures. We explored the ways political and social structures impact teachers' worklives in urban school bureaucracies. We engaged students in educational philosophies as they developed their own teaching philosophy. Although we explored the traditional "methods" of language arts, science, math, and social studies as part of the elementary school curriculum, we framed this work within the politics of knowledge production as well as within the sociocultural context of children's lives. The methods portion of our program was grounded in transformative school practices. Our assumption was that traditional schooling has not been successful in urban/multicultural communities and that teachers must have a wide repertoire of pedagogical and curricular practices to engage students from diverse communities.

The Urban/Multicultural Teacher Education Program was designed for elementary education students who were committed to teaching in urban schools or with students from diverse cultural backgrounds. In keeping with UNITE's goal, the purpose of the program was to prepare highly qualified teachers to work in schools in urban/multicultural settings with children who come primarily from impoverished families. We expected to prepare multicultural educators who were knowledgeable about and able to affirm diversity in all its forms: social class, gender, race and ethnicity, religion, sexual orientation, and differing abilities. The notion of critical muticultural education or anti-racist education was infused throughout the program as preserve teachers examined the sociocultural contexts of schools and communities, child development, curriculum, and pedagogy. The program sought to prepare teachers who could effectively use transformative pedagogical practices in urban schools.[11]

Selecting School Partners

In keeping with the UNITE goal of preparing high quality teachers for urban schools, we looked to the inner-city schools of Knoxville to begin to develop partnerships with principals and teachers. Our partner schools included four elementary and one middle school with populations ranging from 300 to 700 students. Two of the schools had predominantly African-American student bodies (95 percent and 92 percent), two schools were predominantly white Appalachian (85 percent and 83.2 percent) and one school was more racially balanced with 58.5 percent African American and 41.8 percent White Appalachian. Two of the schools had federal housing developments within their school zones. All schools had high percentages of students who qualified for free and reduced lunch (from 85 percent to 99 percent).

In addition to our partnerships with inner-city schools, we formed relationships with four schools about thirty minutes from inner-city Knoxville in a district serving a highly educated, professional community. Although one of the elementary schools was considered an "inner-city" school and had a substantial population of children from low-income families, the district overall, was white and middle class. It was a well-funded, progressive district where teachers were better paid and were expected to use more innovative teaching methods. We worked closely with the administration and teachers in the elementary schools, placing a small number of interns in the schools for the entire year and other interns for 4-6 week rotations during the academic year. Our purpose was to provide a context that was quite different from the city schools so as to encourage more discussion around the political and sociocultural issues that were raised in the program. When students had experience in these starkly different contexts, they were able to critically examine inequities in school funding across districts.

We found that students needed a variety of experiences in their internship year. Lengthy rotations provided experiences in different grade levels and with different teachers. Rotations across school contexts sharpened students' perspectives of the base school. Occasionally interns working in the intensive environments of urban schools needed a short rotation in a less emotionally draining suburban school to regroup and reflect on their experiences. In addition, we found that by placing 4-5 interns in each of our city partnership schools, they were able to build a support system within the school. This approach encouraged students to try out the kinds of non-traditional pedagogies we encouraged. The addition of 4-5 teachers in a school for a year definitely contributed to the work of the faculty and students in the school.

We began our work with clear program goals for our students, the beginnings of collaborative relationships with teachers and administrators in five urban schools, and the belief that we would learn how best to "do teacher education" for urban contexts within the work of the program. Not surprisingly, we found that developing networks of teachers and principals in partnership schools requires intense, sustained effort over time. By maintaining a small number of partnership schools we were able to build trusting relationships with the school staff. We realized the importance of maintaining the same university staff within a school to further develop relationships and contribute to the school community.

Constructing a College Faculty Team

As director of the program, I assembled a small group of doctoral students from social foundations as well as curriculum and instruction programs to serve with me as the instructional team. All graduate students were experienced teachers, some with experience in inner-city schools. Faculty from other departments in the college regularly offered the set of core professional courses including (1) Teachers, Schools, and Society, (2) The Learner, and (3) The Elementary Curriculum. Our small team taught the remainder of the program. We taught together in pairs or teams in an attempt to model quality collaboration in teaching. We offered students an integrated program rather than a set of discrete courses taught separately by different faculty members. We believed that teacher education students model transformative practice only if they have sustained, positive experiences with alternative forms of pedagogy and begin to see them as the norm. Since many students came to our program with traditional banking models of teaching as lecturing in their heads and no experience with alternative, more engaging models, we worked hard to provide them with a repertoire of teaching experiences based in democratic and critical pedagogy.

Selecting Students for Diverse Perspectives and Experiences

The program used a cohort design in which 25 students moved through it from the time they began their pre-internship block of methods courses through the end of their internship year. We expected the cohort to develop into a cohesive community of learners. We believed that by building community, and thus, a support system within the group and with teachers in select partnership schools we could better prepare pre-service teachers to work in these complex and challenging settings. We took care to construct cohorts of students who themselves represented a variety of different ages, cultural and social class backgrounds, and life experiences. By selecting a small, but heterogeneous group of students we hoped to have students challenge each others' assumptions, values and beliefs as they learned to work together, building community across differences.

The selection of students for the program was made within the context of an Admissions Board made up of College of Education professors, partnership school teachers and principals, liberal arts faculty, and current interns. Prior to each set of Fall and Spring Admissions Boards, we held training sessions for all Board members who were to select students to participate in the program. These sessions familiarized Board members with the purposes of the program, the student selection criteria, and qualitative interview strategies we found most successful in our process.

Although the program was open to all students who were committed to teach in urban/multicultural settings, students with backgrounds in the social sciences such as history, sociology, anthropology, African American Studies, women's studies, urban studies, multicultural programs, and other related fields tended to have stronger knowledge bases for this program.[12] We attempted to select students who described themselves as learners, were able to work collaboratively with others, had some experiences with diverse populations, had work experiences, and were open to challenges. Applicants were asked questions specifically about cultural diversity, gender equity, and social justice issues. For example, typical interview questions would be, "Think of a time when you experienced discrimination and tell us about it" or "Think of a time when you experienced conflict and tell us about it." Students who had more limited experiences, but convinced the Admissions Board that they were open to the challenge of learning in urban contexts were admitted to the program. We typically selected only 50 percent of the students who applied for the program.

After students were officially admitted to the College of Education, the mentoring team met with the cohort of pre-intern students during the Fall semester prior to the commencement of the pre-internship spring semester. This meeting was designed to begin to develop a sense of community within the group. Students from the current cohort of interns provided specific information about the program and introduced students to partnership teachers, principals, and current students. Each student was assigned to a peer mentor who was already in the internship year. We encouraged a support system for new students to provide continuity from one cohort group to the next. Peer mentoring enabled students to form bonds with each other across cohorts. New students benefited from the knowledge and experience of the current students; current students looked back at where they were and how much they had grown. The more experienced students often remarked with surprise when they met the incoming group, "Did we really look like that?"

The students who selected and were selected by the Urban/Multicultural Teacher Education Program tended to be risk-takers. They wanted the challenge of working in urban schools. However, despite their different cultural and social class backgrounds, many had grown up in suburban or rural communities within the "Bible Belt" and had limited understandings of difference in its many forms (culture, race/ethnicity, language, religion, gender, sexual orientation, social class, and abilities). We continually engaged students in discussions and projects around difference and diversity. Some students regularly questioned what the sociocultural and political content had to do with anything related to teaching. They were uncomfortable exploring their own sociocultural backgrounds and resisted discussions about inequities in schooling, racism, sexism, and other difficult issues that were raised. Some students resisted doing community-based projects because they could not see the relationship these projects had to their future lives as teachers. They saw schools as separate from communities, preferring to focus on the curricular content or teaching methods with little attention to sociocultural aspects of the communities where the schools were situated. They were so focused on the gathering of methodological "tricks" as they packed their "teaching bags" to be ready for their impending internships, that it took some effort for them to stand back for a broader perspective. The brevity and intensity of the program itself helped to instill this performance anxiety in the students. However, because we selected for diversity in our program, we always had some students who, through personal experiences and insights, could present alternative perspectives and challenge others to reconsider their positions.

Program Components

The Urban/Multicultural Teacher Education Program was and continues to be one of several options for the teacher education students in the college. Although much of the content and pedagogy differed, the curricular components of the program were the same as all other elementary programs in the college. These components are illustrated in Table 1. Diversity was a core component of our program's knowledge base and pedagogical processes. The following bodies of scholarly literature informed our practice in the program: multicultural education, urban teacher education, sociology of education, anthropology of education, qualitative approaches to inquiry, reflective practice, critical/feminist perspectives on schooling, and transformative pedagogies of schooling (integrated curriculum, project-centered learning, case-based instruction, alternate forms of text such as film, fiction, autobiography, etc.).

Table 1

Common Components for all Teacher Education Programs, UTK

Spring Semester	Fall Semester*	Spring Semester*
Teachers, Schools and Society (400-level social foundations course/3 hours)	Internship (4 hours)	Internship (4 hours)
The Learner (400-level educational psychology course/3 hours)	Analysis of Teaching I (2 hours)	Analysis of Teaching II (8 hours)
Elementary Curriculum (400-level curriculum and instruction course/3 hours)	Integrated Elementary Methods II (6 hours)	
Integrated Elementary Methods I (6 hours)		

*All courses during the internship year were at the 500-level graduate courses.

Working through a democratic education model that utilized critical/feminist pedagogy, students were expected to be active learners responsible for working together in a project-centered curriculum. Projects based in qualitative approaches to inquiry such as community/school culture studies, cultural autobiographies, case studies, reflective journals, child study, literacy development study, thematic units were regular components in our program. We used observational and interview techniques to hone students' listening and "kidwatching" skills. The students read African American and Appalachian fiction, poetry, and autobiographical narratives to provide further knowledge and connections with children from those cultural backgrounds. We incorporated pertinent films where appropriate to increase students' understandings of the historical, political, and cultural contexts of diverse communities and to challenge previously held beliefs about these communities. All projects focused students' attention to diversity and community.

During the pre-internship semester in the first Integrated Elementary Methods course, students were involved in project-centered "culture studies" of inner-city communities. Each team of students explored a different community around one of the partnership schools. They interviewed people, learned about the community's culture, history, geography, economy, political structure, and community agencies. At the completion of the project, students shared their knowledge so that this community—one generally quite different from the students' own home communities—became more familiar to all students in the cohort and served as a knowledge base as they began their field experiences and internships within the partnership school communities. The projects provided extensive learning in African American and Appalachian cultures and in the sociohistorical contexts of these particular communities.

Our pedagogy employed a cyclical model of Theory, Observation, Practice, and Reflection (TOPR) where students (1) learned the knowledge base necessary for good elementary educational practice, (2) observed and reflected on what they saw in classroom practice, and (3) tried out for themselves what they were learning in both theory and practice. This model was one in which they continuously reflected on their own process and practices. The field experience portion of the program was tightly woven into the design of our on-campus coursework. All students gained experience in urban partnership schools through a minimum of forty-five hours in a field experience placement during the spring semester prior to the internship year. Supervisors and mentoring teachers provided feedback on the students' progress throughout the spring semester. Each mentoring teacher completed a final evaluation. At the end of this semester of coursework, we asked students to write written reflections on their progress throughout the semester and assess their development as teachers, describing their strengths and weaknesses.

The professional full-year internship followed the public school calendar. Students began to work in their assigned schools from the first day of teacher in- service through to the end of the school year. As indicated in Table 1, in addition to their work in schools, interns took eight hours of graduate work in research and teaching methods. Reflective practice was a cornerstone of this program. One of the aims of this program was to have beginning teachers reflect critically on their own practices in light of their professional knowledge base. Each Friday morning during the fall semester, we began with reflection groups led by faculty facilitators. Students brought to class written reflections about a particular experience that stood out from them during the week. Reflection groups provided an opportunity for interns to discuss what they learned that week about themselves and their work as teachers. This was not to be an "advice-giving session" but a time when students were expected to critically examine school practices and policies and their own perspectives on those practices. We collected the written reflections and audiotapes of the group discussion for use in later assessment of students' development. The remainder of the day was spent in collaborative group work around curricular projects based on issues raised in their school contexts. Interns were responsible for identifying areas of concern and organizing educational programs for the group around those issues. Occasionally we visited community resources to familiarize interns with possibilities for integrating the community with their school practices.

Teacher research was another integral component of the program. As part of their eight graduate hours during the fall semester of their internship year, students took a course called Analysis of Teaching with three major themes: (1) sociocultural contexts of schools and communities, (2) reflective practice, and (3) teacher as researcher. In the first part of the course, students practiced the skills of participant observation and analysis. They examined their school and community contexts systematically and reflected on the relationship of particular contexts and practices as compared to what they have learned from their previous course readings. As the course progressed, students read in the reflective practice literature and begin to write about their own practice. They developed metaphors for themselves as teachers and began to develop a portfolio of their teaching practices that was completed during the spring semester.[13]

A final portion of the course introduced students to teacher inquiry approaches they might use in an action research project. Students developed action research projects in collaboration with school staff that could be of immediate benefit to school faculty, staff, and children. By the end of the semester, students developed a full proposal for their research, including a review of the literature, that was read and approved by both school-based and university faculty. All interns across programs in the college completed their action research projects in the spring semester of the internship year and presented their results to peers, faculty and school colleagues during a Capstone Intern Conference in April of each year. This conference developed into a regular, expected part of the internship year. The conference provided a serious, research-based, reflective culminating activity for the internship year for both students and faculty. Through intensive, sustained, and structured experiences with reflective practice, we students were able to develop habits of reflection and critical inquiry in their professional practice. They became quite open to and adept at critically examining their own practices as well as the school contexts that, in part, shaped their pedagogy.

Final Reflections

My involvement with the Urban/Multicultural Teacher Education Program was during the years of its development and early implementation from 1992–1996. I worked with three cohorts of students as they moved through the program. At the final meeting of the UNITE group,[14] we discussed our progress in meeting our goals of preparing high quality teachers for urban communities. I recall describing our program to my colleagues from other institutions and was particularly struck by a college of education dean from another institution who scoffed at the whole idea of building a program firmly within a social foundations framework. His experiences with social foundations faculty led him to believe that this approach to teacher education could be nothing short of ludicrous. Despite his and others' reservations about the abilities of social foundations faculty to work at the core of teacher education programs, I continue to believe that programs like the one described here are essential if we are to make progress in preparing educators for teaching in diverse communities. I do not expect all social foundations faculty to want to engage in this labor-intensive work with schools and communities. It is exhausting and pulls us away from more traditional forms of scholarship. However, it can move us to think about scholarship that is more entwined with our daily work with teacher education students in school settings. By building bridges with colleagues in curriculum and instruction programs, we can achieve a more collaborative model in which social foundations really is the foundation for our work in teacher education.

Social Foundations within the Current Context of Performance-Based Standards

The National Council for the Accreditation of Teacher Education (NCATE) new 2000 *Standards* as well as the movement toward performance-based standards required by many states move us away from course specific requirements in teacher education. It is becoming difficult to find states that specify particular courses in history, philosophy, or sociology of education as requirements for teacher certification. The shift in state and national regulations away from inputs in the form of coursework no longer serves to protect the field of social foundations by requiring specific courses. In previous years, social foundations faculty could point to the specific courses where "their" content was a required portion of the teacher education curriculum. This safety net is becoming increasingly rare. Current state requirements shift the focus toward requiring teachers to demonstrate their abilities to construct educational environments where "all children can learn." In the following discussion, I provide three state examples followed by examples from NCATE 2000 to illustrate this shift from course specific social foundations requirements to performance outcomes.

The state of Connecticut's current policies for specific coursework in foundations of education are being changed to competency-based standards. The language of current standards specifies coursework in foundations of education in "areas such as: philosophy of education, history of education, and comparative education."[15] In 2003, Connecticut statutes move to a performance model that requires teacher education candidates to "demonstrate competence in recognizing the relationship of school and society and of social-cultural issues as they affect the public school's responsibilities, including the provisions for educational equity and opportunity, and the provisions of special education as defined by state and federal regulations." For competencies for the elementary teacher 1-6, Standard Certificate, the statute is as follows: "Pedagogical Content Knowledge. The effective teacher of elementary education: a. understands the foundations of elementary education and the philosophical, historical and sociological issues in the field, including underlying theories and the value of active learning."[16] In this case, while we see an acknowledgement of social foundations disciplinary knowledge in the statues, there is clearly no requirement for specific social foundations courses in the preparation of teachers.

Arizona does not have a specific requirement for social foundations, but currently has nine broad standards that are to be measured with performance-based assessments. The items in the standards most closely reflective of social foundations content are the following: teachers are expected to link learning with students' prior knowledge, experiences, and backgrounds; incorporate strategies which address the diverse needs of learners, and demonstrate multicultural sensitivity; demonstrate knowledge of the influences of individual development, experiences, talents, prior learning, language, culture, gender, family, and community on student learning; demonstrate knowledge of schools as organizations within the larger community context and the operations of the relevant aspects of the educational system; and demonstrate knowledge of laws and ethics related to student, parent, and teacher rights and responsibilities. Here, again, we see attention to social foundations content as related to diversity, multicultural education, school structure, professional ethics, and legal aspects of teaching but no specific requirement connecting this knowledge to particular social foundations courses.

One final example that is typical of this movement toward a limited number of broad state performance-based standards, can be found in South Carolina. Currently the state has a set of ten broad state standards for teacher education candidates including the following: (1) Long-Range Planning, (2) Short-Range-Planning of Instruction, (3) Short-Range-Planning, Development, and Use of Assessments, (4) Establishing and Maintaining High Expectations for Learners, (5) Using Instructional Strategies to Facilitate Learning, (6) Providing Content for Learners, (7) Monitoring and Enhancing Learning, (8) Maintaining an Environment That Promote Learning, (9) Managing the Classroom, and (10) Fulfilling Professional Responsibilities Beyond the Classroom. Each of these topical areas contains specific competencies for which teachers are expected to demonstrate their abilities. Although one could envision social foundations content and understandings in many of these broad standards, within the eighth standard there is language most closely relevant to social foundations:

Competent professional teachers show an awareness of and sensitivity to individual differences among students, as well as their social and cultural backgrounds. All students are equally encouraged to participate, learn and develop, and to achieve high levels of success. Competent professional teachers create and maintain an environment in which cooperation and teamwork is valued and students learn to respect and appreciate differences among individuals. The beliefs, ideas, opinions, and other contributions of all students are given thoughtful consideration.[17]

South Carolina's standards includes social foundations content, particularly as related to diversity, but contain no specific requirements for the historical, philosophical, and sociocultural knowledge typically included in social foundations courses.

All these state examples are consistent with the new NCATE 2000 Standards that focus on candidate performance. The language of the NCATE 2000 that is most reflective of social foundations knowledge, skills, and dispositions is evident in the conceptual framework as well as in several of the standards. According to the NCATE 2000 Standards, the conceptual framework is no longer included as one of the standards, but is a requirement that serves as the unifying frame that "*establishes the shared vision for a unit's efforts in preparing educators to work effectively in P-12 schools. It provides direction for programs courses, teaching, candidate performance, scholarship, service, and unit accountability. The conceptual framework(s) is knowledge-based, articulated, shared, coherent, consistent with the unit and/or institutional mission, and continuously evaluated.* In other words, the conceptual framework guides the entire work of the unit. The unit's conceptual framework is judged, in part, on the extent to which it includes a diversity component. In the following paragraphs, I have included three of the six standards as well as a bit of the language of the rubrics used to evaluate the extent to which the standard has been met. These excerpts are provided here to illustrate possible connections with social foundations knowledge and understandings in professional education programs.

Standard 1/Candidate Knowledge, Skills, and Dispositions: Candidates preparing to work in schools as teachers or other professional school personnel know and demonstrate the content, pedagogical, and professional knowledge, skills, and dispositions necessary to help all students learn. Assessments indicate that candidates meet professional, state, and institutional standards.

Assessment Rubric: They (candidates) consider the school, family, and community contexts in which they work and the prior experience of students to develop meaningful learning experiences.

Standard 3/Field Experiences and Clinical Practice: the unit and its school partners design, implement, and evaluate field experiences and clinical practice so that teacher candidates and other school personnel develop and demonstrate the knowledge, skills, and dispositions necessary to help all students learn.

Assessment Rubric: All candidates participate in field experiences or clinical practice that include students with exceptionalities and students from diverse ethnic, racial, gender, and socioeconomic groups.

Standard 4/Diversity: The unit designs, implements, and evaluates curriculum and experiences for candidates to acquire and apply the knowledge, skills, and dispositions necessary to help all student learn. These experiences include working with diverse higher education and school faculty, diverse candidates, and diverse students in P-12 schools.

Assessment Rubric: Candidates learn to develop and teach lessons that incorporate diversity and develop a classroom and school climate that values diversity. Candidates become aware of different teaching and learning styles shaped by the cultural influences and are able to adapt instruction and services appropriately for all students, including students with exceptionalities. They demonstrate dispositions that value fairness and learning by all students.

Faculty with whom candidates work in professional education classes and clinical practice have knowledge and experiences related to preparing candidates to work with students from diverse cultural backgrounds, including students with exceptionalities.[18]

The NCATE 2000 performance-based standards require that students and faculty from across programs in colleges of education demonstrate they are able to provide educational environments to meet the needs of diverse students and increase opportunities to interact with diverse communities.

These new state and national standards could actually serve to reposition social foundations faculty within colleges of education to embrace a broader notion of the role of social foundations content knowledge in teacher education. In essence, we are being invited to share our knowledge of the field in all phases of coursework and field experiences within school communities. We may choose to work with curriculum and instruction colleagues with student cohorts in programs such as the one I have described above. There are a range of alternative ways we might participate in this enterprise. There are particular programmatic requirements that could benefit from a social foundations perspective. For example, students are often asked to write an educational philosophy to include in their professional portfolios. Who is better prepared to guide this work than social foundations faculty? I am definitely not suggesting here that we abandon the more traditional social foundations courses for an infused model. Often an infusion approach actually decreases the impact of what we have to offer. I am arguing for both an increased number of social foundations courses as well as an increased presence of social foundations faculty in other courses and program experiences. We might work with our colleagues in curriculum and instruction to redesign programs, tailoring and integrating the pedagogy courses as illustrated in the Urban/Multicultural Teacher Education program so that more courses could be offered to provide students with understandings of the sociocultural and political contexts of schooling that are too often neglected in teacher education programs. For example, it seems reasonable for social foundations faculty to become involved in courses related to parent and community involvement, politics of education, multicultural education, rural and urban schooling, teacher inquiry, reflective practice, and other similar courses requiring knowledge, skills, and dispositions within a social foundations framework.

As we meet the challenges of the new standards to change the way we incorporate social foundations understandings in teacher education, we have an opportunity to provide challenging opportunities for our own graduate students. We can model ways to work across the boundaries so often rigidly in place within colleges. Team teaching with curriculum and instruction or arts and sciences colleagues is one way to disrupt notions of curricular ownership. Engaging in the intense work of field-based teacher education programs is another. Social foundations graduate students who are provided with opportunities to work with us in these ways can develop the dispositions necessary to team teach, work broadly across teacher education programs, and integrate their scholarship into the work of teacher education. These are the individuals who will be able to engage the next generation of scholars in alternatives for the way we "do Social Foundations" in teacher education.

In addition to the actual teacher education programs, social foundations faculty are in the unique position of having the skills and knowledge necessary to work with colleagues across departments to develop the conceptual framework that will guide their efforts. I am not suggesting that colleagues in curriculum and instruction and other departments are not able to construct such frameworks. My point here is that social foundations faculty tend to enjoy working with and engaging in debates around theories, abstractions, and philosophical perspectives—precisely what is needed in thinking through the conceptual framework aspect of the new standards. There are those among us who might be adventurous enough to take leadership roles in shaping the ways we work with the standards both within our own institutions and in the state and national arenas. If we choose to do so, we are in a position in social foundations to make major contributions to shaping the way that teacher education programs do their work.[19]

In conclusion, the Council of Learned Societies in Education's Social Foundations *Standards for Academic and Professional Instruction in Foundations of Education, Educational Studies, and Educational Policy Studies* guide college of education faculty as they undertake their program refinements to meet the new state and national standards. The six principles for educators (located in the appendix of the standards) along with their indicators for demonstrating knowledge, disposition, and performance standards are valuable for shaping our work with colleagues across departments in teacher education. It might be time, once again, to get those standards out and share them with colleagues as we shape our programs to address state and local requirements. More importantly, they provide a strong foundation for our work in preparing pre-service and in-service teachers to provide high quality learning environments for all our students.

EPIOLGUE

In the spring of 2001 when this chapter was first published as an article, George W. Bush had just signed into law the No Child Left Behind (NCLB) legislation. In this brief epilogue, I examine the challenges this legislation as well as other more recent proposed legislation holds for social foundations scholars. Although the context for social foundations was difficult at the time I wrote this article, we are faced now with even more challenges both for our work in schools with teachers struggling to deal with the Bush Administration's repressive policies for K–12 schools as well as new efforts to dismantle colleges of teacher education.

The purpose of Public Law 107-110, No Child Left Behind Act (Title I: Improving the Academic Achievement of the Disadvantaged), is to "to ensure that all children have a fair, equal, and significant opportunity to obtain a high-quality education and reach, at a minimum, proficiency on challenging State academic achievement standards and state academic assessments." Despite promises to provide billions of federal dollars to support local education programs aimed toward meeting these goals, the legislation remains largely unfunded. Teachers and administrators in local school districts are scrambling to meet the requirements of adequate yearly progress (AYP) through the implementation of the following requirements of the law (as quoted from NCLB):

- High-quality academic assessments and accountability systems aligned with challenging state academic standards.
- Improving and strengthening accountability.
- A variety of programs to meet the educational needs of low-achieving children, migratory children, children with disabilities, Indian children, neglected or delinquent children, and young children in need of reading assistance.
- Greater decision-making authority and flexibility to schools and teachers *in exchange for* [my emphasis] greater responsibility for student performance.
- Promoting schoolwide reform and ensuring the access of children to effective, scientifically based instructional strategies and challenging academic content; and affording parents substantial and meaningful opportunities to participate in the education of their children.

Although this law promises to ameliorate issues of education for underserved populations, it ignores the processes of education that are democratic, critical, aesthetic, emotional, and moral—the very aspects of education at the heart of the field of social foundations. These aspects of education can neither be taught nor assessed in ways that are "scientifically based."

Once NCLB was passed, the Bush Administration turned its focus toward teacher education and is now in the process of moving the reauthorization of the Higher Education Act, entitled the Ready to Teach Act (H.R. 2211), through Congress. Passed by the House in July 2003, as I write, it is in the Senate's Committee on Health, Education, Labor, and Pensions. In a press release on July 10, 2003, U.S. Secretary of Education Rod Paige issued the following statement:

> President Bush and I believe that every child in America can learn, every child in America will learn and no child will be left behind. Every child deserves a highly qualified teacher in the classroom, and we can ensure this happens by improving teacher education programs and increasing the number of *highly qualified teachers* [my emphasis] through alternative certification methods. Research shows a strong link between a teacher's content knowledge and student achievement, and a critical component of No Child Left Behind is to strengthen teacher preparation programs. Teaching graduates must be highly qualified with the skills and knowledge needed to ensure student success in today's challenging classrooms. (Paige, 2003)

It is clear from the Ready to Teach Act and statements like these issued by the Bush Administration that "highly qualified teachers" are those that can demonstrate their content knowledge largely through passing standardized tests. Federal legislation such as this paves the way for states to enact new certification rules to speed up the process of teacher and administrator certification through alternative routes. Recent certification rules adopted in February 2004 by the Georgia Professional Standards Commission allow for a "test out" route to initial certification for students with a degree in a "closely related field" and supervised practicum that must be initiated within the first year of certification. Certification policies such as these bypass teacher education programs altogether.

A final aspect to the context is the newly announced study initiated by the U.S. Congress to study the effectiveness of colleges of education. This study, expected to be conducted by the National Research Council with $1.5 million in allocated funding, has as its focus the academic content and field experience preparation of preservice teachers. According to an article in *Education Week* (March 3, 2004), critics of the study "point to Mr. [Reid] Lyon's (Chief of the National Institute of Child Health and Human Development) role in shaping the study as an indication that the information gathered will be used to quash colleges of education" (Blair, 2004, p. 13). The notion behind the study is that although teacher education programs

report some data to state and federal agencies, there is no current requirement that teacher education programs compile data about many aspects of
their programs and make this data public.

What role can teacher educators, particularly those in social foundations,
play in this context? The Council of Learned Societies in Education
Standards[1] stated (1997) that:

> Foundational study, therefore, contains a prescriptive as well as a descriptive
> dimension: to consider in tandem *what schools are doing and what they ought to
> be doing* [my emphasis]. Such study focuses on the ways schools carry out their
> mission of preparing individuals to occupy productive roles in our society. A
> common theme is discernment of educational aims that are implied in cur-
> rent school practices as well as in recommendations for modifying such prac-
> tices. (CLSE, 1997, p. 8)

This statement within the standards points to fruitful avenues for foundations scholars to resist and to work for change in federal and state policies such as those just described. Social foundations researchers might
work closely with colleagues in K–12 settings to document the implementation of NCLB in local schools, sharing the struggles of teachers and administrators with a broader audience. In addition to articles in scholarly
journals, pieces written for local newspapers, presentations to school
boards, and other local efforts could assist to disseminate the concerns of
educators as well as to make recommendations for modifying the practices
of NCLB. Teachers live and work in contexts that are culturally, politically, interactionally, and emotionally messy, complex, and challenging.
As foundations scholars, we can document and share this messiness as well
as the inadequacy of NCLB's accountability measures to assess students
and teachers within these contexts.

In the arena of teacher education, social foundations scholars and
teacher educators are called on to stay vigilant to the moves of the Bush Administration with regard to teacher education. Foundations scholars might
serve in advocacy roles at the local and state level to inform policymakers in
regard to swiftly changing certification rules. We might work for key social
foundations scholars to be included on the National Research Council's
panel to conduct the newly funded research in teacher education. We can
continue to document and disseminate findings from our own work within
and studying high-quality teacher education programs.

The quality of teacher education programs needs to be assessed on a regular basis by those who work within them as well as by state and national accreditation agencies. I encourage colleagues in social foundations to

---

[1]The Council of Learned Societies in Education later changed its name to the National
Council for the Social Foundations.

become involved in continual assessment and improvement processes within their institutions, as well as through agencies such as the National Council for the Accreditation of Teacher Education. Having foundations scholars on state and national accreditation teams and/or working with the accreditation processes in their institutions ensures that the foundations perspectives on teacher education is articulated.

Within our colleges of education, now is the time to work closely and collaboratively with colleagues in curriculum and instruction as well as the arts and sciences to continue to prepare "high-quality" teachers who have the knowledge, skills, and dispositions to understand the complexity of schools and children within diverse settings as well as the ability to create teaching and learning environments that ensure that all children can achieve. High-quality teachers should be much better prepared than those "highly qualified" teachers who merely demonstrate their content mastery on Praxis II exams.

REFERENCES

Blair, J. (2004, March 3). Congress orders thorough study of teacher education programs. *Education Week*, p. 13.
Council of Learned Societies in Education. (1997). *Standards for academic and professional instruction in foundations of education, educational studies, and educational policy studies.* San Francisco: Caddo Gap Press.
Paige, R. (2003, July 10). *Press releases: Paige issues statement on House passage of education bills.* Washington, DC: U.S. Department of Education. http://www.ed.gov/news/pressreleases/2003/07/07102003.html

Notes

1. *Standards*, op. cit, 9.
2. *Standards*, op.cit., xx.
3. *Standards for Academic and Professional Instruction in Foundations of Education, Educational Studies, and Educational Policy Studies*, Council of Learned Societies in Education (Caddo Gap Press). 1997, 8.
4. For the past three years the Committee on Academic Standards and Accreditation (CASA) has presented a State of the States panel discussion at the American Educational Studies Association meetings. Results of state surveys and discussions among AESA members indicated major concerns about (1) the diminishing number of actual social foundations courses required for licensure, (2) the substitution of social foundations courses with Introduction to Education courses, and (3) the lack of preparation in social foundations disciplines among faculty teaching these courses.
5. *Standards*, op. cit, 8.
6. I have reported the success and challenges of this program elsewhere, so will not repeat them here. SeeKathleen deMarrais, Jamie Lewis, & Sally Oran. (1999). Educating teachers for an urban/multicultural context: Growing through diversity. In Marvin Wideen & Paulette Lemma (Eds.), *Ground Level Reform in Teacher*

Education. 1999. (Detselig Enterprises Ltd.). This chapter provides more of the students' perspectives about the program.

7. We have struggled with the terms urban and inner-city. In the work reported here, the UNITE Project focused on urban schools while the district we work in used the term inner-city to describe the school that were our partners. In this paper, we use the labels urban and inner-city synonymously, but are quick to recognize the assumptions and stereotypes that are often associated with the labels.

8. UNITE was a project directed by Kenneth Howey at Ohio State University and was a collaborative effort among eight colleges of education including: Ohio State, Simon Frasier, University of Toronto, Central Connecticut State University, University of Louisville, University of Tennessee, Indiana University, and Miami University.

9. Steve Tozer, Toward a New Consensus among Social Foundations Educators: Draft Position Paper of the American Educational Studies Association Committee on Academic Standards and Accreditation. *Educational Foundations* 7:4 Fall, 1993, 20–21.

10. I use the pronoun we to refer to the students, teachers, and university faculty who worked collaboratively in the design and implementation of this program.

11. Cf. Kathleen deMarrais and Margaret LeCompte, Henry Giroux, Gloria Ladson-Billings, Peter McLaren, Sonia Nieto, Christine Sleeter, Joel Spring, George Wood and many others who write in critical pedagogy, democratic education, and multicultural education.

12. All students admitted to teacher education programs at UTK had degrees in specific fields of study.

13. In reflecting back on the process, this portfolio would be more effective if started during the pre-internship semester.

14. This was a final meeting of the first phase of the UNITE Project; the project was funded for additional years.

15. Connecticut state regulations for teacher certification.

16. New Connecticut state regulations for teacher certification.

17. South Carolina state standards for teacher certification.

18. *NCATE Unit Standards*, 2000.

19. Social foundations scholars such as Erskine Dottin, Douglas Simpson, and Steve Tozer are just a few who are involved in shaping the professional standards. Numbers of social foundations faculty serve on the NCATE Board of Examiners. The Committee on Academic Standards and Accreditation is developing rubrics to assess the demonstration of social foundations principals for educators.

Part IV

SOCIAL FOUNDATIONS AND THE ENGAGEMENT OF CONTESTED POSITIONS

Diversity, Democracy, and Definitions: Contested Positions for the Future of the Social Foundations

Dan W. Butin

Educational discourses position schools as ameliorative institutions. Teaching becomes a "noble calling," where determination and caring mix to create better classrooms, better children, and thus a better society. Preservice teachers embrace this view, positioning themselves as advocates of change, of hope, and of children. Yet most students' previous school experiences are all too often bereft of such sentiments or attention; boredom and lack of meaning permeate much of students' time (National Research Council [NRC], 2003). "That's just the way things are" becomes a standard response.

This is a classic double bind. To suggest that schools might be repressive institutions is to reject one's own trajectory and life decisions to become a teacher, risking one's sense of place within it. To accept the ideology of betterment, though, silences the dissonance of experience and forecloses any real opportunity to reveal and rework the basic building blocks that undergird our system of schooling.

To accept is to be silenced. To reject is to be silenced. The educational double bind is complete. So what allows for the unraveling of this binding? Elizabeth Ellsworth (1997) reminds us that "The crucial element [of the double bind] is not being able to leave the field, or point out the contradiction" (p. 262). If so, what pedagogy supports a questioning that leads to passages into the unknown, fostering a productive doubt that allows us to grasp the contradictions just enunciated (Martesewicz, 2001)?

Let me suggest that the social foundations of education may promote such an unbinding—that the social foundations of education classroom is fundamentally an attempt to help students "leave the field." For what links the chapters of this volume together is a stubborn resistance to being silenced about educational theory, policy, or practice. It is not only Maxine Greene's "imaging how things might be otherwise" or Paulo Freire's demand for praxis through problem-posing education (Freire, 1992; Greene, 1978). The social foundations of education classroom is, I argue, about a passionate engagement with contested positions.

Undergraduates come to college deeply immersed in the hidden curriculum of schooling; they are "naive experts" of the educational process, having spent over 16,000 hours internalizing the normative boundaries of what it means to teach and learn (Jackson, 1968). Moreover, most coursework within teacher education programs is driven by a technical formalism committed to imparting "best practices" to produce "highly qualified" teachers.

Yet the educational process is a highly complex, unstable, and furiously interactive task—what Churchman (1971) described as a "wicked problem." Traditional paradigms of teaching as a causal and linear process are thus inadequate in explicating the micropolitics and micropractices of classroom life. Dewey (1910) argued that all deep educational encounters must begin from a condition of doubt, a "forked-road situation," "which is ambiguous, which presents a dilemma ... [which] involves willingness to endure a condition of mental unrest and disturbance" (pp. 11, 13). It is in this disturbance of the normal, of the seemingly "natural," that deep assumptions become visible, that paradigmatic perspectives shift, that our expectations are redefined. And it is in the cracks of the disruption that avenues for teaching about highly contentious issues (e.g., oppression, social justice, identity construction) becomes possible (Apple, 1999; Britzman, 1998).

An engagement with contested positions shows that the possible extends beyond the "commonsensical." Whether this is through disciplinary depth, methodological rigor, or epistemological doubt, social foundations classrooms are usually the only spaces within which preservice teachers may be able to increase the sphere of possibilities about what is "normal" and "natural" in teaching. Engaging with contested positions allows us to work through the uncertainties, the doubts, and the transformations necessary for understanding schooling practices.

Historical or cross-cultural studies, for example, may show how schools act as sites of socialization; student-led in-depth community-based research may foster greater understanding of the linkages between socioeconomic status, schools, and political leverage; feminist readings may reveal the skewed emphasis on "truth," "neutrality," and "outcomes" as inherently male obsessions. Each of these examples is not about revealing the "truth" of education so much as laying out contested positions to question the implicit hegemony of what it means to do schooling.

Contested positions can be understood against the backdrop of the "modern trinity" of social science research—class, race, and gender—or through the postmodern absorption with issues of identity, knowledge, and power. So what are the contested positions? What is it that we should be teaching and researching within the social foundations of education?

I find three distinct strands within this volume that I would like to expand on: engaging with diversity; demonstrating democracy; and, defining social foundations for ourselves and for others.

ENGAGING WITH DIVERSITY

The U.S. Census (1996) projected that by 2050 Whites will be a numerical minority within the United States. This is already the case in California's public schools (Lopez, 2003). Although much of the population growth of Hispanic and Asian populations will continue to occur in urban metropolitan areas, the lure of jobs and the serendipity of migration decisions has already created such seeming cultural incongruities as the Hmong in Minneapolis/St. Paul, Hispanic-majority towns in North Carolina, and the "Indian" saturation of Silicon Valley.

Many of the contentious consequences of such population diversity can already be expected: debates over curricular content, over the diversity of teaching methods and learning styles, and over cultural clashes between communities and schools are sure to increase. Educators, policymakers, and the public at large have begun to realize that the "melting pot" model of assimilation so common at the turn of the 20th century is no longer applicable or helpful to the plurality and politicization of American society (Sleeter & Grant, 1999). Difference multiculturalism and critical multiculturalism with their metaphors of mosaics and inequitable playing fields, respectively (Butin, 2003), have taken hold.

It seems incumbent on social foundations scholars to teach and research such issues. Irrespective of actual numbers, our society continues to operate within a "culture of power" seemingly at odds with the values and practices of nondominant groups (Delpit, 1995). School policies and practices continue to act as implicit and powerful gatekeepers for our most valued cultural possessions.

Social foundations scholars have deep theoretical traditions by which to examine such policies and practices. From anthropological examinations of schools as mechanisms of acculturation to sociological analysis of stratification practices to historical examinations of the failure of educational reform, the social foundations field has been examining such issues for almost a century.

Another implication that foundations scholars may be poised to analyze is the redefining of multiculturalism and multicultural education. In one respect this necessitates the continued analysis of ongoing debates around long-standing political skirmishes such as affirmative action and the education of English language learners. At a deeper level, though, lies a fundamental rethinking of what diversity entails and implies.

Multicultural education is grounded on an uneasy tension: It must use the status of categories (e.g., the inequity of achievement between White and African American youth), while arguing for the rejection of the categorization of the other. Yet such dichotomizations (e.g., Black/White) have been deconstructed not only theoretically but pragmatically. As the U.S. Census finally acknowledges that race is a social construct and as a media-driven, consumerist culture permeates American culture, there is very little ballast left for notions of radical and incommensurate cultural differences.

How is difference thus to be conceptualized in a post-race world (Alexander, 1996; Gilroy, 2003)? To what extent can multiple, overlapping, and highly situational identities be reconciled, categorized, and/or understood (Ellsworth, 1997)? How do we begin to understand the "internal cultural segmentations, the internal frontlines" of identity politics within and across racial boundaries that were all too rigid just a decade or two ago (Hall, 2000)? Is DuBois's (1995) argument that "the problem of the twentieth century is the problem of the color line" no longer applicable to the 21st century? Does race no longer matter even when de facto segregation pervades inner city schools throughout the United States (Orfield, 2002)? These are crucial questions with no simple answers.

Likewise, our notions of diversity are shibboleths for the myths of American radical individualism. They are dependent on the self as a stable, internal, and bounded entity—an entity that is easy to assess, to categorize, and to sort. The reconstitution of diversity thus has potential to disrupt the tyranny of the bell curve and to reject the mystification of inequitable achievement as by-products of bad genes, bad habits, and bad people. To grapple with the redefinition of diversity is truly an engagement with contested positions, and one, I would argue, overdue within the social foundations of education.

DEMONSTRATING DEMOCRACY

In chapter 1, Tozer and Miretzky quote R. Freeman Butts discussing the intensive meetings held by Teachers College faculty during the 1949–1950 academic year that reexamined the social foundations program: "It need hardly be said that this [the reconstitution of the social foundations program at Teachers College] is an effort to make a discipline of the democratic process, particularly as this becomes the concern of educators in a democracy." Butts suggests a seemingly audacious equivalence: the foundations program as democratic practice. Let me take this equivalence seriously to expand on this notion: namely, that the social foundations of education classroom can promote the basic attributes of liberal democratic societies—the ability to articulate and think through conflicting conceptions of the good (Rorty, 1998).

I do not mean here to enter into the theoretical debates between communitarian, critical, postmodern, utilitarian, and liberal notions of the "good society." What is of relevance is that such political discussions are generally absent in educational discourses about the moral life of schools (Oakes, 2002). The educational double bind referred to at the beginning of this chapter survives and succeeds exactly because no modes of critical discourse are available to question the purposes and practices of schools as societal mechanisms of socialization and stratification.

But one cannot simply "talk" about democracy. At a deep level one must enact it. This is not a retreat toward "student-centered" learning, as if there was such a thing in an educational apparatus finely tuned for teachers' work. This is the difficult endeavor of creating classrooms where students are actually developing "habits of mind" that are meaningful. As Gene Provenzo in chapter 3 and Mary Bushnell Greiner in chapter 5 demonstrate, such practices are exhilarating and exhausting to implement.

Deliberative classrooms centered on democratic principles foster students' exploration and creation of linkages and dialogues across academic, institutional, psychological, and emotional borders. In so doing, such classrooms highlight rather than obscure the consequential and contested aspects of certain "truths," knowledges, and perspectives. Provenzo's students learned how governments use textbooks to construct histories; Greiner's students learned how artistic endeavors help us to understand what is meaningful about education.

Such practices, it should be noted, place the teacher in a highly precarious position. The teacher's privileged status as the gatekeeper of knowledge becomes exposed as the subjective construction of what "truths" students should be exposed to and participate in. Yet this is also a liberating predicament, for the positioning can be reversed. A democratic classroom makes visible and thus debatable what knowledge is learned and why. It allows for the full participation of all members in the self-reflexive decision making of how we come to decide what it means to be educated.

This is a radical departure from and a threat to the technical proficiency propounded in much of teacher education. Performance-based outcome measures prevalent in education schools all too easily become focused only on measurable and quantifiable models of nonambiguous progress. Such instrumentalism—devoted to the completion of a clear product—ignores the questions and dilemmas at the heart of deliberative democratic communities: Whose goals are we meeting? To what cause? For whose benefit? With what level of foreknowledge?

The practices of the social foundations of education field are in and of themselves contested positions for their proclivity to foster rather than constrain questioning and critical exploration. This is even more the case if we are to acknowledge that most classrooms consist almost exclusively of student–teacher conversations. True student-student dialogue and debate is virtually nonexistent (if we discount those conversations enacted for teacher approval—and that desist as soon as the teacher is out of hearing). Until I explicitly modified my teaching practices, for example, my students did not know even half of the names of the other students in the class; they (the names and, by extension, the individuals) were deemed not relevant to the supposed learning ongoing in the classroom.

Demonstrating democracy in social foundations of education is thus the construction of learning environments where content and context convey analogous messages of inclusive and sustained academic engagement. It is an attempt to create classrooms where learning is deliberate, the outcomes are meaningful, and the presuppositions transparent for investigation.

DEFINING SOCIAL FOUNDATIONS

Finally, I would argue that probably the most contested position for social foundations within teacher education is that theory matters. The anti-intellectualism of education schools is a long-standing by-product of education's liminal status within the academy (Labaree, 2004). Education's "pre-professional" designation promotes a seeming disdain of theory for the sake of theory and a deep distrust of theory's ability to provide useful input to teacher education programs committed to a technical formalism.

In one respect this may be a valid critique of the role and value of theory within the academy; the advocacy of theory can no longer be understood as the academician's trump card. Theory is a limited tool. It cannot prevent wars or overcome political maneuvering. Theory cannot predict the future; nor can it fully explain the past. As Mitchell (2004), the long-time editor of *Critical Inquiry*, lamented, "How can one take Edward Said's advice and speak truth to power when power refuses to listen?" (p. 327). Mitchell suggested that perhaps it must come from a "medium theory": "Our theory crisis demands a crisis theory that can maintain its equilibrium over the long haul, neither euphoric nor dystopic" (p. 334).

But if the center cannot hold, if singular meta-narratives have been replaced by a cacophony of micronarratives, of what use is social foundations? Social foundations seems to be exactly about examining the theoretical groundings of educational policies and practices. This, it seems to me, is something to be embraced.

Education cannot be analyzed through singular, monofocal lenses. Or to put it more precisely, no single lens does justice to the complexity of schools and classrooms embedded within American society. Theory matters, whether it is operationalized in specific conceptual frameworks or through methodological procedures. The contributions to this volume have offered a diverse perspective of both methodological and conceptual perspectives—critical theory, postmodernism, ecojustice, aesthetic education, action research, feminism, and constructivism, among others.

This is not a smorgasbord of pseudo-postmodernist radical relativism claiming anything goes. As Richard Rorty has remarked, "Nobody, not even the most far-out post-modernist, believes that there is no difference between the statements we call true and those we call false. Like everybody else, post-modernists recognize that some beliefs are more reliable tools than others" (Rorty, 1997, p. 23). The point is not that nothing is legitimate; the point is rather that no claim has sovereign authority to claim ultimate legitimacy. All truth claims are what Foucault termed "regimes of truth" and Wittgenstein (less politically) "language games." All ideologies are thus to be contested.

The contributors to this volume engage exactly in such a dynamic, questioning and interrupting what we usually think of as a "normal" social foundations classroom. Engaging contested positions, though, is not simply a destructive move. In one respect there is a certain accuracy to the postmodern nihilistic tendency to disrupt the centered subject and the claim of objective knowledge. Such metanarratives may hide more than they reveal about our world. The meta-narratives of the IQ, of "all children can learn," and of the "at-risk" student certainly foreclose alternative conceptualizations (Fine, 1995). The deconstruction of such categories is to be fostered.

But deconstructions may be also thought of as displacements rather than destructions. The contributors to this book offer productive strategies and theoretical positions from which social foundations scholars can challenge students to rethink and revise their notions of how we think about schools. And here the insularity of the social foundations field must also be critically contested. As Eric Bredo asked in chapter 2, to what extent can we use the tools of our field to better understand and work on ourselves?

How we define ourselves as informed by and through theory is itself the engagement of a contested position. Put simply, social foundations must take the contested position that contested positions are worthy of inclusion within teacher education. Only here do the issues previously mentioned—diversity and democracy—truly come to life.

To engage in contested positions is to refuse to be silenced; it is to refuse complacency. Dewey argued that at the heart of democracy is a conversation. But a conversation can only be had with those with whom one is willing to have discussions (Rorty, 1989). Without that sense of willingness to confront an other, one all too easily moves into the realm of categorizing the other as something that cannot be imagined: as a monster (Kearney, 2003). Richard Kearney (2003) persuasively argued that the Western tradition has pushed our engagement with monsters into the realms of art and religion, such that "the Other has passed from the horizon of reflective understanding into the invisible, unspeakable, unthinkable dark" (p. 7).

Let me thus conclude by suggesting that it is exactly such "monsters" that social foundations can and must confront. To discuss them is to keep them on the table, open for debate, analysis, and revision. Often we find that the monsters are not out there, but inside: in the ways we speak, define, and categorize (Foucault, 1973). This is a difficult realization to acknowledge: that we are often complicit in the realities we rail against. Yet it is this self-reflective stance—the ability to speak of the systems within which we work—that I find to be of the most value within the social foundations of education field.

This volume can be seen as exactly such an attempt: to bring together a wide range of scholars to discuss the systems that social foundations of education functions within, for, and against. This discussion is not meant to eradicate the system; it is meant to expose it. In so doing, I hope that it provides fruitful opportunities to both tame and to deconstruct how and why we do social foundations. Both steps, it appears to me, are necessary for the continued enrichment of our field.

REFERENCES

Alexander, C. (1996). *The art of being Black.* Oxford: Oxford University Press.

Apple, M. W. (1999). *Power, meaning, and identity: Essays in critical educational studies.* New York: P. Lang.

Britzman, D. (1998). *Lost subjects, contested objects: Towards a psychoanalytic inquiry of learning.* Albany, NY: SUNY Press.

Butin, D. (2003). The limits of categorization: Re-reading multicultural education. *Educational Studies, 34*(1), 59–67.

Churchman, C. (1971). *The design of inquiring systems.* New York: Basic Books.

Delpit, L. D. (1995). *Other people's children: Cultural conflict in the classroom.* New York: New Press.

Dewey, J. (1910). *How we think.* Boston: D. C. Heath.

Dubois, W. E. B. (1995). *The souls of Black folk.* New York: Signet.

Ellsworth, E. (1997). Double binds of Whiteness. In M. Fine, L. Weis, L. Powell, & L. M. Wong (Eds.), *Off White: Readings on race, power, and society* (pp. 259–269). New York: Routledge.

Fine, M. (1995). The politics of who's "at risk." In B. B. Swadener & S. Lubeck (Eds.), *Children and families "at promise"* (pp. 76–94). Albany, NY: SUNY Press.

Foucault, M. (1973). *The order of things: An archaeology of the human sciences.* New York: Vintage Books.

Freire, P. (1992). *Pedagogy of the oppressed.* New York: Continuum.

Gilroy, P. (2001). *Against race: Imagining political culture beyond the color line.* Cambridge, MA: Harvard University Press.

Greene, M. (1978). *Landscapes of learning.* New York: Teachers College Press.

Hall, S. (1996). *Stuart Hall: Critical dialogues in cultural studies.* New York: Routledge.

Hall, S. (2000). Old and new identities, old and new ethnicities. In J. Solomos & L. Back (Eds.), *Theories of race and racism.* London: Routledge.

Jackson, P. (1990). *Life in classrooms.* New York: Teachers College Press.

Kearney, R. (2003). *Strangers, gods, and monsters: Interpreting otherness.* London: Routledge.

Labaree, D. (2004). *The trouble with ed schools.* New Haven: Yale University Press.

Lopez, A. (2003). Mixed-race school-age children: A summary of Census 2000 data. *Educational Researcher, 32*(6), 25–37.

Martusewicz, R. A. (2001). *Seeking passage: Post-structuralism, pedagogy, ethics.* New York: Teachers College Press.

Mitchell, W. (2004). Medium theory. *Critical Inquiry, 30,* 324–335.

National Research Council. (2003). *Engaging schools: Fostering high school students' motivation to learn.* Washington, DC: National Academies Press. Http://www.nap.edu/books/0309084350/html

Oakes, J. (2002). *Becoming good American schools: The struggle for civic virtue in education reform.* New York: Wiley and Sons.

Orfield, G. (2002). *Race, place, and segregation. Harvard Civil Rights Project.* http://www.civilrightsproject.harvard.edu/research/metro/three_metros.php

Rorty, R. (1989). *Contingency, irony, and solidarity.* New York, Cambridge University Press.

Rorty, R. (1997). *Truth, politics and "post-modernism."* Amsterdam: Van Gorcum.

Rorty, R. (1998). *Truth and progress.* New York: Cambridge University Press.

Sleeter, C., & Grant, C. (1999). *Making choices for multicultural education: Five approaches to race, class, and gender* (3rd ed.). New York: John Wiley & Sons.

U.S. Census. (1996). *Current population reports: P25-1130 Population projections of the United States by age, sex, race, and Hispanic origin: 1995 to 2050.* http://www.census.gov/prod/1/pop/p25-1130/

APPENDIX:
COURSE SYLLABI

Social Foundations of Education Syllabus

Dan W. Butin
EDUC 209, sections A&B
Social Foundations of Education
Spring 2004

Professor Dan W. Butin

105 Weidensall Hall

717-337-6553 (w)

717-653-4469 (h)

dbutin@gettysburg.edu

http://www.gettysburg.edu/~dbutin

office hours: tue.–fri., 10–11 a.m.; 1–2 p.m.

Times: Wednesdays & Fridays

ED 209A—11:00 a.m.–12:15 pm., in Weidensall 302

ED 209B—2:10 p.m.–3:25 p.m., in Weidensall 301

COURSE OVERVIEW

The social foundations of education course is an exploration and analysis of the underlying issues within contemporary educational policies, practices, and theories. It is an attempt to ground the day-to-day realities of the class-room within a larger philosophical, historical, anthropological, political, and sociological context. Such an interdisciplinary perspective will allow students to begin to reflect upon the structures and practices of American education and provide a foundation from which to continue becoming reflective and critical educational practitioners and leaders. It is also an opportunity to investigate the role of schooling and education within a democracy.

Through classic and contemporary texts, this class will explore numerous issues at multiple levels: classroom, school, and school system. Overarching questions of multiculturalism, inequity, identity formation, the role of schooling, and issues of power will be discussed. So will more specific issues, such as tracking, educational reform, dropouts, community–school relations, and affirmative action. Moreover, the class will make use of field observations in schools, service learning, and experiential learning activities to highlight and reinforce the relationship between the theory and practice of education.

A fundamental component of this course is student involvement and debate. To this end, the course will make use of diverse methods to help students grapple with the many issues of our educational system. This course will be run on the principle of a "guide on the side" rather than a "sage on the stage"—discussions, debates, questions, and silence will be the rule, not the exception.

COURSE GOALS

1. To give students a deeper multidisciplinary perspective from which to interpret, question, reflect on, and engage with the underlying issues within contemporary educational theory and practice.
2. To nurture and promote the art of dialogue (written and oral) inside the classroom and civic responsibility outside of it.
3. To link the theory of the texts with the lived reality of students in their schools and communities.
4. To make explicit and begin to question the implicit norms of radical individualism and in the process foster students' self-reflexivity toward who we are and what we do and subsequent implications on teaching and learning.

COURSE TEXTS

- Deborah Meier, *The Power of Their Ideas*, 2002.
- Jay Macleod, *Ain't No Makin' It*, 1995.
- Richard Rodriguez, *Hunger of Memory: The Education of Richard Rodriguez*, 1983.
- All of the other readings are available as e-reserves on CNAV, through online databases, or on the Internet. Please refer to the syllabus and the professor's web site for specific information.

COURSE EVALUATION (SUMMARY)

Critique papers	50 points
Service-learning project	15 points
In-class engagement	10 points
Text discussions	10 points
Quizzes	10 points
Concluding thematic presentation	5 points
	100 points

This is a graded course. The following scale will be used:

97+	A+	87–89	B+	77–79	C+	67–69	D+
93–96	A	83–86	B	73–76	C	63–66	D
90–92	A–	80–82	B–	70–72	C–	60–62	D–

COURSE EVALUATION (DETAILED)

Critique Papers

Four critique papers will be due. Each should be submitted to the professor (either as an e-mail or in class) and archived on your personal web page. The overarching goal of each critique is to synthesize your thinking on the readings in relation to your experiences outside of class (e.g., service learning, classroom observations) and your own interest in being a teacher. This will be facilitated, in the first three critiques, through a set of guiding questions to be taken up, analyzed, questioned, and expanded on. The guiding questions are attached.

Each subsequent critique will be worth more points as you come to learn my expectations for writing a critique. Thus the 1st critique will be worth 5 points, the 2nd critique 10 points, the 3rd critique 15 points, and the final critique 20 points. This does not connote that the content of the 4th critique is more important than the content of the 1st critique; rather, it simply signifies the expectation that you will be able to write a concise, articulate, and thoughtful critique by the end of the term. I expect critiques to be analytical, reflective, critical, and synthesizing. By this I mean that I do not want a description of the texts (I have already read them), nor a negative analysis. A grading rubric for how I will grade critique papers is attached.

Each critique should be between 1,000 and 2,000 words (approximately 3–6 pages). It should be double-spaced, 12-font, have page numbers, and be stapled. All citations of the texts should be footnoted. Late papers will be downgraded one letter grade (e.g., from an "A" to a "B") for each week late. Any papers not handed in by the due date of the next paper will be given a grade of zero (0).

You have the opportunity to hand in a draft of each paper to the professor. The draft must be submitted at least 48 hours before the due date. The draft should be either e-mailed to the professor or given as a paper copy. I will try to respond with comments as soon as possible.

Service Learning Project

This course has a service-learning component. Service learning in this course is defined as the integration of community-based service and academic classroom work. Some of the primary foundations for service learning are *reciprocity* between the college and community, *respect* for those being served, and *relevance* of content both to the teacher education students and to the youth and community organization partnered with.

The service-learning project will be focused on the issue of access to higher education. Specifically, you will be working with migrant, immigrant, and low-income ninth-grade students at Gettysburg High School. This will be a class project. The goal for the class will be to help these students begin the process of thinking about higher education. This will consist of three distinct components: (a) after-school tutoring, (b) college access, and (c) community relations. It is up to the entire class to determine the allocation of tasks among you.

The class will be required to provide a minimum of 5 hours per week of after-school tutoring to a group of students at Gettysburg High School. This will occur at Gettysburg High School from ~3 to 4 p.m. You will be helping students with their homework, study skills, and general academic skills (reading, writing, math). This tutoring may be one-on-one, in small groups, or a combination of the two.

The class will also be required to provide an introduction to college to the group of students. This should include, at minimum, the following: (a) a visit to a social/cultural event at Gettysburg College (dinner at Servo, a sporting event, a lecture), and (b) a presentation of a "road map to college" for the students and, potentially, their parents. The class is encouraged to come up with additional ideas (which should be discussed with the professor). All activities must be approved by the professor prior to implementation.

Finally, the class will be responsible for developing and implementing a community component. By this is meant that your work should be accessible to the general public, above and beyond the students you will be working with. While this will most likely be the students' parents, the actual audience could be much larger (local schools, general public, etc.). Some examples of a community component might include: a panel presentation of current Gettysburg students discussing their experiences of college; a formal presentation from the admissions office; the development of an informational web site on college access, the financial aid process, etc.; the completion of a ropes course with the students to develop leadership and collaboration skills.

Your grade will be based on: your level of participation in the service-learning project (irrespective of which part you focus on); your peers' assessment of your level of participation in the service-learning project; the overall quality of the three components of the service-learning project. Detailed checksheets and rubrics will be handed out in class.

In-Class Engagement

In-class engagement implies both personal contributions and thoughtful contemplation of peers' points. Although the extremes—constant contributions and complete meditative silence—are obviously discouraged, everything in between is acceptable. Regular attendance is expected. Any absences must be made up through a one-page writeup of the texts due for that day. The writeup should be both descriptive and analytical. The writeup will be due on the following class. Three or more absences without such a writeup will result in lowering your in-class engagement grade by one letter grade. Five or more absences, regardless of whether a writeup was submitted, will also result in lowering your in-class engagement grade by one letter grade. Exceptions will not be made except under extraordinary circumstances as determined by the professor.

Text Discussions

A "text discussion" will be conducted at the beginning of each class by a group of students. A text discussion consists of three things: (a) a text outline, (b) a *discussion* of the text outline within the context of a guiding question, and (c) *questioning/critique* of the text, text outline, and/or answer to the guiding question. It is up to each group of students to determine how the completion of these tasks are to be allocated within the group.

The *text outline* is a summation of a text or a set of texts through bullet points, a concept map, or some other notational method. It should be no more than one page, double-sided. This outline is to be handed out at the beginning of the class such that other students can use it as a reference for the day's texts.

The *discussion* should consist of a short summation of the text outline (not a direct reading of it) and a discussion of the guiding question. This discussion should be about 5 minutes. It is an opportunity for the group to articulate some of their major points and ideas about the texts and the guiding question.

The *questioning and critique* is to consist of several questions of the text, text outline, and/or answer to the guiding question. Answers to the questions are not expected.

Additionally, there will be several out-of-class experiential learning activities in the latter half of the course that will serve as the "texts" for the text discussions. These activities are meant to challenge you and your ability to think "out of the box" concerning what we mean by teaching and learning. You are to treat these activities as any other text to be "read" and analyzed within the context of this course. Although none of the activities are illegal, immoral, or dangerous, some students may feel uncomfortable doing them. As such, students may ask the professor for an alternative assignment(s) to fulfill this part of the course.

Overall, the text discussions are an opportunity for students to directly guide the teaching and learning process in the class. As such, all aspects of the text discussions should be thoroughly prepared: for example, text discussions should be succinct, clear, informative, challenging, and entertaining. You will be graded at the end of the semester both by the professor and by your peers in the group on these qualities and your contributions to the group effort. Please contact the professor ASAP if you are having any problems or issues in regards to your group.

Quizzes

Two short quizzes will be given in this course. They will focus on your ability to clearly and succinctly articulate the main themes of our readings. Both quizzes are take-home "open book" quizzes; in other words, you may use your readings, notes, etc.

Concluding Thematic Presentation

You will be required to present a concluding thematic presentation during the final exam date. An executive summary/synopsis should be submitted to the professor (either as an e-mail or in class) and archived on your personal web page.

The concluding thematic presentation is an opportunity for you to review and synthesize your writings, projects and reflections over the course of the semester. You are to review your notes, papers, journals, and any other materials as preparation for this presentation. The presentation should be 5–10 minutes in length. The presentation should have an overarching theme (e.g. "what I have learned," "how I have changed," "the most important strand of this course has been," "how I see myself as a teacher") and should be informative, concise, and engaging. A grading checksheet is attached.

Additional Notes & Requirements

1. *Classroom Observations*—The education department requires that all students in the education minor complete a total of 40 hours of classroom observations before they begin their student teaching semester. All students must therefore complete a minimum of 10 hours of classroom observations during this course. Secondary students must also complete an additional 10 hours of observation; this may be done either during or after this semester. A minimum of 5 of these hours must be done at a school and with a cooperating teacher to be assigned to you. You do have the option of completing these observations at another school and with another teacher. All other hours may be completed in a variety of ways, such as a classroom assistant, as a tutor in an after-school pro-

gram, etc. Your service-learning hours may count toward these hours as well. You will receive a classroom placement in the first weeks of the semester as well as a detailed outline of how to proceed with these observations. Make sure to keep track of your hours using the blue cards available in the Educational Department office.

2. *Personal web page*—You will be required to develop a personal web page if you do not already have one. This is the site where you will archive all of your writings and reflections—journals, critique papers, and concluding presentation synopsis. You should think of this web page as the start of your education portfolio, as you will make use of this site and the writings on it throughout your progress through the education department. Detailed instructs for the construction and maintenance of this site will be given in class. You will also have full support from the college's IT department for the construction, maintenance, and troubleshooting of this site.

A Journey (from *Those Who Ride the Night Winds*, by Nikki Giovanni, 1983)
It's a journey … that I propose … I am not the guide … nor technical
assistant … I will be your fellow passenger …
Though the rail has been ridden … winter clouds cover …
autumn's exuberant guilt … we must provide our own guideposts … I have
heard … from previous visitors … the road
washes out sometimes … and passengers are compelled …
to continue groping … or turn back … I am not afraid …
I am not afraid of rough spots … or lonely times … I don't fear …
the success of this endeavor … I promise you nothing … I accept your
promise … of the same we are simply riding … a wave …
that may carry or crash … It's a journey … and I want … to go …

COURSE SCHEDULE

Fri. Jan. 23	Class Introduction & Overview
Wed. Jan. 28	Philosophical Foundations—Goals of Education I

Wed. Jan. 28 — Philosophical Foundations—Goals of Education I
  • A. S. Neill, Summerhill, pp. 3–34 [e-reserve]
  • E. D. Hirsch, Jr., "The Core Knowledge Curriculum—What's Behind Its Success?," Educational Leadership, 1993, May, pp. 23–30. [Online database]
  • E. D. Hirsch, Jr., "Why General Knowledge Should Be a Goal of Education in a Democracy" and "Why Core Knowledge Promotes Social Justice" [web site]

Fri. Jan. 30 — Philosophical Foundations—Goals of Education II
  • John Dewey, Democracy and Education, Chapters 1 and 24 [web site]
  • John Dewey, My Pedagogical Creed [web site]

Wed. Feb. 4 — Philosophical Foundations—Critical Perspectives

- Paulo Freire, Pedagogy of the Oppressed, pp. 57–74 [e-reserve]
- Jules Henry, Culture Against Man, pp. 283–293 [e-reserve]

Fri. Feb. 6   Philosophical Foundations—Feminist Perspectives

- Nel Noddings, "Teaching Themes of Care," Phi Delta Kappan, 1995, 76, pp. 675–679. [Online database]
- Nel Noddings, "The Care Tradition: Beyond 'Add Women and Stir,'", Theory into Practice, 2001, 40(1), pp. 29–34 [online database]

Wed. Feb. 11   Philosophical and Historical Foundations—Synthesis

- Phillip Jackson, Life in Classrooms, pp. 3–37 [e-reserve]
- John Goodlad, A Place Called School, pp. 123–129 [e-reserve]

Fri. Feb. 13   Philosophy of Education–Synthesis

- **1st Critique Paper Due** [Experiential Learning Activity—in-class]

Wed. Feb. 18   Sociological and Multicultural Foundations—Introduction

- Jonathan Kozol, Savage Inequalities—East St. Louis & Chicago, IL [web site]
- NAACP Call For Action in Education [web site]

Fri. Feb. 20   Sociological and Multicultural Foundations—linkages with service-learning

- Richard Rodriguez, Hunger of Memory, Chapter 1 and Service Learning
- **Quiz 1 handed out**

Wed. Feb. 25   Sociological and Multicultural Foundations—Language, Ethnicity and Identity

- Hunger of Memory, rest of book
- **Quiz 1 due**

Fri. Feb. 27   Sociological and Multicultural Foundations—Issues of Race

- Lisa Delpit, Other People's Children, pp. 21–47 [e-reserve]
- John Ogbu, "Adaptation to Minority Status and Impact on School Success," Theory into Practice, 1992, 31(4), pp. 287–295 [online database]

Wed. March 3   Sociological and Multicultural Foundations—Issues of Race and Class

- Jay Macleod, Ain't No Makin' It, Part I

Fri. March 5   Sociological and Multicultural Foundations—Issues of Race and Class

- Jay Macleod, Ain't No Makin' It, Part II

Wed. March 10   Sociological and Multicultural Foundations—Tracking

- Maureen Hallinan & Jeannie Oakes, "Exchange on Tracking," Sociology of Education, 1994. 67(3), pp. 79—91 [online database]
- Alfie Kohn, "Only For My Kid", Phi Delta Kappan, 1998, April, 79(8). Pp. 568–577 [online database]

Fri. March 12   Sociological and Multicultural Foundations—Synthesis

- **2nd Critique Paper Due** [Experiential Learning Activity—in-class]

Wed. March 24   Anthropological Foundations—Introduction

- George Spindler, "The Transmission of Culture," pp. 141–178. [e-reserve]
- Horace Miner, "Body Ritual Among the Nacirema," American Anthropologist, 1956, 58(3), pp. 503–507 [online database]

Fri. March 26   Anthropological Foundations—Questioning Gender

- David Sadker, "Gender Equity: Still Knocking at the Classroom Door," Educational Leadership, 1999, 56(7), pp. 22–26 [online database]
- Judith Kleinfeld, "Student Performance: Males versus Females," The Public Interest, 1999, Winter, pp. 3–20 [online database]

Wed. March 31   Anthropological Foundations—Questioning Gender II

- Blythe McVicker Clinchy, "Toward a More Connected Vision of Higher Education," New Directions for Teaching and Learning, 2000, 82, pp. 27–35 [online database]
- Adrienne Rich, "Toward a Women-Centered University,", pp. 328–355 [e-reserve]
- Dorte Marie Sondergaard, "Poststructuralist approaches to empirical analysis." Qualitative Studies in Education, 15(2), pp. 187–204. [e-reserve]

Fri. April 2   Anthropological Foundations—Questioning Success

- George D. Spindler, "Beth Anne—A Case Study of Culturally Defined Adjustment and Teacher Perceptions," pp. 111–126. [e-reserve]
- George and Louis Spindler, "There Are No Dropouts Among the Arunta and Hutterites," pp. 181–190 [e-reserve]

Wed. April 7   Anthropological Foundations—Questioning Culture

- Nancy Ukai, "The Kumon Approach to Teaching and Learning," Journal of Japanese Studies, 1994, 20(1), pp. 87–113. [Online database]
- G. Victor Sogen Hori, "Teaching and Learning in the Ritual Zen Monastery," Journal of Japanese Studies, 1994, 20(1), pp. 5–35. [Online database]

* **Quiz #2 handed out**

Wed. April 14   Anthropological Foundations—Questioning Our Selves

* Out-of-class experiential learning activities
* **Quiz #2 due**

Fri. April 16   Anthropological Foundations—Synthesis

* **3rd Critique Paper Due** [Experiential Learning Activity—in-class]

Wed. April 21   Socio-Political Foundations—Education in a Democracy

* Deborah Meier, The Power of Their Ideas

Fri. April 23   Socio-Political Foundations—Education and Reform

* Larry Cuban & David Tyack, Tinkering Towards Utopia, pp. 85–109. [e-reserve]

Wed. April 28   Socio-Political Foundations—Education as a Political Act

* James Baldwin, "A Talk to Teachers,", pp. 131–137 [e-reserve]
* John Taylor Gatto, "A Different Kind of Teacher,", pp. 158–167 [e-reserve]
* Bell hooks, "Ecstasy", pp. 201–207 [e-reserve]

Fri. April 30   Socio-Political Foundations—Education as a Category

* Ray McDermott & Hervé Varenne, "Culture as Disability," Anthropology & Education Quarterly, 26(3), pp. 324–348. 1995 [e-reserve]
* Michel Foucault, The Order of Things, pp. Xv–xxiv. 1970 [e-reserve]

Wed. May 5   Socio-Political Foundations—Synthesis

* **4th Critique Paper Due** [Experiential Learning Activity—in-class]

Fri. May 7   Conclusions

Tue. May 11   ED 209B Final Exam—8:30–11:30 a.m.

* Concluding thematic presentations

Sat. May 15   ED 209A Final Exam—8:30–11:30 a.m.

* Concluding thematic presentations

CRITIQUE PAPER QUESTIONS

1st Critique paper: The readings in the philosophical foundations articulate very different philosophies of education. They put forward differing educational goals (e.g., freedom, cultural literacy, lifelong learning), and suggest highly divergent means by which to achieve such goals. What is your own philosophy of education? What do you see as the goal(s) of education? How should such a goal(s) be accomplished? How does your perspective compare/contrast to these authors? How, moreover, do these philosophical goals relate to the realities of the classroom? Refer to at least two of the authors from the readings within your paper.

2nd Critique paper: The readings in the sociological and multicultural foundations suggest that American education may not be truly equitable; it may not be a place where all children have access to an excellent education. Issues of race, ethnicity, class, and gender (among others), are intertwined in complex ways to students' academic achievement and sense of self. As Jay Macleod would argue, American education may be better understood in terms of structural determinism rather than radical free agency. Analyze one or more of these issues. For example, to what extent do we have free will to pursue our educational aspirations, regardless of our race, gender, or ethnic group? Is education the primary variable in a successful future? Is American education a "level playing field"? Your paper should ideally work on explicating interrelations: (a) between readings (e.g., Delpit, Ogbu, and/or Macleod); (b) between variables (e.g., race, class, and/or gender); or (c) between discourses (e.g., readings, your educational experiences, and/or service-learning project).

3rd Critique paper: The readings and activities in the anthropological foundations question the implicit and seemingly "natural" norms by which we think and act concerning education. How we act, what we say, and how we think (whether it is about success, gender, or critical thinking skills) is culturally determined. Put otherwise, we become habituated (and habituate ourselves) into believing that our actions, thoughts, and beliefs are our own individual, unique, and "correct" way to think about something. The readings and activities challenge this. In "academic speak," "reality" and "self" are social constructions rather than natural givens. Analyze this perspective by linking a specific issue (e.g. gender, success, intelligence, well-adjusted, (dis)ability) to one of the experiential learning activities. You should refer to at least two readings and you may also consider having additional linkages (to, e.g., your own educational experiences, the service-learning project).

4th Critique paper: Choose a topic/issue of your choice and analyze it. You may choose to focus on one or more readings throughout the semester, your own educational experiences, your service-learning project, the experiential learning activities, and/or your classroom observations. Regardless of your focus, your paper must make some direct reference and linkage to class readings and other activities engaged in throughout the semester (e.g., service learning, classroom observations).

RUBRIC FOR GRADING CRITIQUE PAPERS

A critique does not denote a negative analysis. Instead, a critique involves a sensitive and thorough reading of the texts in question. This reading should not be for its own sake; in other words, while an accurate, concise, and well-articulated description of the texts is critical to your paper, such a description should be a first step to deeper analysis, reflection, critique, and synthesizing. By this I mean that the paper should be able to engage one or more of the following:

Analytic:

- What is the purpose of the reading?
- What is the main argument?
- How does the author support his/her position?
- What are the implications of this argument?
- How is this argument supported, extended, and/or contradicted by other readings?

Reflective:

- Where do you stand on the author's position?
- What aspects of your own experiences as a human being and as a student support and/or contradict this author's perspective?
- Why do you believe as you do on these points?
- What are your assumptions and presuppositions?
- How has this reading affected your position and/or understanding of this issue?

Critical:

- What are the assumptions of the reading?
- What is glossed over in the reading?
- What (or who) is kept silent/silenced in the reading?
- What are some unintended consequences of the conclusions of the reading?
- What are some of the limitations of the conclusions of the reading?
- Do other readings support, extend, and/or contradict this argument? What are the implications if there is major disagreement and/or contradiction in the readings?

Synthesizing:

- How does this reading relate to other course readings? To classroom observations? To the service-learning project? To the experiential learning activities? To your own educational experiences?
- What implications does this reading have upon your classroom observations, experiences, etc.?
- What implications does this reading have upon your perspectives concerning the issues brought out?
- If accurate, how does the reading modify and/or support your perspectives concerning teaching and learning? To the functioning of a school? To the goals of education for our society?

Your paper may take any shape or form, use a formal or informal voice, be first- or third-person, etc. You may want to make use of Gettysburg's writing center. In general, though, your paper should have the following components:

1. *Purpose*—this is where you outline what you are going to write about and why.
2. *Main thesis*—this is where you state, clearly and succinctly, the main argument/point you are discussing. Note that even if your paper does not reach a firm final conclusion on a specific issue (and many times there are no firm conclusions on the most important and complex issues), you should still be able to articulate the issue on which you cannot reach a conclusion.
3. *Elaboration*—this is where you spend more time articulating your main thesis. You may do so through multiple examples, in relation to other readings, through different perspectives, etc.
4. *Support/evidence*—this is where you support your thesis by referring to other discourses, be they class readings, personal experiences, etc. Be aware that neither your subjective opinions ("I think this ...") nor received knowledge ("Dewey says this ...") are valid support in and of themselves. You must be able to show why your and/or others' perspectives are helpful to the discussion, what limitations they may have, etc.
5. *Evaluation*—this is where you take a harder, deeper, and more critical look at your argument and the arguments of others you may have put forward. This is also where you begin to make some tentative and/or firm conclusions and implications of such conclusions.

Your paper will be graded based on the following rubric:

70%   Clear and succinct description of the texts. Able to articulate the position of the author and the main point(s). No analysis. No questioning. No reflection based on personal perspective. No linkage to other readings. No synthesis and extension of reflection, critique, and other readings.

80%   Clear and succinct description and analysis of the texts. Able to articulate the position of the author and the main point(s) and able to analyze it and/or reflect upon it. Rudimentary questioning and linkage to other readings. No synthesis and extension of reflection, critique, and other readings.

90%   Clear and succinct description, analysis, critique, and linkage of the texts. Able to analyze, reflect, and question the author and the main point(s) based on personal perspective and/or other readings. Rudimentary synthesis and extension of reflection, critique, and other readings.

100%   Clear and succinct description, analysis, critique, linkage and extension of the texts. Able to synthesize readings and personal perspectives in order to effectively argue for one's position. Able to show how the central issue is related to other major issues.

Note. Your critique papers should be double-spaced, 12-font, have page numbers, and be stapled. All citations of texts should be footnoted. Moreover, it should be free of spelling and grammatical errors. While you will not receive extra points for this, you will be downgraded if these are not present. Excessive problems in one or more of these areas will result in the downgrading of your paper by one letter grade.

RUBRIC FOR GRADING CONCLUDING THEMATIC PRESENTATION

Your concluding thematic presentation is your opportunity to review and synthesize your writings and reflections over the course of the semester. You are to review your notes, papers, journals, and any other archived materials (e.g. photographs) as preparation for this presentation. This is also an opportunity to share your thoughts as they have developed over the course of semester with your peers in the class as well as other potential visitors.

Your presentation should be approximately 5–10 minutes, and include time for a question-and-answer period. You can structure the presentation in any way you like. Some examples may be based on a theme throughout the journals, on an experience you had while tutoring, some reflection of how the class readings may relate to your own background or how this has affected your perceptions of being a teacher, and/or based on a reading/activity/discussion from class. No matter how it is structured, though, the presentation should have a clear introduction, some discussion of how it relates to the social foundations of education class and your own personal philosophy of education, some discussion of what you have learned, and a strong conclusion.

Keep in mind the following tips when preparing your presentation:

- Have an agenda. Your audience wants to know where you are going in your presentation.
- Be engaging. Your audience does not want to be lectured at for 10 straight minutes. Therefore, be sure to change the pace, present materials in different formats, etc.
- Make sure you have a conclusion. Make sure that your conclusion relates to your introduction.

You will be graded on the following points:

Presentation Skills
_____ Articulate and clear delivery utilizing proper grammar
_____ Conveys enthusiasm and confidence, involves the audience
_____ Maintains eye contact & posture
_____ Pacing and speed of delivery
_____ Demonstrates professionalism

Organization
_____ Prepared
_____ Organized with a strong theme or clear main ideas
_____ Respects assigned time
_____ Creative/Interesting/Original
_____ Designs appropriate closure for remarks
_____ Includes professional visuals and variety that make the presentation more meaningful

Content
_____ Demonstrates educational philosophy in presentation
_____ Adequately articulates the main points (as discussed above)
_____ Uses self reflection

INTASC STANDARDS	In-class read-ings	In-class participation	Written work	Field experiences— Classroom observations	Field experiences— Service-Learning	Final presenta-tions
1. The teacher understands the central concepts, tools of inquiry, and structures of the discipline(s) he or she teaches and can create learning experiences that make these aspects of subject matter meaningful for students.						
2. The teacher understands how children learn and develop and can provide learning opportunities that support their intellectual, social, and personal development.	X	X	X	X	X	X
3. The teacher understands how students differ in their approaches to learning and creates instructional opportunities that are adapted to diverse learners.	X	X	X	X	X	X
4. The teacher understands and uses a variety of instructional strategies to encourage students' development of critical thinking, problem solving, and performance skills.	X	X	X	X	X	X
5. The teacher uses an understanding of individual and group motivation and behavior to create a learning environment that encourages positive social interaction, active engagement in learning, and self-motivation.					X	
6. The teacher uses knowledge of effective verbal, nonverbal, and media communication techniques to foster active inquiry, collaboration, and supportive interaction in the classroom.					X	

(continued on next page)

INTASC STANDARDS	In-class readings	In-class participation	Written work	Field experiences— Classroom observations	Field experiences— Service-Learning	Final presentations
7. The teacher plans instruction based upon knowledge of subject matter, students, the community, and curriculum goals.					X	
8. The teacher understands and uses formal and informal assessment strategies to evaluate and ensure the continuous intellectual, social, and physical development of the learner.	X	X	X	X	X	X
9. The teacher is a reflective practitioner who continually evaluates the effects of his/her choices and actions on others (students, parents, and other professionals in the learning community), and who actively seeks out opportunities to grow professionally.						
10. The teacher fosters relationships with school colleagues, parents, and agencies in the larger community to support students' learning and well-being.				X	X	

Teaching and Learning 101 Syllabus

Eugene F. Provenzo, Jr.
School of Education
University of Miami
Department of Teaching and Learning
Fall 2003
Teaching and Learning 101

SOCIAL FOUNDATIONS UNIT

Monday, Wednesday and Friday
Section B–9:00–9:50
INSTRUCTOR:
Eugene F. Provenzo, Jr.
Office 222 D Merrick

Merrick Building 316

Office Hours:
M 10:00–12:00
T &R 10:45–12:00

Office hours change after the midterm break.
provenzo@miami.edu
Telephone: 305-284-5102

Bulletin Description: A combined social and psychological introduction to education. The social component of the course includes an historical, philosophical, and sociological analysis of the school in American society. The school as an institution responsible to social, economic, and political change is emphasized. The psychological component of the course focuses on factors affecting the teaching-learning process in the classroom.

Conceptual Framework: This course covers all four areas of the School of Education's conceptual framework including: Technology; Diversity; Integration of Disciplinary Knowledge; and Reflective Practice.

Florida 12 Accomplished Practices Emphasized in this Course: #2 Communication; #3 Continuous Improvement; #4 Critical Thinking; #5 Diversity; #6 Ethics; #8 Knowledge of Subject Matter; #9 Learning Environments; #11 Role of the Teacher; and #12 Technology.

Honor Code: This course conforms to the policies outlined in the University of Miami Undergraduate Honor Code.

Policy on Instructional Modifications for Students with Disabilities: All efforts are made in this course to provide reasonable adaptations of course materials and evaluations to students with special needs.

Policy on Cell Phones: Cell phones are not to be used in the classroom. If cell phones are brought into the classroom they are to be turned off. Students in violation of this rule will be required to participate in the recreation of a nineteenth century writing exercise.

Copyright Notice: © Eugene F. Provenzo, Jr., PhD as to this syllabus, handouts, sample textbook materials, online materials and lectures. Students are prohibited from providing, either for a fee or for free—except to a fellow classmate missing a lecture or needing study help—notes or online material of this course to any person or commercial firm, without the express written permission of Professor Provenzo.

Texts:

Eugene F. Provenzo, Jr., *Teaching, Learning and Schooling in American Culture: A Twenty-First Century Perspective* (Boston: Allyn & Bacon, 2002).

The web site for this book is located at:

www.ablongman.com/provenzo

Eugene F. Provenzo, Jr., *The Internet and the World Wide Web for Teachers* (Boston: Allyn & Bacon, 2001, 2nd edition).

The web site for this book is located at:

www.ablongman.com/provenzo2e

Jana Noel, *Notable Selections in Multicultural Education* (Guilford, CT: Dushkin/McGraw-Hill, 2000).

Course Web Site: The web site for this course is located at:

http://www.education.miami.edu/ep/TAL101/home.html

In addition to an online version of this outline, hyperlinked reference sources, study activities and instructional web-based activities are available at the class web site. Instructions on the use of the Internet and the World Wide Web are provided by the instructor, in your text, *The Educator's Brief Guide to the Internet and the World Wide Web*, and are also available at the web site or at:

http://www.education.miami.edu/ep/iworkshop

Grade and Course Requirements: The TAL 101 course is divided into two instructional units with different instructors for each unit. For the Foundations unit each student in the course will be evaluated on the basis of his or her involvement in: (1) class discussion, (2) performance on quizzes, (3) the completion of a credo statement or philosophy of education, and (4) selected Internet based activities (Digital Research Basics). Attendance is taken. More than one unexcused absence during the course of the semester can lead to points being subtracted from the student's course average. Excessive unexcused absences (3 or more) will automatically lead to the lowering of the student's grade by one grade (a grade of B, for example, would be lowered to a C). Students in this course are subject to the rules and regulations of the university's undergraduate honor code. Total course grade will be divided in half (50%) for each unit of the course (Social Foundations Unit and Psychological Foundations Unit).

Grading Policy: The Social Foundations Unit will constitute 50% of the course grade. Students will be evaluated on the basis of their performance for the following requirements:

A. 3 quizzes	40 points each	= 80 points
B. 1 writing assignment (Credo)		= 10 points
C. Digital Research Basics		= 10 points
		= 100 points

* Students will only be excused from taking a regular quiz with the permission of the instructor. The decision to accept an excuse will be at the discretion of the instructor. Makeup quizzes will be conducted following the final quiz during exam week

Schedule for Writing Assignments and Quizzes.

Quiz 1:	Monday, September 29, 2003
Quiz 2:	November 12, 2003
Makeup Quiz:	During the second hour of final
Digital Basics:	Monday following Thanksgiving
Writing Assignment (Credo):	Friday, October 31, 2003
Final Exam	Friday, December 12, 2003
	8:00–10:30 in 316 Merrick

Course grades (* criterion-referenced):

A	93–100%
A–	90–92
B+	86–89
B	83–85
B–	80–82
C+	76–79
C	73–75
C–	70–72
D+	66–69
D	63–65
D–	60–62
E	59% or below

I. Prologue

LECTURE #1.   Wednesday, August 27, 2003

General Introduction

  Outline of requirements. Education as reflecting the culture of which it is a part. Paideia—changes in definition and meaning. *The New England Primer* as an educational artifiact. Bias in testing materials reflecting cultural values and belief systems. Examples of racism in photographs from the Farm Security Administration (1930s). How is education culturally specific? Emile Durkheim's recognition of schools as being instruments for recreating a culture or society. Reflections on the meaning of what we have discussed.

Introduction of the students. Instructions on completion of information sheets for web system.

Read: "Preface," and Chapter 1, "Introduction," in Eugene F. Provenzo, Jr., *Teaching, Learning and Schooling in American Culture: A Twenty-First Century Perspective*, pp. xv–12; and Eugene F. Provenzo, Jr., *The Internet and the World Wide Web for Teachers*, pp. iv–86.

II. General Issues Concerning Schools and American Society

LECTURE #2.   Friday, August 29, 2003

 **General Issues Concerning School and Society**

On what does the educational process focus? Education
and the records of teachers and their work as evidence
of a culture. What is taught and why is it taught? Environment. Values. Henry Giroux and the idea of "border crossing." Contemporary culture as a "Protean Culture." Defining postmodernism.
Post-Fordism. The relationship between postmodernism and schooling.
Observing schools. What is included and excluded? What is the focus of
the curriculum? How is education culturally specific? The Pledge of Allegiance. What values are taught in American schools? Education as a cultural act. How do students learn? Who educates? Education as polyphasic.
Hidden curriculum. Null curriculum. The Great School Legend. What is
the scope of American education? Black versus White in Dade County.
What should we expect from the public schools?

Read: Chapter 2, "Schools as Cultural Institutions," in Eugene F. Provenzo,
Jr., *Teaching, Learning and Schooling in American Culture: A Twenty-First Century Perspective*, pp. 13–28; and Eugene F. Provenzo, Jr., *The Internet and the
World Wide Web for Teachers*, pp. 87–154.

Labor Day

Read: In Jana Noel, *Notable Selections in Multicultural Education*, RONALD
T. TAKAKI, from *A Different Mirror: A History of Multicultural America*, pp.
3–10; and JOEL SPRING, from *Deculturalization and the Struggle for Equality: A Brief History of the Education of Dominated Cultures in the United States*,
2nd ed., pp. 11–19; EDWARD T. HALL, from *The Silent Language*, pp.
81–83; HENRY T. TRUEBA, from "The Dynamics of Cultural Transmission," in Henry T. Trueba et al., *Healing Multicultural America: Mexican Immigrants Rise to Power in Rural California*, pp.84–92; and JOE L.
KINCHELOE AND SHIRLEY R. STEINBERG, from *Changing Multiculturalism*, pp. 272–279.

LECTURE #3.   Wednesday, September 3, 2003

The Aims of Education

 What are the goals and purposes of education and schooling? Creating a just and sustainable culture. Jefferson and the Rockfish Gap Report (1818). Schools as ecological systems.

Discussion Assignment: Review and be prepared to discuss the "Critical Questions About the Nature and Purpose of Schooling," pp. 43–46 of your textbook. Be prepared to defend one question as being the most important to discuss in this course. Hint: Professors sometimes have pop quizzes at about this point in class to make sure students are critically engaged in the materials for the course.

LECTURE #4.   Friday, September 5, 2003

Teaching in a Historical Context

 Teaching in America. Historical development. Colonial Traditions. Women as educators in the nineteenth century. The feminization of the profession. Contemporary implications.

Read: Chapter 6, "Local, State and Federal Involvement in U.S. Education," in Eugene F. Provenzo, Jr., *Teaching, Learning and Schooling in American Culture: A Twenty-First Century Perspective*, pp. 113–114.

LECTURE #5.   Monday, September 8, 2003

Education and Cultural Literacy

 Education as Cultural Capital. Knowledge as power. E. D. Hirsch and cultural literacy. The Culture Wars of the 1980s. Questions about knowledge and its construction and meaning. Hirsch's list. Provenzo's Counter Cultural Literacy list. Culturally specific questions.

DISCUSSION #1.   Wednesday, September 10, 2003

 Questions About the Nature and Purpose of Schooling

Read: Chapter 3, "Sustaining Our Culture and the Goals of Education," in Eugene F. Provenzo, Jr.'s, *Teaching, Learning and Schooling in American Culture: A Twenty-First Century Perspective*, pp. 29–49.

Read: Chapter 4, "Education and American Society, " in Eugene F. Provenzo, Jr.s, *Teaching, Learning and Schooling in American Culture: A Twenty-First Century Perspective*, pp. 51–70.

LECTURE #5.   Friday, September 12, 2003

Education and American Society

 Education and American Society. America's commitment to education. Sources for statistics on education. Gallup Poll. America's commitment to public schooling. Expenditures on schools. What Americans think of their schools. Paulo Freire. Banking models of education. Colonial models of education. Education and hegemony. The work of Antonio Gramsci. Jurgen Habermas and a systems approach to schooling.

Read: Chapter 5, "Teachers in American Society, " in Eugene F. Provenzo, Jr., *Teaching, Learning and Schooling in American Culture: A Twenty-First Century Perspective*, pp. 71–111.

Discussion Assignment: Read the online *The New England Primer*. Be prepared to discuss how its content and the content of other textbooks reflect the social, cultural and political values of a culture. You can find the *Primer* online at: http://www.education.miami.edu/ep/neprimer/

DISCUSSION #2.   Monday, September 15, 2003

 Looking at the Cultural Content of Textbooks

Assignment: Visit the Lowe Museum. Come to class on Monday with a one paragraph statement describing a piece you particularly liked. Turn it in to Professor Provenzo on Monday. Students not completing this assignment will have 5 points deducted from their course grade. Late assignments will only be accepted with the permission of the instructor.

LECTURE # 6.   Wednesday, September 17, 2003

Teachers in American Society I

 The professional socialization of teachers. Who becomes a teacher? Teacher supply and demand. What do teachers do? The teacher in popular culture sources such as film, television and cartoons. Rewards and satisfaction for teachers. Are teachers professionals? Unions.

Discussion Assignment: Write a one page, double spaced essay describing your "best" and "poorest" teacher. Emphasize the characteristics that made you view them in either a positive or a negative light. Students not completing this assignment will have 5 points deducted from their course grade. Late assignments will only be accepted with the permission of the instructor.

Turn in Lowe essay to Dr. Provenzo.

LECTURE #7.   Friday, September 19, 2003

Teachers in American Society II

 The teacher as a social force. The empowerment of teachers. Teacher freedom, authority and power. Teachers and vulnerability. Teachers as intellectuals. Teachers and resistance. Postmodern trends and their implications for the work of teachers. Social/ecological perspectives. Lortie's attractions to the profession.

Discussion Assignment: Write a one page, double spaced essay describing your "best" and "poorest" teacher. Emphasize the characteristics that made you view them in either a positive or a negative light. Students not completing this assignment will have 5 points deducted from their course grade. Late assignments will only be accepted with the permission of the instructor.

DISCUSSION #3.   Monday, September 22, 2003

Discussion of Experience With and Perception of Teachers

Assignment: View one of the following films about teachers: *The Dead Poet's Society, Teachers, Stand and Deliver*.

LECTURE #8.   Wednesday, September 24, 2003

Schools as Bureaucracies

Schools as Bureaucracies. Classical definitions of a bureaucracy. The work of Max Weber and others. How do schools function as bureaucracies? Implications for teachers. What are the problems and advantages underlying bureaucratic systems? Functioning within a bureaucratic context. Political and social realities. Analysis of the Dade County Public Schools as a bureaucratic system. Local, state and federal control of public schools. Judicial decisions affecting school funding. Resistance to control.

Read: Chapter 7, "Private Education and Religion in the United States," in Eugene F. Provenzo, Jr., *Teaching, Learning and Schooling in American Culture: A Twenty-First Century Perspective*, pp. 145–161.

LECTURE #9.   Friday, September 26, 2003

Federal Involvement in Schooling

Federal involvement in American education. Early federal involvement. The Land Grant College Act of 1862. The U.S. Office of Education. Patterns of federal influence. Federal control of education. The federal government and equality of educational opportunity. Postmodern realities and the control of local and federal education. Social/ecological perspectives.

Assignment: Study for Quiz #1.

Quiz #1.   Monday, September 29, 2003

Time remaining after the quiz (approximately 20 minutes) will be used to review general issues related to the course.

Read: Chapter 8, "Immigration, Education and Multiculturalism, " in Eugene F. Provenzo, Jr., *Teaching, Learning and Schooling in American Culture: A Twenty-First Century Perspective*, pp. 163–197.

III. Equity and Diversity

LECTURE #10.   Wednesday, October 1, 2003

Immigration and Cultural Inclusion in the United States

The Founding Myth of the American Republic. Voluntary pluralism. The Inclusivist immigration tradition. The United States as a nation of nations, a people of peoples—a tossed salad of cultures rather than a melting pot of people. Stir fry models of culture—i.e. the blending of cultures. Pluralism and American society. Who have been the immigrant groups in the United States? Historical. Contemporary. Anti-immigrant sentiments. Anti-Catholic prejudice and Nativisim. Restrictions on people of color. Asian immigration and restrictions in the 19th century. Mexican immigration and restrictions. Restrictions on European groups in the early decades of the twentieth century. Reasons for exclusion. The persistence of xenophobia and racism.

LECTURE #11.   Friday, October 3, 2003

Cultural Pluralism and Education

The Americanization of immigrants. Anti-immigrant sentiment in 19th-century editorial cartoons. Cultural pluralism—historical perspective. Cultural pluralism—contemporary perspective. Restrictions on immigration. The "new immigration." Multicultural education. Immigrant cultures as dominated cultures. Culture and ethnicity. A survey of ethnics. Bilingualism and American education. English only. Legal issues and bilingualism. Postmodern realities: The end of ethnicity? Social/ecological perspectives.

Assignment: Outline your family history in a one to two page essay , double spaced, going back to your great grandparents. List their names, country of origin and how their ethnic and cultural background have shaped you and your immediate family. Be prepared to discuss what you have put together in class. Note: This assignment may require a call to your parents or grandparents. Students not completing this assignment will have 5 points deducted from their course grade. Late assignments will only be accepted with the permission of the instructor.

Remember to attend the Michael Apple lecture on Tuesday October 5, 2003, at 12:15 in Merrick 316.

DISCUSSION #4.   Monday, October 6, 2003

Discussion of Family History Essays

Turn in family essay to Professor Provenzo.

LECTURE #12.   Wednesday, October 8, 2003

Defining a Philosophy of Education

 Overview of major educational philosophers: Freobel and Dewey. Modern theorists: Maxine Greene and Nel Noddings. Why does a philosophy and personal position concerning education and schools matter?

Writing Assignment: Begin to work on a three to four page, double spaced essay outlining your philosophy of education and teaching (credo). This essay is due Friday, October 31, 2003. Unexcused late essays will have one grade level deducted for each class session they are not turned in.

LIVETEXT TRAINING   Friday, October 10, 2003

LECTURE #13.   Monday, October 13, 2003

What is Multiculturalism?

 Race, Socio-Economic Class, Gender, Language, Culture, Sexual Preference, Disability. "...general lack of awareness that race, class, gender and sexuality are non-synchronous and criss-crossed by vectors of privilege and relations of inequality, and hence are constructed by a *materiality of forces*" (Pe-

ter McLaren, 1998). Liberal multiculturalism as representing a displacement of the contextual specificity of difference leading to a new type of colonialism under the guise of democracy (Kincheloe and Steinberg, 1998). Conservative multiculturalism/monoculturalism, Liberal multiculturalism, Pluralist multiculturalism, Left essentialist multiculturalism, Critical multiculturalism.

LECTURE #14.   Wednesday, October 15, 2003

Religion and American Education

 Public schooling and the separation of church and state. Judicial decisions. In God We Trust. Fundamentalism and the schools. A moment of silence. Fundamentalism and Secular Humanism. Rights of Christian schools. Postmodern realities—social/ecological perspectives.

Discussion Assignment: Read John Dewey's "My Pedagogic Creed," You can find Dewey's Creed online at: *http://www.rjgeib.com/biography/credo/dewey.html* or for a second source go to *http://www.users.globalnet.co. uk/~infed/e-texts/e-dew-pc.htm*

Read: Chapter 10, "Race and American Education," in Eugene F. Provenzo, Jr., *Teaching, Learning and Schooling in American Culture: A Twenty-First Century Perspective*, pp. 219–257.

Friday, October 17, 2003

Meeting with Area Coordinators and Advising for the Education Program

LECTURE #15.   Monday, October 20, 2003

Read: Jana Noel, Notable Selections in Multicultural Education, PAULO FREIRE, from Pedagogy of the Oppressed, pp. 171–175; HENRY A. GIROUX, from "Insurgent Multiculturalism and the Promise of Pedagogy," in David Theo Goldberg, ed., Multiculturalism: A Critical Reader, pp 176–184. **Be prepared to discuss these readings in class.**

Ivan Illich and Paulo Freire

 Overview of the work of Ivan Illich and Paulo Freire. Traditions of critical pedagogy. Other contemporary educational theorists dealing with education and culture.

Developing an Educational Credo (Discussion of John Dewey's "My Pedagogic Creed").

Assignment: Catch up on any reading you might have fallen behind on.

LECTURE #16.   Wednesday, October 22, 2003

African-Americans and the Schools.

 Slavery and its legacy. History of Black education. African Americans and American education. The Civil Rights struggle. Key court cases. Desegregation and its consequences. Compensatory education. The role of schooling for African-Americans. Assimilation or pluralism? Postmodern realities and the meaning of Race. Social/ecological perspectives.

Read: Jana Noel, *Notable Selections in Multicultural Education*, KENNETH R. HOWE, from "Liberal Democracy, Equal Educational Multicultural Opportunity, and the Challenge of Multiculturalism," *American Educational Research Journal*, pp. 31–37; MAXINE GREENE, from "The Passions of Pluralism: Multiculturalism and the Expanding Community," *Educational Researcher*, pp. 38–46; SAMUEL BOWLES, from "Unequal Education and the Reproduction of the Social Division of Labor," in Martin Carnoy, ed., *Schooling in a Corporate Society: The Political Economy of Education in America*, 2nd ed., pp. 47–53; JOHN U. OGBU, from "Adaptation to Minority Status and Impact on School Success," *Theory into Practice*, pp. 54–61; JONATHAN KOZOL, from Savage Inequalities: Children in America's Schools, pp. 62–68.

Fall Break October 24, 2003

LECTURE #17.   Monday, October 27, 2003

Booker T. Washington and W. E. B. Du Bois: A Biographical Exploration

 Washington and the Hampton model. The Atlanta Exposition Speech. Accomodationism. Du Bois and *The Souls of Black Folks*. The Niagara Movement and the origins of the NAACP. Links to Civil Rights movment of the 1950s and 1960s.

Read: In Jana Noel, *Notable Selections in Multicultural Education*, BOOKER T. WASHINGTON, from a Speech During the Atlanta Exposition, Atlanta,

Georgia, September 18, 1895, pp. 20–24; and W. E. B. DU BOIS, from *The Souls of Black Folk*, pp. 25–30.

Outline, in a half page summary, each of the main points of the philosophies of both Washington and Du Bois. Students not completing this assignment will have 5 points deducted from their course grade. Late assignments will only be accepted with the permission of the instructor.

DISCUSSION #7.   Wednesday, October 29, 2003

 **Discussion of Washington and Du Bois**

Turn in position paper Washington and Du Bois.

Read: In Jana Noel, *Notable Selections in Multicultural Education*, GORDON W. ALLPORT, from *The Nature of Prejudice*, pp. 93–101; GLENN S. PATE, from "Research on Prejudice Reduction," *Educational Leadership*, pp. 102–108; CORNEL WEST, from *Race Matters*, pp. 109–114; PEGGY McINTOSH, from "White Privilege: Unpacking the Invisible Knapsack," *Peace and Freedom* , pp. 115–120; and CHRISTINE SLEETER, from "White Racism," *Multicultural Education*, pp. 121–126.

Assignment: Credo due next class.

DISCUSSION #8.   Friday, October 31, 2003

 **Viewing and Discussion of bell hooks's video "Cultural Criticism and Transformation" (Media Education Foundation)**

Read: Chapter 9, "Childhood, Adolescence and the Family," in Eugene F. Provenzo, *Teaching, Learning and Schooling in American Culture: A Twenty-First Century Perspective*, pp. 199–218.

Turn in Credo

LECTURE #18.   Monday, November 3, 2003

Childhood, Youth, the Family and Education

 The great change in Childhood. Childhood and contemporary culture. The child as adult. Youth culture and contemporary society. Traditions of adolescent rebellion. The family as educator. The family and compulsory education. The changing American family. The increase in the number of working women. The growth in the divorce rate. The changing family and its impact on schools and teachers. Postmodern realities: the reconstitution of the American family—social/ecological perspectives.

Read: Chapter 11, "Gender and Education," in Eugene F. Provenzo, *Teaching, Learning and Schooling in American Culture: A Twenty-First Century Perspective*, pp. 259–280.

LECTURE #19.   Wednesday, November 5, 2003

Women and Education.

 Women and the history of American education. Sexism and language. Gender roles and culture. Women and contemporary education. Sexual discrimination in the classroom. Failing at fairness. Sexism and video games. Sexism in children's books and textbooks. Postmodern realities and the meaning of gender—social/ecological perspectives.

Read: Chapter 12, "The Education of Students with Special Needs," in Eugene F. Provenzo, *Teaching, Learning and Schooling in American Culture: A Twenty-First Century Perspective*, pp. 281–302.

LECTURE #20.   Friday, November 7, 2003

Educating Students with Special Needs.

Students with special needs and historical perspective. The growth in special education since the 1950s. The Vocational Rehabilitation Act of 1973. Public Law 94-142. Mainstreaming. Equal access. Labeling as a social issue.

Read: Chapter 13, "Textbooks and the Curriculum," in Eugene F. Provenzo, *Teaching, Learning and Schooling in American Culture: A Twenty-First Century Perspective*, pp. 303–327.

IV. Mass Culture, Media and Schooling

LECTURE #21.   Monday, November 10, 2003

The Social Content of Textbooks.

What is curriculum? Curriculum as cultural capital. The hidden curriculum. Textbooks as a business and industry. 18th- and 19th-century textbooks. Ethnocentrism in 19th-century geography texts—a case study. Contemporary conflicts: Kanawha County, West Virginia. Censorship and education. Cultural diversity—different views about education. State adoptions of textbooks. Ideological content of textbooks. Sexism and racial bias in textbooks. The "Dick and Jane" readers. Contemporary conflicts over textbooks. Issues for the future. Textbooks and the curriculum in a postmodern culture —social/ecological perspectives.

Assignment: Study for Quiz #2

Quiz #2   Wednesday, November 12, 2003

LECTURE #22.   Friday, November 14, 2003

Education and Popular Culture.

Popular culture sources and what they tell us about contemporary American schooling. What are the sources for popular culture—the masses or the media? Television. Film. Comics. Popular culture as shaping the culture's consciousness about teaching and schooling.

Read: Chapter 14, "Media, Computers and Education," and "Conclusion" in Eugene F. Provenzo, *Teaching, Learning and Schooling in American Culture: A Twenty-First Century Perspective*, pp. 329–362.

LECTURE #23.   Monday, November 17, 2003

Toys, Creativity and Object Learning

 Historical development of toys. The emergence of pedagogical toys in the Eighteenth and Nineteenth centuries. Natural Magic and Victorian scientific toys. Froebel and Montessori. Toys as learning devices. Video games and culture.

Read: In Jana Noel, *Notable Selections in Multicultural Education*, AMERICAN ASSOCIATION OF UNIVERSITY WOMEN, from *How Schools Shortchange Girls: A Study of Major Findings on Girls and Education* I, pp. 187–194; CAROL GILLIGAN AND JANE ATTANUCCI, from "Two Moral Orientations: Gender Differences and Similarities," *Merrill-Palmer Quarterly*, pp. 195—205; GLORIA LADSON-BILLINGS, from "But That's Just Good Teaching! The Case for Culturally Relevant Pedagogy" *Theory into Practice*, pp. 206–216; KAREN SWISHER AND DONNA DEYHLE, from "Adapting Instruction to Culture," in John Reyhner, ed., *Teaching American Indian Students Notable*, pp. 217–226; ALICIA PAREDES SCRIBNER, from "Advocating for Hispanic High School Students: Research-Based Educational Practices," *The High School Journal*, pp. 226–235; VALERIE OOKA PANG, from "Asian-American Children: A Diverse Population," The *Educational Forum*, pp. 236–243; JIM CUMMINS, from *Empowering Minority Students*, pp. 244–252; LILY WONG FILLMORE AND CONCEPCION VALADEZ, from "Teaching Bilingual Learners," in Merlin C. Wittrock, ed., *Handbook of Research on Teaching*, 3rd ed. , pp. 253–260; JEAN ANYON, from "Social Class and School Knowledge," *Curriculum Inquiry*, pp. 261–271; LOUISE DERMAN-SPARKS, from "Empowering Children to Create a Caring Culture in a World of Differences," *Childhood Education*, pp. 283–290; JAMES A. BANKS, from "Transforming the Mainstream Curriculum," *Educational Leadership*, pp. 291–298; SONIA NIETO, from Affirming Diversity: The Sociopolitical Context of Multicultural Education, 2nd ed., p. 299; NCSS TASK FORCE ON ETHNIC STUDIES CURRICULUM GUIDELINES, from "Curriculum Guidelines for Multicultural Education," *Social Education*, pp. 308–314.

Doing Online Library Research   Wednesday, November 19, 2003
in Education

(Workshop session)

Doing Online Library Research   Friday, November 21, 2003
in Education

(Workshop session)

Complete all Internet activities
by next class.

LiveText Training   Monday, November 24, 2003

Review of Credos   Wednesday, November 26, 2003

THANKSGIVING BREAK

LECTURE #24.   Monday, December 1, 2003

Television and Education

The new media. The merging of television and computers. Postmodernism and post-typographic cultures. Television and learning in the classroom. How television has
changed family life. Television's perceived promise as educator. Effects of
children's programming on learning. Television and the socialization of the
child. Ethnic, racial, and sex-role stereotyping. Television as a type of learning. TV viewing, violence, and aggression. Advertising and television. Video
games and the emergence of interactive television.

Read: "INTASC Standards " in Eugene F. Provenzo, *Teaching, Learning and
Schooling in American Culture: A Twenty-First Century Perspective*, pp. 363–378.

LECTURE #25.   Wednesday, December 3, 2003

Computers and Education

Computers and education. The computer as the children's machine. The new teaching machines. Hypertext
and other innovations. Tutor, tool, or tutee? Computer
literacy. Equal access and the microcomputer. Augmenting human intellect
via computers. Teaching in the computer age. What is the role of the
teacher in a computer-mediated curriculum? Media and computers in a
postmodern culture. Social/ecological perspectives.

Friday, December 5, 2003

Concluding Remarks by Dr. Provenzo

Social issues facing postmodern America as it enters the next millennium. What are the obligations and duties of the culture to its citizens? The idea of a social safety net. The realities of poverty in our society (the Homeless, Urban Poor, Migrant Workers). Do the schools have a role in creating greater social equity? Training Children for the workplace of the future. What will be the jobs of the 21st century? Who will work and why? The loss of the craft tradition. The "dumbing down" of the work force elite and nonelite populations. Who should control knowledge in a democratic society? Health, AIDs education, alcohol and drug abuse. Teen pregnancy. Raising the consciousness of future generations. Issues of consensus. Issues of contention. What issues are we willing to address in the schools? (abortion? environment? etc.) What role can the schools play in creating a new social order? Critical thinking through reflecting on society. The teacher in the classroom during the first years of the new millennium. Potentials and limitations.

Assignment: Prepare for Final. Makeup quizzes will be done immediately after the final exam.

Final Questions for Reflection.

1. **What is taught in the schools?** Who determines the curriculum? Does the content reflect a specific social or political set of values? Is the censorship of certain ideas necessary to protect students from "dangerous" or inappropriate ideas? What should textbooks include or not include?
2. **Should the schools act as agents for social change or as a means of maintaining the status quo?** To what extent should teachers act as agents for promoting change or maintaining the dominant values and beliefs of the culture? Should teachers be restricted in what they are allowed to teach their students?
3. **Who is to be educated?** In a democratic society such as the United States is equal education either possible or desirable? Does the gifted child need the same support and resources as the average child or the handicapped child? What is equitable? Should ethnic

groups and language minorities receive different training from other groups?

4. **What makes a good school?** Does the definition of a good school differ depending on the social and economic background of its students? Can schools with different types of clients who have different types of needs be compared?

5. **What types of obligations do the schools have beyond simply educating students?** Should schools address the moral development of students? Should they provide health services?

6. **Should schooling be compulsory?** It so, for how long? What is considered a sufficient education? Should students be compelled to learn things they or their parents oppose on moral and personal grounds?

7. **Should private schools be encouraged or discouraged?** Should they receive direct or indirect support from the government?

8. **What role should religion play in schooling?** Should selected religious practices or sects be allowed in the schools? Should certain religious groups be excluded? What is equitable?

9. **Who should control the schools?** Should schools be controlled by parents, administrators, or state and federal governments? Who is capable of making the most informed decisions concerning what is needed by the educational system?

10. **What constitutes the necessary and proper means of training teachers?** Who should be allowed to teach? To what extent should teachers have the right to act according to the dictates of their own values?

11. **To what extent should the schools be used as a means of correcting or compensating for past social injustices?** Should the schools be used to desegregate the society and bring about greater equality?

12. **To what extent should the schools provide instruction that has in the past been provided by the family and other social groups?** Should subjects such as sex education or personal ethics and values be taught by the schools?

13. **To what extent is the media—in the form of television, movies, popular music, video games and computers—taking the place of more traditional family and school-based instruction?** Is most of the education children receive coming from media sources? How is this type of education different from other types of learning? How is it related to the commercial interests of our society?

14. **Who do new educational technologies like computers most benefit?** Do the privileged have the most to gain from new computer technologies like the Internet? Are there differences in the services provided individuals based on their social or economic class? Are boys encouraged to use technology more than girls?

15. **What is considered useful knowledge?** Whose knowledge is taught in the classroom? Is there a "canon" that is taught? Where is it from?
16. **How does race affect what goes on in the schools?** Does the racial background of the student affect how and what they are taught?
17. **How does ethnicity affect what goes on in the schools?** Are certain ethnic groups treated differently based on their background and experience? Are all ethnic groups treated the same?
18. **How does gender affect what goes on in the schools?** Are men educated differently than women? Are women subjected to different treatment and experiences than men?
19. **How does social class affect the experience of students in the schools?** Are students from lower social-economic groups treated differently than children whose parents are part of the culture's power bloc?
20. **What types of citizens do our schools want to create?** What knowledge is necessary to make people active and productive citizens?
21. **What constitutes good teaching?** How are teachers trained? What is considered good teaching?
22. **Why are the majority of teachers women?** Why are there fewer men and minorities in the teaching profession than in the general population?
23. **Should schools provide social services?** Is it the obligation of schools to provide free lunch and health care programs for students in need?
24. **What are the rights of teachers?** What can teachers do or not do? How much control should the society have over teachers in the classroom? Over their private lives?
25. **What is the role of business in shaping and influencing the content of education?** What type of influence should business have in shaping the curriculum of the schools? Should students be trained for specific jobs demanded by the business system?

Course Outline Revision: August 2003.

EDL 204: Sociocultural Studies in Education
Spring 2003 syllabus
Kathleen Knight Abowitz
Department of Educational Leadership
Miami University

I. INTRODUCTION TO THE COURSE

EDL 204, Sociocultural Studies in Education, is an introduction to the social foundations of education that applies a cultural studies approach to the investigation of selected educational topics. The course serves as the social foundations of education requirement for undergraduate education majors, and as an introductory course in the cultural studies thematic sequence, Cultural Studies and Public Life, and as a humanities course under the Miami Plan foundations requirement.

EDL 204 is a theme-based course that draws on different disciplines and fields of study to address certain fundamental questions and issues in the sociocultural study of education. We consider this a trans-disciplinary course (rather than inter-disciplinary) because we are less interested in the study of specific disciplines (e.g., the history, sociology or philosophy of education) and more interested in examining problems and issues in the sociocultural study of education. It might be helpful to understanding the nature of this course by introducing the three major fields upon which the course is drawn: the social foundations of education, cultural studies, and the humanities.

The social foundations of education is a field of study that draws on the disciplines of history, sociology, philosophy, and anthropology to study and debate the foundation of educational practice and ideas. In a social foundations of education class, students examine, critique, and explain education in light of its origins, major influences and consequences, by utilizing three perspectives: the analytical, interpretive, and normative perspectives. We will study the nature of these perspectives in more detail as the course proceeds. As an introductory course in the social foundations of education, EDL 204 offers students the opportunity to study those socio-cultural conditions, including social institutions, processes, and ideals, which underlie educational ideas and practices.

EDL 204 also introduces students to themes and concepts of cultural studies, an area of study where we study culture as something that is actively produced and debated by different people in different social contexts. Culture is viewed as a process that is constructed out of the power relations, debates, and negotiations of the wide range of people who make up a society.

243

Because culture is seen as the result of relations between people (and not merely a fixed, abstract thing), then cultural studies is also intrinsically concerned with the analysis of power relations between people. Who is in more of a position of authority and power to influence what culture is? Who is in less of a position of power, and is, therefore, powerless about defining or controlling culture? The field of cultural studies presents a number of methods of analysis of studying culture, and students will be introduced to those methods in this course, in particular the use of textual analyses of original narratives on American education and culture. Through explorations of written and visual texts, students will study the construction of and the meaning of social texts and culture, and will explore the ways in which educational goals and practices are influenced by those constructed texts and discourses. Students will learn that education and schooling as we know it today have been and continue to be actively constructed, and are not, in and of itself, a neutral "fact" or undebateable quality.

The cultural studies emphasis of the course is closely linked to the humanities approach of the course, because in both areas of study, we examine the cultural meaning of personal and public narratives and arts. As a humanities course, EDL 204 begins not with a social science approach to understanding impersonal educational institutions, but by inviting students to analyze and reflect on the way in which people have created ideals, images, and constructs of education as part of American culture. In other words, the readings in the course are representative of the cultural *meaning* that people give to education (as opposed to social science studies of what actually happens in education.) As in any humanities class, for example, English Literature or Art, students will be asked to understand how meaning is created within the text. Like any reading of a Charlotte Bronte novel or a Picasso painting, educational texts are cultural constructs that reflect a combination of cultural beliefs, images, common practices, hopes, and dreams.

II. COURSE OBJECTIVES

1. Students will be able to understand the key concepts of the course as raised through the assigned readings, classroom discussions, and other learning activities in the class; students will and use the concepts to address and explore the Lead Question raised each week.
2. Students will engage in debates about the purposes of education in a democratic society, and will critically analyze the role of schools in creating citizens, social behaviors, and workers.
3. Students will learn to think critically about the ways in which schools address such issues as diversity and difference in their curriculum, philosophies, and purposes.

4. Students will consider all of the above objectives by analyzing the written and visual assigned texts, by taking part in educational projects outside of the classroom, and by reflecting on their own experiences as students and citizens.

III. ASSIGNMENTS AND EVALUATION

(See the Assignment Due Date and Description sections for further descriptions—note that individual instructors may have additional assignments)

(1) Reading and writing on assigned texts. Students will regularly reflect upon the assigned readings through short papers assigned by instructors. These papers are designed to helps students make meaning of course concepts and assigned readings through the writing process.

(2) Group Pedagogical Project. (Field experience assignment) In the field experience assignment students participate and observe in the world outside of the classroom, applying concepts and skills learned in the course to a specific project. In the Group Pedagogical Project, students work in small cooperative groups to identify and study the way in which educational text is constructed in a local community, group, or organization. [This will serve as a minimum of 4 hours of field experience for professional education majors.] There are several subtasks involved in the project:

    a. **Annotated Bibliography (worked on and turned in by group).** This is a collection of sources, with brief descriptions of each source, that group members have consulted to become educated on the topic chosen for the group project.

    b. **Text analysis paper (worked on and turned in as individuals).** This paper should be an analysis of one text related to the pedagogical project topic. Using the text analysis approach described in our Reader and course materials, students will examine the text using the analytical, interpretive, and normative lenses.

    c. **Pedagogical Project Analysis Papers (worked on and turned in by group).** This paper—or set of papers, depending on how each individual instructor assigns this project—is a text analysis of carefully selected artifacts relating to the project topic. These artifacts should *not* be texts that have already been analyzed in the text analysis paper written by group members.

(3) Cultural Interview (final exam). (Field experience assignment) Students interview a peer from a different cultural, ethnic, class, or racial background about their experience of schooling. Students then write a paper analyzing the idea of cultural difference—the difference between the interviewee 's experiences in school and the author's own experiences in school. Using course concepts, assigned texts, and other materials from the course, students will make meaning of the differences and similarities between self and interview subject, and the implications for these differences and similarities for schooling practice and policy.

IV. COURSE OUTLINE

Part One: The Cultural Context of Schooling

Week 1: Culture

Lead Question: What is culture and why does it matter in education?

Concepts:

culture	Cultural studies
canon	Social foundations of education

Readings:

- "The Great Game of High School," by Nathan Dutton, Rick Quantz, and Nolan Dutton (2000)
- "What Is Culture and Why Does It Matter?" by Don Lavoie and Emily Chamlee-Wright (2000)
- "Opening the American Mind," by William E. Cain (2001)
- "Multicultural Teacher Introspection," by Nitza M. Hidalgo (1993)

Weeks 2 How to read texts

Lead Question: Why do we "de-code" texts? What does it mean to examine texts critically?

Concepts:

Education vs. schooling	Popular culture
Mediated society	texts
claim	discourses
evidence	ideology
rhetoric	Political interests

narrative
icon
Metaphors   similes

Visual texts:
"Ethnic Notions"
"Slim Hopes"
"Killing Screens"

Readings:

- "The Reading of Texts" by Kate Rousmaniere, Richard Quantz, and Kathleen Knight Abowitz(1995)
- "Are Disney Movies Good for Your Kids?" by Henry Giroux (1998)
- "Text analysis: Harry Potter and the Sorcerer's Stone," by Ruthann Mayes-Elma (2002)

Part Two: Philosophies of Education

Week 3/4: Comparing philosophies of education

Lead Question: What are the different visions of, and purposes for schooling as articulated by American philosophers and educators?

Concepts:
perennialism   Critical theory and critical pedagogy
essentialism   Ethic of care
progressivism   behaviorism
Social reconstructionist

Readings:

- "Comparing Philosophies of Education," Sadker and Sadker (2001)
- "The Basis of Education," by Robert Hutchins (1953)
- "The Paideia Proposal: Rediscovering the Essence of Education," by Mortimer J. Adler (1982)
- "An Essentialist's Platform for the Advancement of American Education," by William C. Bagley (1938)
- "A Nation at Risk" (1983)
- "The Council for Basic Education's Program" (1959)

- "My Pedagogic Creed," by John Dewey (1897),
- "Experience and Education," by John Dewey (1938)
- "Art and Imagination," by Maxine Greene (1995)
- "A New Approach to Indian Education," by Paul Conklin (1967)
- "Dare the School Build a New Social Order?" by George S. Counts (1932)
- "Teaching for Democracy," by George H. Wood (1990)
- "An Ethic of Care and Its Implications for Instructional Arrangements," by Nel Noddings (1988)
- "Caring and Respect: Key Factors in Restructuring a School," by Dennis Littky (1990)
- "The Sanctuary of School," by Lynda Barry (1992)

Part Three: Purposes of School

Week 5: The Social Construction of a Nation and its Citizens

Lead Question: In what ways have American culture and its social institutions—especially its schools—helped to construct the norms, ideals, and practices of citizenship?

Concepts:

citizenship	Educational construction of citizens
nationalism	patriotism
Cultural pluralism	Melting pot
angloconformity	assimilation
multiculturalism	

Visual Texts:

"School: The Story of American Public Education" part 1 or 2

Readings:

- "New York Teachers' Oath" (1934)
- "Opposition of the American Association of University Professors to Loyalty Oaths for Teachers" (1937)
- "Children May Not Be expelled from School for Refusing to Salute the National Flag" (1943)
- "Multicultural Citizenship" by Will Kymlicka (1995)
- "What Does It Mean to Be an American?" by Michael Walzer (1990)
- "The Children's Story," by James Clavell (1963)

Week 6: Schooling for Literacy

Lead Question: How have cultural commentators defined "literacy," and what political purposes do these various definitions serve?

Concepts:

Banking education	Critical literacy
Functional literacy	hegemony
Cultural literacy	Media literacy

Visual texts:

"Cultural Illiteracy"

Readings:

- "Massachusetts School Law of 1647"
- "Mississippi Law Forbidding Education of Slaves or Free Negroes" (1823)
- "Bill for the more general diffusion of knowledge," by Thomas Jefferson (1779)
- "Restoring Cultural Literacy in the Early Grades," by E. D. Hirsch, Jr. (1988)
- "The People Speak Their Word: Learning to Read and Write in São Tomé and Principe," by Paulo Freire (1981)
- "Adult Literacy: The Ingenuous and the Critical Visions," by Paulo Freire (1985)
- "Liberty and Literacy," by Tozer-Violas-Senese (2001)
- "A Third of the Nation Cannot Read These Words" by Jonathan Kozol (1985)
- "Invisible Minority: The Growing Crisis of Illiterate America" by Jonathan Kozol (1985)

Week 7: Schooling and Socialization

Lead Question: In what ways have American commentators understood schooling to educate people for social life, or for the role(s) they are to play in society?

Concepts:

socialization	Hidden curriculum
ritual	community
Social solidarity	

Visual texts:

"The heart broken in half"

"Straight up rappin'"

Readings:

- "Senator Daniel Webster on the Schools as a 'Wise and Liberal System of Police'"(1820)
- Selections from The Scott, Foresman Readers (1955)
- "Old Miami," words by A. H. Upham, music by R. H. Burke (1921)
- "Lift Every Voice and Sing" by James Weldon Johnson (1900)
- "Schooling, Socialization, and Social Problems" (2001) by Arends-Winitzky-Tannenbaum
- "What our rituals tell us about community on campus" by Peter Magolda (2001)

Week 8: Schooling for Economic Purposes

Lead Question: In what ways have American commentators understood schooling to educate people for economic life?

Concepts:

capitalism	Human capital
Social efficiency	Vocational education & guidance
consumerism	

Visual texts:

"Affluenza"

"All the Right Stuff"

Readings:

- "Intellectual Education as a Means of Removing Poverty and Securing Abundance," by Horace Mann (1848)
- "The Factory System," by Margaret Haley (1923)
- "Resisting Educational Standards," by David Labaree (2000)
- "The Dangers of Market Rhetoric," by Jeffrey Henig(1996)
- "Education and Human Capital," by Joel Spring (2002)
- "Why I Said No to Coca-Cola," by John Sheehan (1999)

Part Four: Social Categories and Schooling

Week 9: Schooling and the construction of racial identity

Lead Question: How do schools, among other social and political institutions, help to construct race? What are some implications of these constructions?

Concepts:

race

racism   Racial formation

double-consciousness   Whiteness

representation   Afrocentrism

Visual texts:

"The Tiger Woods Effect"

"A Class Divided"

"America in Black and White"

Readings:

- "Of Our Spiritual Strivings," by W. E. B. DuBois (1903);
- " Racial Formation, " by Michael Omi and Howard Winant (2001)
- "How Americans Became White: Three Examples," by Werner Sollors (1997)
- "Introduction: Race Matters," by Cornel West (1993)
- "Defining Racism: Can We Talk?" by Beverly Tatum (1999)
- "Just Walk on By: A Black Man Ponders His Power to Alter Public Space," by Brent Staples (1986)
- "Interview with Peter Soderstrom," by Studs Terkel (1992)
- "Universal Freckle, or How I Learned to Be White," by Dalton Conley (2001)

Week 10: Schooling and Gender

Lead Question: How do schools, as social and political institutions, help to construct gender? What are the implications for boys and girls?

Concepts:

Gender versus sex

Masculinity/femininity as binary oppositions

feminism

Visual texts:

"Dreamworlds II"

"Girls Like Us"

"Tough Guise"

Readings:

- "Female Influence"(1795)
- "White Privilege and Male Privilege: A Personal Account of Coming to See Correspondence Through Work in Women's Studies," by Peggy McIntosh (1989)
- "Rethinking Masculinities: New Ideas for Schooling Boys," by Michael C. Reichert (2001)
- "The Case for Nurture," by Richard A. Lippa (2002)
- "How the Schools Shortchange Girls"(1995)
- "The 'F' Word," by Carissa Marie Nelson (2000)
- "Within the Hurricane-Depression," by Mary Pipher (1994)
- "Inside the World of Boys: Behind the Mask of Masculinity," by William Pollack (1998)

Week 11: Schooling and Social Class

Lead Question: How do schools help to construct and reproduce class differences?

Concepts:

class

Social reproduction

Cultural capital

Visual texts:

"A Portrait of Two Urban Schools"

"Children in America's Schools"

"People Like Us"

Readings:

- "Parent and Community Expectations," by Barbara Benham Tye (2000)
- "A Touchy Subject," by Paul Fussell (2001)
- "Tired of Playing Monopoly?" by Donna Langston (1988)
- "Coming to Class Consciousness," by bell hooks (2000)

Week 12: Schooling and Sexuality

Lead Question: How do schools help to construct sexual identity among students and educators? What implications do these constructions have?

Concepts:
homophobia
hetereosexism

Visual texts:
"It's Elementary: Talking About Gay Issues In School"

Readings:

- "Gay teens finding more support amid hostile school hallways," CNN (2000)
- "Thinking About the Gay Teen," by Gerald Unks (1995)
- "What Do We Say When We Hear Faggot?" by Lenore Gordon (1995)
- "Why Should We Care About Gender and Sexuality in Education?" by Susan Shurberg Klein (1992)
- "Voices from the Glass Closet: Lesbian and Gay Teachers Talk about Their Lives" by Rita Kissen (1993)

Week 13: Schooling and Ethnicity

Lead Question: How is ethnicity constructed within schools?

Concepts:
ethnicity
Americanization
harrassment

Visual texts:
"Silent Minority" (Appalachian culture)
"In Whose Honor?"

Readings:

- "A Call for the Americanization of Mexican-American Children," by Merton Hill (1928)

- An Editorial in 'The Massachusetts Teacher' on the Irish Immigrant (1851)
- "Education of a Hopi boy" (c.. 1899)
- "Prohibited Racial or Ethnic Harassment—Reminders of Responsibility under the Title VI of the Civil Rights Act of 1964" (2001)
- "Ethnicity," by Kimberly P. Martin (1997)
- "I'd Like to Be Considered Lebanese," by James Karam,(1992)
- "On Being a Mexican-American," by Joe I. Mendoza (1994)
- "A Chicano in Philadelphia," by Danny Romero (1997)

Part Five: Differentiated Education

Week 14: Religion and Schooling

Lead Question: How do issues of religion and schooling intersect? How are these two institutions historically, culturally, and politically connected and conflicting?

Concepts:

The First Amendment to the Constitution

Public/private schools

vouchers

Readings:

- "Selections from The McGuffey Readers" by William Holmes McGuffey (1879)
- "Decision on Busing of Children to Religious Schools at Public Expense" (1947)
- "The Catholic School: The Stronghold of Christian Life" (1919)
- "A Parent's Dilemma: Public vs. Jewish Education," by Svi Shapiro (1996)

Week 15: Bilingual Education

Lead Question: What historical, social, cultural, and political factors have contributed to today's debates about bilingual education?

Concepts:

Bilingual education

Language submersion, transitional approach, immersion approach

English-Only movement

Visual texts:

"English Only in America?"

"Richard Rodriguez: Victim of Two Cultures"

Readings:

- "Decision on the Teaching of Any Subject Except in English," (1919)
- "Bilingual Education" by Sadker and Sadker (2001)
- "Firsthand Experience in Educating Language Minorities," by Rosalie Pedalino Porter (1996)
- "Language," by James Fallows (1983)
- "Hunger of Memory: The Education of Richard Rodriguez" by Richard Rodriguez (1982)

Week 16: Segregation, Integration, and Resegregation

Lead Question: How has segregation, specifically based on race, ethnicity, and class, been an ongoing issue in American educational debates?

Concepts:

"Separate but equal" doctrine   Brown v. Board of Education

segregation   desegregation

Visual texts:

"The Road to Brown"

"School: The Story of American Public Education"—part 3

"The Lemon Grove Incident"

Readings:

- "Resolution of the San Francisco School Board," (1905)
- "The San Francisco Chronicle on Segregation of Japanese School Children" (1906)
- "Brown v. Board of Education, 347 US 483" (1954)
- "Deepening Segregation in American Public Schools: A Special Report from the Harvard Project on School Desegregation," by Orfield, Bachmeier, James, and Eitle (1997)
- "Would African-Americans Have Been Better Off Without Brown v. Board of Education?" by Jack M. Balkin (2002)
- "A Dream Deferred," by Gloria Ladson Billings (1994)

- Selection from "Warriors Don't Cry," by Melba Patillo Beals (1994)

Week 17: Tracking

Lead Question: How does tracking, as a historical and contemporary practice in education, both cause and support difference?

Concepts:
tracking
Ability grouping

Visual texts:
"Off Track Classroom: Privilege for All"

Readings:

- "The Superintendent of the Choctaw Academy Recommends Vocational Education for Indian Youth," letter from Thomas Henderson to Lewis Cass (1832)
- "Tracking," by Jeannie Oakes (1985)
- "Social-Class Differences in Education," by Joel Spring (2000)
- "In Search of Reality: Unraveling the Myths About Tracking, Ability Grouping and the Gifted,"
- by Fiedler, Lange, and Winebrenner (1993)
- Selection from "The Bee Season" by Myla Goldberg(2000)

SOFD 328
SCHOOLS IN A MULTILCULTURAL SOCIETY
Fall 2003

Professor: Dr. Rebecca A. Martusewicz   **Office Hours:** Wed. 12–2:00, TH 12:00
Office: 314 F Porter   2:30, or by appointment
Email: rmartusew@emich.edu   **Phone:** 487-7120, ext. 2624

CREDITS: 3

PREREQUISITES: Admission to the College of Education

EMU PROGRAM THEME:
Eastern Michigan University teacher preparation programs develop knowledgeable professionals who are caring, reflective decision makers in a culturally diverse, democratic society and who can provide successful learning experiences for all children.

CATALOG DESCRIPTION:
A study of the interactive relationship between schools and society, and the development of a culturally responsive pedagogy. Special emphasis on educational equity and the theoretical foundations of multicultural education. (This course was formerly called Social Aspects of Teaching.)

PURPOSE/RATIONALE:
The purpose of this course is to enhance an understanding on the part of preservice students about the complex interactions between schooling and factors such as race, gender, sexual identity, social class, religion, politics and exceptionality. The impact of these interactions is then refocused on the responsibilities of citizenship in a democracy, and the nature and goals of change in the context of a culturally diverse, democratic society.

OUTCOMES/OBJECTIVES:
The course objectives are 1) to understand the concepts and theoretical perspectives that describe the patterns of interaction between a) schooling and b) different personal, social, ecological, and situational factors; 2) to apply concepts and theoretical perspectives in the critical analysis of education; and 3) to conceptualize informed opinions about educational goals, policies and practices. Students will be engaged in making informed, normative judgments about educational aims and practices orally and in writing, and they are required to defend such judgments with reasoned argument and evidence from

257

the relevant scholarship and from their own experiences. The ultimate aim, therefore, is to produce knowledgeable professionals who are caring, reflective decision makers in a culturally diverse and democratic society.

ON A PERSONAL NOTE:
Dear 328 students,

I want to begin the course by sharing a quote with you that sums up quite nicely how I approach teaching and what you may expect from me this term. The words are historian Howard Zinn's.

> "This is not an 'objective' course. I will not lie to you, or conceal information from you because it is embarrassing to my beliefs. But I am not a 'neutral' teacher. I have a point of view about war, about racial and sexual inequality, about economic [and ecological] injustice—and this point of view will affect my choice of subject, and the way I discuss it. I ask you to listen to my point of view, but I don't expect you to adopt it. You have a right to argue with me about anything, because, on the truly important issues of human life there are no 'experts.' I will express myself strongly, as honestly as I can, and I expect you to do the same. I am not your only source of information, of ideas. Points of view different from mine are all around, in the library, in the press. Read as much as you can. All I ask is that you examine my information, my ideas and make up your own mind."
>
> Howard Zinn, *Failure to Quit*.

REQUIRED TEXTS:

Daniel Quinn, *Ishmael: An Adventure of the Mind and Spirit*. New York: Bantam, 1992.

There will also be a required course pack available at Mike's bookstore.

COURSE REQUIREMENTS:

I. CLASS PARTICIPATION

Attend all class meetings, complete all readings, and be prepared to discuss them in class. Your attendance and contribution to the discussions is required, and as I've always found, will play a **very important** part in what we all learn in this course. I expect each student to try to articulate his/her questions and responses to the readings, lectures and films in the context of this class, as a means of illuminating the complexity of the issues we will be discussing. You will all be responsible for the knowledge that gets made in this course, thus, I believe there is an important equity issue related to class attendance. Those who are there will be doing the work of producing knowledge with others in the class. You cannot contribute to this democratic process if you are not in class. Therefore, I will grade you accordingly. See the Rubric below:

A Attended all classes and participated fully and regularly in class discussions (this means you made a genuine effort to contribute to the ideas in the class by freely offering comments and asking questions. Your questions are very important to stimulating the thinking that we will be doing, so *please* ask!).

B Missed one class but participated regularly in class discussions.

C Missed more than one class, or was late to class more than once, or did not participate fully and regularly in class discussions.

D Missed more than one class and seldom participated in class discussion.

E Never participated in class.

Additionally:

1. Students missing more than one class will lose will lose all rewrite privileges (i.e., I will not read your second draft of the Vision Statement/Critical Analytical Essay).
2. Students missing more than two classes will be given a full letter grade reduction in their final grade. No excuses accepted. There is simply not enough time in the semester to miss classes, and ultimately it isn't fair to anyone.
3. Students **late** to more than two classes will also lose all rewrite privileges.
4. An attendance list will be circulated at the beginning of each class. Students are responsible to sign in. Since I only have this system to go by, failure to sign in will result in being considered absent.
5. In spite of this tough policy, I am very open and sensitive to the difficulties that arise in crisis situations. So please let me know when you are in a bind, or have experienced something so trying that it interrupts your studies. We'll do our best to help you stay on track.

II. WRITTEN ASSIGNMENTS

1. *Ishmael* **Discussion Questions and Brief Response Paper:** To facilitate discussion of the novel *Ishmael*, I have developed a list of guiding questions to help you keep track of the main ideas. You must respond to half the questions on the list, either all the odd or all the even numbered questions. Please do so in writing and be prepared to hand in your responses. You do not have to type or answer in complete sentences; notes are sufficient, but be sure they are legible. For the final question, I do expect a word-processed response. This should be a brief essay containing your thoughts and insights in response to the prompt questions. See the question sheet for the grading rubric for this assignment. This assignment is worth 15%.

2. Online journal/class discussion: Under **Groups** in My Emich, you will find SOFD 328, Martusewicz. Follow the directions to get into the Group designated for this course. Each week you will write responses to questions that I've posted there as well as respond to at least two of your peer's comments. I expect you to use this online discussion to 1) prepare for the in-class discussion and activities, 2) study and respond to the issues and ideas discussed in the course materials, 3) engage with your class mates around these issues and 4) prepare for the written essay and final group project. I will not respond to each of your entries individually, but will monitor the discussion closely and respond generally to the entries each week. I will grade you according to how carefully you respond to the texts using the questions, as well as according to your willingness to respond to others. This requirement is worth 20%.

3. Midterm Concept Quiz: In Mid October you will be given an in-class writing assignment that will assess your understanding of the primary concepts used in the course to that point. This assessment is worth 15%.

4. Vision Statement/Critical Analytic Essay: Public Schools in a Democratic Society You will write a critical analytic essay responding to the following questions:

What is your vision of the purposes of public schools in a diverse and sustainable, democratic society? How do today's schools stack up to this vision? How will you contribute to this vision in your own classroom?

This assignment is worth 20% of the final grade.

VSCA Guidelines
To help you answer these question, the following guidelines are offered:

Today's schools:

1. Critically examine the current condition of public schools, using the following questions for help.

- Drawing on the analyses of inequality offered by Valencia, Ryan, Anyon, Kozol, Orenstein, and others in your course pack, discuss who benefits most from public schooling and why. What theories and related ideologies are used to justify the ways children from different social groups are treated? How are schools organized to support those ideas? What specific school practices are used to reproduce these educational relations and conditions?
- To what degree do the practices and policies in public schools prepare citizens who value diversity? Be sure to address both cultural diversity and biodiversity. Who seems to be valued most in public schools? Give good evidence from the course readings.
- Are schools democratic, or organized to teach students the fundamental principles supporting democratic relationships in everyday life?
- Are schools organized to support the ecologically sustainability of communities?
- Given this critique, and using theoretical resources from the course, what would you say the purpose of public education is today? In whose interest and for what purpose are schools organized?

Your vision: If we are to live in diverse and sustainable democratic society, what ought the purposes of public schools be?

1. Defining each term carefully, describe what you think a diverse and sustainable democratic society would be like. What are its primary characteristics, and what principles guide its organization (You are encouraged to use the online discussion for this part of your essay. If you use someone else's ideas from this discussion cite the author, the date it was written and the online class discussion group it was written for).
2. What ought the responsibility of schools to democracy, sustainability and diversity be?
3. What ought to be a teacher's primary ethical responsibility in such schools? Discuss the notion of teachers as political and ethical agents in diverse, democratic and sustainable communities, giving examples of how you personally can act as an ethical agent utilizing the principles laid out in your vision in your community, school, and classroom.

Directions for Form and Style:
This assignment must be typed, double-spaced, **paginated** and follow the citation guidelines of one of the following stylistic forms: American Psychological Association (APA), or Chicago Style, MLA, or Turabian. Please indicate the style of referencing you are using on the bottom right corner of your references or endnotes page. For help with these styles, go to My Emich, Study and Information Tools, Writing Style Guide for information

regarding how to use either APA or Chicago style. Use the guidelines strictly! Do not try to make it up or guess.

Please use Times or Courier font in 12 point. Use 1-inch margins. Staple essays and do not use plastic covers.

The essay will be graded for grammatical accuracy, attention to audience, and style, as well as coherency and strength of the argument presented including appropriateness of evidence, logic, and the accurate use of appropriate theoretical sources. I will give you a rubric in addition to the guidelines in the syllabus.

Rewrite and evaluation policy: Students are allowed to rewrite the Vision Statement/Critical Analytic Essay to your satisfaction. I encourage you to hand in drafts of each section but I will not require drafts or rewrites. I have put suggested draft dates on the course outline to guide you.

You will find that I am a tough reader, but don't despair! You may always argue with my grading/editing of your work. I'm a good negotiator, especially if your case is strong. I feel very strongly that teachers (or anyone for that matter) should be able to write, and therefore think clearly and effectively, so *I will push you* and coach you to do so. I am also aware of stylistic differences, although, as I said, you may sometimes have to argue your case. Writing will be graded on the basis of grammatical soundness as well as the clarity of your thesis or argument and the strength of the evidence presented to support it (see the attached rubrics). In the major assignment, you must demonstrate that you can *use theory* accurately and connect it appropriately to classroom or community practices. In other words, you must demonstrate that you can communicate an idea clearly using the work of other scholars in the field to support your argument. **The final essay MUST include at a minimum eight authors from this course.** Additional outside sources are also welcome.

Note: Students missing class more than once without a signed doctor's note or other official document indicating a crisis or emergency will not be allowed to rewrite any assignments.

III. EARTH CHARTER GROUP ASSIGNMENT and PRESENTATION

This assignment is a collaborative project to be presented to the class orally. It is designed to get you thinking about how to use the Earth Charter in your own classrooms and communities and to get you out in the community talking with people who are actively working to educate people in their cities, towns and neighborhoods about various aspects of and relations between democracy, ecological sustainability, and environmental justice, and their relationship to healthy communities. Most of these organizations are not directly involved in the schools but perhaps should be.

1. You will choose one organization from the following list, and research and critically assess what they do in their respective communities to support the principles and goals laid out in the Earth Charter.
2. Further, imagining that you are a team of teachers from the same school or district you will devise a plan for your prospective district, school or classroom to work in concert with that organization to use the Earth Charter and to get students actively learning about and involved in working for their community's social and ecological well-being. Each group will present their findings and their plans during the final class period.

Formal Guidelines and a rubric will follow. This project is worth 20% of your final grade.

Local Groups:

CPR Detroit (Committee for the Political Resurrection of Detroit), contact Dr. Charles Simmons in the Journalism Dept.

Environmentally Concerned Citizens of South Central Michigan (ECCSCM), contact Dr. Janet Kauffman in the English Dept.

The Ecology Center, contact Mike Garfield or Tawney Gapinski

The South Eastern Michigan Land Conservancy, contact Heather Rorer

Huron Valley Watershed Council, contact

The Boggs Center in Detroit, contact Jim Embery at Jgembr0@cs.com

Detroit Sierra Club, contact

Note: It is the responsibility of the student to inform the professor of any special needs or disabilities that may require alteration of these requirements. I will be happy to meet with students in private at our mutual convenience to discuss such needs or issues. Please see the university guidelines on this matter for more information.

COURSE OUTLINE:

Week 1: Introduction to the Course

Sept. 3/4
Discussion: What is a community? How are we to live together as communities on this planet, and what does education have to do with it?

Week 2: Diversity, the Community of Life, and Education

Sept. 10/11
Reading: Quinn, *Ishmael*

Discussion Questions and short response paper due

Week 3: Principles for Healthy Communities

Sept. 17/18
Reading: The Earth Charter, go to www.earthcharter.org
Wendell Berry, "The Conservation of Communities" handout
Barber, Public Talk and Civic Action

Questions for the Online Discussion: Reading through the Earth Charter, can you come up with a definition of Sustainability using the principles as a guide? Are there principles that you would not have thought about before? Are there some that seem to go together better than others, or that you would not have considered as going together before? Are there any that you do not agree with? Why? How would you revise this document?

What is Wendell Berry primarily concerned with, and how does he think we'll get there? How does he define community and how does this relate to principles in the Earth Charter?

Film: Ancient Futures: Learning from the Ladakh

Week 4: Diversity, Democracy and the Purposes of Public Schooling

Sept. 24/25
Reading:
Glickman, Excerpts from *Revolutionizing America's Schools*
Barber, Benjamin R., "Strong Democracy: Politics as a Way of Living."
Questions for the Online Discussion: What are the fundamental principles of democracy and what do they have to do with education? How do these influ-

ence decision making? What does Barber mean by Strong Democracy? How can democracy be "a way of living?" Where do the principles of democracy intersect with diversity as a condition of life?

Week 5: Sustainable Communities, Culture, and The Purposes of Education

Oct. 1/2
Reading:
David Orr, selections from *Earth in Mind*
C. A. Bowers, handout

Questions for the Online Discussion: What is education for, according to Orr? What *ought* it be for? What does Orr mean when he says that ignorance cannot be overcome? If schools were organized to meet the needs of a Taker society, what would this require? How does Orr propose we should shift that form of organization and what would that mean for creating democracy as a way of life? What are the primary elements of education for ecojustice that Bowers outlines? How do these help us to rethink "community" and democracy?

Suggested Draft Deadline (if you're starting with "what ought to be" or a vision of schooling for a diverse and sustainable, democratice society)

Week 6: Schooling as Deculturalization

Oct. 9/10
Reading:
Spring Handouts
Gregory Cajete handout

Questions for the Online Discussion: Discuss the concept "deculturalization." How did schooling contribute to the deculturalization of Native Americans in this country. Why was this kind of education seen as necessary? What economic interests was it related to? What ideological definitions of Native Americans helped to justify these educational processes?

What are the primary educational purposes in Indigenous education described by Cajete? How do these differ from what your experiences of education have been? How does Cajete's work help to shed light on the ecological implications of deculturalization?
Film: *In the White Man's Image*

Week 7: Schooling and the Reproduction of White Privilege

Oct. 16/17
Reading:
McIntosh, "White Privilege: Unpacking the Invisible Knapsack"
Delpit, "The Silenced Dialogue," handout
Delpit "Seeing Color"

Questions for the Online Discussion: In what ways have you been touched by White privilege? Can you think of any specific experiences where White privilege was in operation? How does White privilege contribute to what Delpit calls the silenced dialogue.

Film: *Eyes on the Prize: Fighting Back*

Online Response to the Film: What were your general responses to this film? What connections to the readings so far can you make? Choose two readings and use the concepts therein to comment on this film.

Week 8: Schooling and the Reproduction of Deficit Thinking

Oct. 23/24
Ryan "The Art of Savage Discovery"
Pearl, Arthur, 1997, "Democratic Education as an Alternative to Deficit Thinking"

Questions for the Online Discussion: What are the basic ideas in deprivation theories or deficit thinking? Can you relate deficit thinking to the way Taker communities relate to life? How do these theories blame the victim? How do they interfer with democratic and sustainable communities? How is individualism implicated in these theories?

Week 9: Schooling and the Reproduction of Class Differences

Oct. 30/31
Reading:
Anyon, Jean, 1981, "Elementary Schooling and Distinctions of Social Class"
Rethinking Our Classrooms (p. 115 in course pack):
Clark, L. C., 1994. "Expectations and 'At Risk' Children: One Teacher's Perspective"
Schwabe, Molly, "The Pigs: When Tracking Takes its Toll"
Meirer, Terry, 1994, "Why Standardized Tests are Bad"
Karp, Stan, 1994, "Detracking Montclair High School"

Oakes, Jeannie, 1994, "Tracking: Why Schools Need to Take Another Route"

Questions for the Online Discussion: In what specific ways does Anyon see school practices reproducing social inequality? How is the organization of tracks related to what Anyon and Ryan are talking about. What is the relation between Anyon's perspective on inequality in schools what the Rethinking Our Classrooms authors have to say about testing, teacher expectations, tracking, and so on? Can you see how the deprivation theories were operating in the schools Anyon discusses?

Concept Quiz Given

Film: *Children in America's Schools*

Online Response to the Film: What were your general responses to this film? What connections to the readings so far can you make? Choose two readings and use the concepts therein to comment on this film

Week 10: Schooling and the Reproduction of Gender Inequality

Nov. 5/6
Reading:
Sadker and Sadker, readings from *Failing at Fairness*
Orenstein, readings from *School Girls*
Bravo and Miller, "What Teachers can Do About Sexual Harrassment"
Stein and Sjostrom, "Flirting vs Sexual Harrassment"

Questions for the Online Discussion: What specific factors lead to the unequal educational experiences and outcomes for boys and girls? How does sexual harassment impact a democratic society? Why does it matter for a democratic society to look at how girls and boys are socialized in schools? Can you relate personally to any of these authors' descriptions?

Suggested VSCA Draft deadline

Week 11: Schooling and Heterosexism

Nov. 12/13
Reading:
Martino, Wayne, 1998, "'It's Ok To be Gay': Interrupting Straight Thinking in the English Classroom"
Questions for the Online Discussion: How do homophobia and heterosexism operate in schools and classrooms across the country? Is it the responsibility

of teachers to try to interrupt behaviors associated with discrimination against homosexuality? How does Martino's article deal with this question and what is your response to these practices?

Film: *It's Elementary*

Week 12: So What Do We Do? Teaching for Social and Ecological Justice

Nov. 19/20
Reading:
Joseph Kiefer, "Stories from Our Common Roots"
Williams and Taylor, "From Margin to Center"
Bigelow and Peterson, *Rethinking Globalization*, read through this whole section particularly for the teaching ideas

Questions for the Online Discussion: What were the primary ideas behind the Common Roots project in Vermont and what do you think about this approach? What do Williams and Taylor mean by from margin to center, and do you think such an approach is important, feasible? Can you foresee bringing such practices into your own classroom or school? How do the essays and teaching ideas in the Rethinking Globalization (Bigelow and Peterson) section help us teach about the relation between culture and ecological devastation? Which ideas in the Rethinking Globalization section do you think are most adaptable to your own teaching? If none appeal, say why they don't. How might any of these ideas help us to teach students to become active democratic citizens?

Film: *Common Roots*

THANKSGIVING BREAK! YIPPEE!

Week 13: Teaching for Social and Ecological Justice, cont.

Dec. 3/4
Reading:
Sapon Shevin and Schneidewind, "Cooperative Learning as Empowering Pedagogy"
Alschuler, "Schools in which it is Easier to Love" (optional), "Liberating People From Conflict" (required)
Wood, Teaching for Democracy handout
Questions for the Online Discussion: Can you relate cooperative learning to teaching for democracy? How will classroom management be organized

democratically using Alschuler's ideas? Are there connections between these ideas and the Common Roots project we discussed last week? How are teaching for sustainability and teaching for democracy related in classroom practice?

Film: *The World in Claire's classroom*

Last Day to hand in a VSCA draft

Week 14: Teaching for Social and Ecological Justice, cont.

Dec.10/11
Reading: Orenstein, "Anita Hill Is a Boy"

Final VSCA Papers due

Week 15: Earth Charter Community Organization Projects

Dec. 17/18

Author Index

Subject Index